CONTENTS

Household Strategies for Survival 1600–2000:
Fission, Faction and Cooperation

Edited by
Laurence Fontaine and
Jürgen Schlumbohm

Household Strategies for Survival: An Introduction
Laurence Fontaine and Jürgen Schlumbohm   1

Negotiating a Living: Essex Pauper Letters from London, 1800–1834
Thomas Sokoll   19

"It Is Extreme Necessity That Makes Me Do This":
Some "Survival Strategies" of Pauper Households in London's
West End During the Early Eighteenth Century
Jeremy Boulton   47

Using Microcredit and Restructuring Households: Two
Complementary Survival Strategies in Late Eighteenth-Century
Barcelona
Montserrat Carbonell-Esteller   71

Poor Jewish Families in Early Modern Rural Swabia
Sabine Ullmann   93

Industrious Households: Survival Strategies of Artisans in a
Southwest German Town during the Eighteenth and Early
Nineteenth Centuries
Dennis A. Frey, Jr   115

Individualization Strategies Among City Dwellers in Contemporary
Africa: Balancing the Shortcomings of Community Solidarity
and the Individualism of the Struggle for Survival
Alain Marie   137

Finding the Right Balance: Financial Self-Help Organizations
as Sources of Security and Insecurity in Urban Indonesia
Hotze Lont   159

Stepping on Two Boats: Urban Strategies of Chinese Peasants
and Their Children
Danyu Wang   179

NOTES ON CONTRIBUTORS

Jeremy Boulton, Department of History, Armstrong Building, University of Newcastle, Newcastle-upon-Tyne NE1 7RU, UK; e-mail: J.P.Boulton@ newcastle.ac.uk

Montserrat Carbonell-Esteller, Departament d'Història i Institucions Econòmiques, Universitat de Barcelona, Diagonal 696, E-08034 Barcelona, Spain; e-mail: montcar@eco.ub.es

Laurence Fontaine, Département d'histoire et civilisation, Institut Universitaire Européen, villa Schifanoia, via Boccaccio 121, I-50133 Firenze, Italy; e-mail: fontaine@datacomm.iue.it

Dennis A. Frey, Jr, Mercer County Community College, Division of Liberal Arts, PO Box B, Trenton, NJ 08690, USA; e-mail: freyd@mccc.edu

Hotze Lont, ASSR, Oude Hoogstraat 24, 1012 CE Amsterdam, The Netherlands; e-mail: lont@pscw.uva.nl

Alain Marie, Université de Paris 1–IEDES (Institut d'Études du Développement Économique et Social), 45 bis, avenue de la Belle Gabrielle, F–94130 Nogent sur Marne, France

Jürgen Schlumbohm, Max-Planck-Institut für Geschichte, Postfach 2833, D-37018 Göttingen, Germany; e-mail: schlumbohm@mpi-g.gwdg.de

Thomas Sokoll, Historisches Institut, FernUniversität Hagen, Feithstrasse 140, D-58097 Hagen, Germany; e-mail: thomas.sokoll@fernuni-hagen.de

Sabine Ullmann, Bayerische und Schwäbische Landesgeschichte, Philosophische Fakultät II, Universität Augsburg, Universitätsstrasse 10, D-86135 Augsburg, Germany; e-mail: Sabine.Ullmann@Phil.Uni-Augsburg.de

Danyu Wang, Department of Anthropology and Center for Studies in Demography and Ecology (CSDE), University of Washington, 104D Savery, Box 353340, Seattle, WA 98195–3340, USA; e-mail: dwang@ u.washington.edu

International Review of Social History 45 (2000), pp. 1–17
© 2000 Internationaal Instituut voor Sociale Geschiedenis

Household Strategies for Survival: An Introduction

LAURENCE FONTAINE AND JÜRGEN SCHLUMBOHM*

FROM THE STUDY OF POVERTY TO THE STUDY OF SURVIVAL STRATEGIES

In early modern Europe, as in developing countries today, much of the population had to struggle to survive. Estimates for many parts of pre-industrial Europe, as for several countries in the so-called Third World, suggest that the majority of the inhabitants owned so little property that their livelihood was highly insecure.[1] Basically, all those who lived by the work of their hands were at risk, and the reasons for their vulnerability were manifold. Economic cycles and seasonal fluctuations jeopardized the livelihood of the rural and urban masses. Warfare, taxation, and other decisions by the ruling elites sometimes had far-reaching direct and indirect repercussions on the lives of the poor. This is also true of natural factors, both catastrophes and the usual weather fluctuations, which were a major factor affecting harvest yields. Equal in importance were the risks and uncertainties inherent in life and family cycles: disease, old age, widowhood, or having many young children.

On calculating both the incomes and the subsistence needs of the "labouring poor",[2] economic historians discovered that, according to this type of accounting, a large section of the rural and urban population would have been unable to survive. In years of dearth, wages were insufficient to feed a family.[3] In many parts of Europe, even the majority of peasant farms did

---

* Lee Mitzman has translated pp. 10–17, written by Laurence Fontaine in French. She has also reviewed Jürgen Schlumbohm's English, pp. 1–10.

1. Robert Jütte, *Poverty and Deviance in Early Modern Europe* (Cambridge, 1994), pp. 46–50; revised German version; *idem, Arme, Bettler, Beutelschneider. Eine Sozialgeschichte der Armut in der Frühen Neuzeit* (Weimar, 2000), pp. 59–64; Stuart Woolf, *The Poor in Western Europe in the Eighteenth and Nineteenth Centuries* (London [etc.], 1986), pp. 4–8; cf. Bronislaw Geremek, *Geschichte der Armut. Elend und Barmherzigkeit in Europa* (Munich [etc.], 1988), pp. 131–152, translated into English as: *Poverty: A History* (Oxford, 1994); Laurence Fontaine, "Pauvreté et crédit en Europe à l'époque moderne", in Jean-Michel Servet (ed.), *Exclusion et liens financiers* (Paris, 1999), pp. 28–43.

2. According to a famous contemporary definition, the "labouring poor" were "those whose daily labour is necessary for their daily support", and "whose daily subsistence absolutely depends on the daily unremitting exertion of manual labour": Frederic Morton Eden, *The State of the Poor, or an History of the Labouring Classes in England from the Conquest to the Present Period [...]* (London, 1797), vol. 1, p. 2.

3. Wilhelm Abel, *Massenarmut und Hungerkrisen im vorindustriellen Europa* (Hamburg [etc.], 1974) pp. 26–27; Jean-Pierre Gutton, *La société et les pauvres. L'exemple de la généralité de Lyon 1534–1789* (Paris, 1971), pp. 69–78; Richard Gascon, "Economie et pauvreté aux XVIe et XVIIe siècles: Lyon, ville exemplaire et prophétique", in Michel Mollat (ed.), *Etudes sur l'histoire de la pauvreté* (Paris, 1974), vol. 2, pp. 747–760. Abel noted (pp. 294–295) that, already in the mid-

not yield enough income for the owner's household to subsist.[4] Historians studying poor relief, on the other hand, have found that the help provided by these institutions was clearly not enough to overcome the misery of the masses. Despite broad variations between different cities, towns, regions, and countries, and the major changes in welfare institutions between the sixteenth and the eighteenth centuries, the number of people receiving support and the amount of help per person or family, were generally too low to make up for the shortfall. This is true even of England, which, under the Old Poor Law, has been called a "welfare state in miniature" and probably had "the most comprehensive system of public support" in the early modern period.[5]

Findings like the ones described above, together with more general changes in historiography, and current social and political problems such as the welfare state's transformation and possible dismantling, have shifted the focus of research. Instead of trying to delineate a broad aggregate picture of the poor or showing the proliferation of welfare institutions and unveiling their disciplining purposes, scholars have started looking more closely at what the people on the margin of subsistence actually did to survive. In the process, historians quickly discovered that many of the labouring poor had not just one occupation but several, and that they shifted from one activity to another in a seasonal pattern, or according to periods of upswing and downturn or over the course of the life cycle. In some respects, this patchwork picture of premodern lives seems to mirror the current debate about the imminent end of lifelong vocations in postmodern society. Olwen Huf-

nineteenth century, a period of mass poverty in many parts of Europe, statisticians were puzzled by similar findings in studies about contemporary working-class families. This made them wonder whether they should assume that the labouring poor could balance their household budgets only by "running into debt, by begging and stealing".

4. Friedrich-Wilhelm Henning, *Dienste und Abgaben der Bauern im 18. Jahrhundert* (Stuttgart, 1969), pp. 171–173; cf. Pierre Goubert, *Beauvais et le Beauvaisis de 1600 à 1730*, 2 vols (Paris, 1960), vol. 1, p. 182.

5. The quotations are from Mark Blaug, "The Poor Law Report Reexamined", *Journal of Economic History*, 24 (1964), pp. 229–245, 229; and Thomas Sokoll, *Household and Family Among the Poor: The Case of Two Essex Communities in the Late Eighteenth and Early Nineteenth Centuries* (Bochum, 1993), pp. 290–291; cf. Paul Slack, *Poverty and Policy in Tudor and Stuart England* (London [etc.], 1988), pp.73–80, 207; *idem, The English Poor Law 1531–1782* (Basingstoke [etc.], 1990), pp. 29–34; Lynn Hollen Lees, *The Solidarities of Strangers: The English Poor Laws and the People, 1700–1948* (Cambridge, 1998), pp. 43 ff.; and the articles by Jeremy Boulton and Thomas Sokoll in this volume. Data from other countries and regions concerning the proportion of the population receiving poor relief and the amount of relief appear in, e.g., Jütte, *Poverty and Deviance*, pp. 50–57, 142; Gutton, *La société et les pauvres*, pp. 51–56; Martin Dinges, *Stadtarmut in Bordeaux 1525–1675: Alltag, Politik, Mentalitäten* (Bonn, 1988), esp. pp. 164–165, 524–527; Catharina Lis, *Social Change and the Labouring Poor: Antwerp, 1770–1860* (New Haven, CT, [etc.], 1986), pp. 102–114; Marco H.D. van Leeuwen, *The Logic of Charity: Amsterdam, 1800–1850* (Basingstoke [etc.], 2000), pp. 103–133.

ton's term "economy of makeshifts"[6] has often been used to show how, in the past, people pieced together their livelihoods from many different sources. Moreover, researchers have envisaged households, rather than just individuals, as the organizational units of the struggle for subsistence. Careful scrutiny has revealed how sources like census lists are often misleading, in that they frequently list the occupations of heads of households only. Feminist scholars and others have underlined the importance of women's work for poor households in early modern Europe, as in developing countries today. In fact, in most families all members had to contribute, including young children. In many cases, however, the poor did not have an integrated family economy in which all household members cooperated in the same home-based activity, be it agricultural or craft production. More often than not, the members of a single household were active in a variety of fields: market and subsistence production, wage labour outside the home, trade, credit, and services. Richard Wall's term "adaptive family economy" highlights the importance of flexibility in the efforts of household members to tap a variety of sources.[7]

HOUSEHOLDS, STRATEGIES, SURVIVAL – COMBINING THREE PROBLEMATIC CONCEPTS

By examining the multiform activities of the labouring poor in towns and villages,[8] economic historians have illustrated the concept of an "economy of makeshift". Their focus on economic activities, however, has often depicted the household as an unproblematic unit that allocates time and labour, pools income, and distributes it fairly evenly among all members. Although this vision is quite compatible with the models of Gary Becker's

---

6. Olwen H. Hufton, *The Poor of Eighteenth-Century France 1750–1789* (Oxford, 1974), pp. 69–127.
7. Richard Wall, "Work, Welfare and the Family: An Illustration of the Adaptive Family Economy", in Lloyd Bonfield *et al.* (eds), *The World We Have Gained: Essays Presented to Peter Laslett* (Oxford, 1986), pp. 261–294. Cf. the debate about the proto-industrial family economy: Peter Kriedte *et al.*, *Industrialization before Industrialization: Rural Industry in the Genesis of Capitalism* (Cambridge [etc.], 1981), pp. 38–73; *idem*, "Proto-industrialization Revisited: Demography, Social Structure, and Modern Domestic Industry", *Continuity and Change*, 8 (1993), pp. 217–252; Ulrich Pfister, "The Proto-industrial Household Economy: Toward a Formal Analysis", *Journal of Family History*, 17 (1992), pp. 201–232.
8. See e.g. Rainer Beck, *Unterfinning. Ländliche Welt vor Anbruch der Moderne* (Munich, 1993), esp. pp. 553–575; Valentin Groebner, *Ökonomie ohne Haus. Zum Wirtschaften armer Leute in Nürnberg am Ende des 15. Jahrhunderts* (Göttingen, 1993); *idem*, "Black Money and the Language of Things: Observations on the Economy of the Labouring Poor in Late Fifteenth-Century Nuremberg", *Tel Aviver Jahrbuch für deutsche Geschichte*, 22 (1993), pp. 275–291; Marco H.D. van Leeuwen, "Logic of Charity: Poor Relief in Preindustrial Europe", *Journal of Interdisciplinary History*, 24 (1994), pp. 589–613, 600 ff.

importance of size of family

"New Household Economics",[9] it has been subject to considerable criticism more recently. Scholars interested in family conflicts and gender problems, in Western and developing countries alike, find models of cooperative or noncooperative bargaining within households more realistic and more useful.[10] Economic historians who have tried to take into account demographic factors have often treated them as exogenous variables: the size and structure of a household put certain constraints on, or offered specific chances to, its economic activities. Chayanov and most of his followers exemplify this approach.[11]

The thriving industry of the "history of household and family", on the other hand, has tended to treat economic factors as a fixed situation over which the household and its members had little control. After focusing initially on comparing average household sizes across countries and over extended periods, scholars showed, for example, that household size and composition varied according to the amount of property held and the head's occupation.[12] A limitation that may be even more serious arises from the type of sources preferred in this research. As long as household lists, whether compiled by civil or ecclesiastical authorities, are the chief sources of information, determining the exact nature of a "household" will be difficult. Most researchers have simply taken the smallest group of persons listed, without questioning what the members of this group actually had in common or considering the meaning of the borderline distinguishing this unit from other groups and larger networks.[13]

This volume aims to take up these different approaches, to help remove

9. Some of Becker's seminal articles are reprinted in Gary S. Becker, *The Economic Approach to Human Behavior* (Chicago, 1976); cf. *idem*, *A Treatise on the Family* (1981), 2nd ed. (Cambridge, MA, 1991).
10. See, e.g., Caroline O.N. Moser, *Gender Planning and Development: Theory, Practice and Training* (London [etc.], 1993), pp. 18–27; Theodore C. Bergstrom, "A Survey of Theories of the Family" in Mark R. Rosenzweig and Oded Stark (eds), *Handbook of Population and Family Economics*, vol. 1a (Amsterdam [etc.], 1997), pp. 21–79, 31–44.
11. Daniel Thorner (ed.), *A.V. Chayanov on the Theory of Peasant Economy* (Homewood, IL, 1966).
12. An excellent study comparing households of the poor to other households and based on record linkage between household lists and other sources is Sokoll, *Household and Family Among the Poor*.
13. Peter Laslett, who defined the household as the "coresident domestic group", was not oblivious to the problems associated with comparing this unit across cultures and over extended periods. Nonetheless, he basically assumed that those compiling household lists in the past used criteria similar to those of modern researchers: Peter Laslett, "Introduction: The History of the Family", in Peter Laslett and Richard Wall (eds), *Household and Family in Past Time*, 2nd ed. (Cambridge, 1974), pp. 1–89, 24–25; E.A. Hammel and Peter Laslett, "Comparing Household Structure Over Time and Between Cultures", *Comparative Studies in Society and History*, 16 (1974), pp. 73–109, 76–77. For some of the later criticisms, see E. A. Hammel, "On the *** of studying household form and function", in Robert McC. Netting *et al.* (eds), *Households: Comparative and Historical Studies of the Domestic Group* (Berkeley, CA [etc.], 1984), pp. 29–43; Winfried Freitag, "Haushalt und Familie in traditionalen Gesellschaften: Konzepte, Probleme und Perspektiven der Forschung", *Geschichte und Gesellschaft*, 14 (1988) pp. 5–37; Michel Verdon, *Rethinking Households: An Atomistic Perspective on European Living Arrangements* (London, 1998), pp. 24–46.

the barriers remaining between them, and to attempt to integrate them into a more comprehensive research strategy by showing fruitful crosslinks. The object is to analyse the complete range of economic choices and activities pursued by the members of a single household, *and* to consider the structure, composition, and even definition of the group called "household" as a matter of negotiation. Recent work in economic anthropology and sociology of developing countries shows that this approach is both feasible and fruitful.[14] Regarding households as the basic organizational units of the struggle for survival seems like a useful point of departure. But how this group was actually defined, who the members were, what they shared – living space, food, other items of consumption, work, property, debts, income – and to what extent this group was isolated from or interwoven with other social groups or networks (like neighbourhood, kin and community) requires careful investigation in each case.[15] In addition to the broad variation between cultures and periods of history, the criteria for pooling contributions and liabilities and for redistributing resources were often subject to negotiation and struggle even at the microlevel, within a household.[16] Moreover, a household's formation and breakdown, as well as changes in its composition, were crucially linked to economic survival. Demographic events like the death of a husband or wife had a paramount impact on the household's economic prospects, and economic considerations mattered in decisions about forming, leaving, or joining a domestic group. Of course, the same has often been assumed of "traditional" marriages, but it can be shown – perhaps even more clearly – for conflicts within families. Many court records reflect quarrels between spouses about who was to be the "master of the purse strings", and how much a single member, more often than not the head, could use for his or her individual purposes, e.g. drinking. This type of conflict was one of the major causes indicated in requests for divorce or separation.[17]

It is therefore not enough to discuss strategies *of* families and households, as has become quite common during the last twenty-five years. Examining strategies *within* households is equally necessary. If households act as units

14. To cite just two examples: Caroline O.N. Moser, *Confronting Crisis: A Comparative Study of Household Responses to Poverty and Vulnerability in Four Poor Urban Communities* (Washington DC, 1996); Richard R. Wilk, *Household Ecology: Economic Change and Domestic Life Among the Kekchi Maya in Belize*, 2nd ed. (DeKalb, IL, 1997).
15. See, e.g., the articles by Danyu Wang on the rural household (*hu*) in China, by Thomas Sokoll and by Montserrat Carbonell-Esteller in this volume. For changes in the use of the terms "family" and "household" cf. Naomi Tadmor, "The Concept of the Household-Family in Eighteenth-Century England", *Past and Present*, 151 (1996), pp. 111–140.
16. See, e.g., the article by Sabine Ullmann in this volume.
17. David Warren Sabean, *Property, Production, and Family in Neckarhausen, 1700–1870* (Cambridge, 1990), pp. 163–182; cf. Sylvia Möhle, *Ehekonflikte und sozialer Wandel: Göttingen 1740–1840* (Frankfurt/M., 1997); Catharina Lis and Hugo Soly, *Disordered Lives: Eighteenth-Century Families and Their Unruly Relatives* (Cambridge, 1996), pp. 94ff.

in some respects, they are a forum for centrifugal and centripetal forces alike in others. Under certain circumstances they emerge as a unified group toward the outside world, whether because of the head's superior power or as a result of multilateral negotiations, or – perhaps most frequently – for a combination of these reasons. In other instances they are an arena of struggle between individual members or subgroups pursuing their own strategies, which may well entail leaving or dividing the household or threatening to do so.

Admittedly, endogenizing too many variables may present a methodological problem. Almost everything becomes uncertain, subject to negotiation, change, and decision, and nothing is an established fact. This situation, however, reflects the actors' point of view. On the other hand, the actors are of course not completely free in their choices. It is precisely in the interaction among choices, risks, uncertainties, and constraints, that the concept of strategies has proven fruitful as an analytical tool. For over half a century it has been transferred from the military field to economics, particularly by game theory. There, the term strategy is used for modelling sequences of decisions, by an actor pursuing a certain goal under set rules or constraints, by trying to anticipate future consequences of specific steps, and by taking into account the actions and reactions of other players.[18]

The concept of strategy has reached historians, at least historians of families and households, through the work of Pierre Bourdieu. Tracing these roots would be worthwhile, precisely because the word has become so common in recent years that in some texts it seems to have lost its cutting edge, whereas other authors strive to impose highly restrictive definitions. Bourdieu's 1972 article on marriage strategies, as part of the strategies of biological, cultural, and social reproduction, published in the *Annales*, has been particularly influential. He expressed a programmatic appeal for a "language of the strategy" instead of a "language of the rule". Blaming structuralism for treating practice as a mere execution of rules, he argued vehemently in favour of dealing with practices in their own right. In this way, he shifted the focus to the actors, their aims, the principles guiding their choices of means, i.e. their strategies in the game, which may include playing with the rules. Although Bourdieu underlined that actors usually have a choice between different strategies to achieve a goal, he was by no means an unequivocal advocate of freedom of choice for the actors. This has often

---

18. This brief remark obviously does not convey the varieties of approaches devised over half a century. The seminal book in this field was John von Neumann and Oskar Morgenstern, *Theory of Games and Economic Behavior* (Princeton, NJ, 1944). Interestingly, the article on "strategy" in the *International Encyclopedia of the Social Sciences*, vol. 15 (1968), pp. 281–288, dealt exclusively with the military meaning of the term and noted only in passing that it had been "applied also to numerous other kinds of competitive situations, including commerce and games". The date of this change was described as "comparatively recent, occurring mostly since World War II" (p. 281).

been ignored by historians who have taken up the concept of strategies. In trying to overcome the opposition between structure and action, Bourdieu devised the concept of *habitus*, "a system of schemes structuring every decision without ever becoming completely and systematically explicit". As a specific way of thinking and acting rooted in persons, the *habitus* mediates between constraints and actors. The "strategies are the product of the *habitus*" and are therefore usually implicit and hardly ever discussed.[19] In fact, Bourdieu warned anthropologists that what the natives tell them about their strategies can be quite misleading.[20]

In the meantime, many historians dealing with households and families have adopted the term "strategy". Louise Tilly, Tamara Hareven, and Giovanni Levi have been among the more influential ones.[21] Frequently, however, the use of the concept of "family strategies" depicts the family as a homogenous unit. This may echo a section of Bourdieu's seminal article, where he seemed to consider the family father as the only player in the "game" of marrying off children, and the children as "cards" in his hand.[22] This bias, however, is by no means inherent in the strategies concept. The opposite fallacy, attributing strategies exclusively to individuals, as suggested by methodological individualism, is to be avoided as well. The point is to use the concept in a complex way, for transactions within *and* between households and the "outside world".[23]

Not surprisingly, some debate exists, as the contributions to this issue reveal, as to whether, or under which conditions, the strategies concept is useful in history and the social sciences. Some scholars support restricting the concept's use to situations where there is evidence of deliberate and explicit choices of actors. Such an approach would of course severely limit

19. Pierre Bourdieu, "Les stratégies matrimoniales dans le système de reproduction", *Annales ESC*, 27 (1972), pp. 1105–1127; English translation "Marriage Strategies as Strategies of Social Reproduction", in Robert Forster and Orest Ranum (eds), *Family and Society* (Baltimore, MD [etc.], 1976), pp. 117–144. A revised version appeared in Pierre Bourdieu, *Le sens pratique* (Paris, 1980), pp. 249–270; English translation *The Logic of Practice* (Cambridge, 1990). Interestingly, in the 1960s Bourdieu had written a first analysis of this ethnographic material in a language of the "logic" (of marriages) and not yet in a language of the strategy: *idem*, "Célibat et condition paysanne", *Etudes rurales*, 5–6 (1962), pp. 32–135.

20. *Idem, Outline of a Theory of Practice* (Cambridge [etc.], 1977), pp. 18 ff.

21. Louise A. Tilly, "Individual Lives and Family Strategies in the French Proletariat", *Journal of Family History*, 4 (1979), pp. 137–152; Tamara Hareven, *Family Time and Industrial Time: The Relationship between the Family and Work in a New England Industrial Community* (Cambridge, 1982); cf. *idem*, "A Complex Relationship: Family Strategies and the Processes of Economic and Social Change", in Roger Friedland and A.F. Robertson (eds), *Beyond the Marketplace: Rethinking Economy and Society* (New York, 1990), pp. 215–244; Giovanni Levi, *Inheriting Power: The Story of an Exorcist* (Chicago, IL [etc.], 1988), esp. pp. xv–xvi.

22. Bourdieu, "Marriage Strategies", pp. 122, 126–127. He did not overlook conflicts within the family, though, see, e.g., pp. 129–130.

23. Cf. Leslie Page Moch *et al.*, "Family Strategy: A Dialogue," *Historical Methods*, 20 (1987), pp. 113–125.

its applicability in historical research. As a counterargument, the use of concepts like "reproductive" and "survival strategies" by neo-Darwinian sociobiologists, who apply them not only to animals but also to plants, is probably less convincing to historians and social scientists than Bourdieu's point that strategies are usually implicit and are the product of the *habitus* rather than of deliberate reasoning.

   To some extent, this argument may comfort historians concerned that they rarely have any direct evidence for strategic reasoning, planning, and acting by people in the past. More often than not, they have to infer actors' strategies from documents mirroring only the results of behaviour, whereas anthropologists not only observe but also question the persons they study. For example, historians usually infer household strategies from census lists reflecting the composition of domestic groups and economic strategies from the distribution of property as recorded in probate inventories.[24] Court records or pauper letters are clearly closer to what the poor actually thought and wanted.[25] They have, however, their own biases, since they are themselves part of strategies for mobilizing support. There, people presented their case in ways they considered appropriate to the addressee's categories and not simply according to their own ideas and motives. If, for example, a wife seeking separation or divorce knew that the authorities were concerned about good householding, she would complain about her husband's drinking and bad management instead of mentioning emotional issues.[26] Likewise, a pauper asking the overseers for support would emphasize his Christian family values to present himself as one of the deserving poor, as a person striving for his family's economic survival and respectability.[27] In recent years, historians have increasingly discovered ego-documents, diaries, and autobiographical texts written by ordinary or even poor people. They range from fully-fledged autobiographies and multi-volume diaries, like those of the famous Swiss smallholder, soldier, and yarn pedlar, Ulrich Bräker, to the few papers that a common beggar carried with him when he was arrested.[28] Although writing down such texts was fairly exceptional for

24. In research on survival strategies, another shortcoming of this type of sources is that they give information about those who are integrated into sedentary communities – even if they have to struggle not to be forced out – rather than about those who really live on the margin of subsistence, like propertyless vagrant people. Cf. the articles by Sabine Ullmann and Dennis Frey in this volume.

25. Thomas Sokoll (ed.), *Essex Pauper Letters, 1731–1837*, Records of Social and Economic History, new series (Oxford, in press).

26. Cf. Sabean, *Property, Production, and Family in Neckarhausen*, pp. 128 ff.; Lis and Soly, *Disordered Lives*, pp. 83–84.

27. Cf. the articles by Thomas Sokoll and Jeremy Boulton in this volume.

28. Ulrich Bräker, *Lebensgeschichte und natürliche Ebentheuer des armen Mannes im Tockenburg* (Zürich, 1789), available in numerous later editions; *idem, Sämtliche Schriften*, vols 1–3 (Munich, 1998) contain the diaries 1768–1798. On the beggar, see Otto Ulbricht, "Die Welt eines Bettlers um 1775: Johann Gottfried Kästner", *Historische Anthropologie*, 2 (1994), pp. 371–398.

poor people in early modern Europe, these documents clearly reflect the thoughts, wishes, and efforts of their humble authors. Nevertheless, they are also shaped by the anticipated expectations of the readers. Ego-documents can provide deep insights into strategic rationales of their authors, but they should not simply be taken at face value. What is described as a purely economic survival strategy may well have arisen from more varied motives than the author wants his audience to believe.[29] While no single type of evidence offers direct access to people's strategies, historians face the usual situation of many different types of sources offering relevant, albeit partial, insights.

Another controversial point is whether the concept of strategies is meaningful only if actors have a considerable margin of choice and are not subject to overly severe constraints. Even some survivors of Nazi concentration camps, however, have found the term "strategies" useful in trying to explain why some were able to survive. Researchers have adopted this analytical tool in spite of the fact that the camps aimed at reducing human beings to a state of utter dependency and exposed them to the arbitrary threat and omnipresent reality of death. The strategies analysed in this context range from watching systematically for an extra piece of bread or for a few seconds of rest during devastating work loads, to trying to follow, in everyday camp life, the maxim of not letting oneself be reduced to the level of an animal.[30]

The notion of survival seems straightforward but is, in fact, just as complex as the strategies concept. Even if, for a moment, we think of nothing

---

29. A fine example appears in the autobiography of the propertyless tailor, who presented his decision to remarry as a purely economic strategy, motivated by the insight that, as a widower with two children, "I could not possibly keep house without a wife". He proved his case by explaining that he married his second spouse, suggested by a woman relative, only two weeks after he met her. The parish registers, however, show that a child was born less than seven months after the wedding, and that, in the marriage entry, the bride was not called "virtuous virgin", which was otherwise usual. See Jürgen Schlumbohm, "'Weder Neigung noch Affection zu meiner Frau' und doch 'zehn Kinder mit ihr gezeugt': Zur Autobiographie eines Nürnberger Schneiders aus dem 18. Jahrhundert", in Axel Lubinski *et al.* (eds), *Historie und Eigen-Sinn: Festschrift für Jan Peters zum 65. Geburtstag* (Weimar, 1997), pp. 485–499, 492.

30. Zenon Jagoda *et al.*, "Das Überleben im Lager aus der Sicht ehemaliger Häftlinge von Auschwitz-Birkenau" (1977), in *Die Auschwitz-Hefte. Texte aus der polnischen Zeitschrift 'Przegląd Lekarski'*, vol. 1 (Weinheim [etc.], 1987), pp. 13–51, 19; Anna Pawełczńska, *Values and Violence in Auschwitz: A Sociological Analysis* (Berkeley, CA, [etc.], 1979), esp. pp. 103, 107; Sybil Milton, "Women and the Holocaust: The Case of German and German-Jewish Women", in Carol Rittner *et al.* (eds), *Different Voices: Women and the Holocaust* (New York, 1993), pp. 213–249, 227; Myrna Goldenberg, "Memoirs of Auschwitz Survivors: The Burden of Gender", in Dalia Ofer *et al.* (eds), *Women in the Holocaust* (New Haven, CT [etc.], 1998), pp. 327–339; Herbert Obenaus, "Der Kampf um das tägliche Brot", in Ulrich Herbert *et al.* (eds), *Die nationalsozialistischen Konzentrationslager: Entwicklung und Struktur*, vol. 2 (Göttingen, 1998), pp. 841–873, 852 ff.; Christoph Daxelmüller, "Kulturelle Formen und Aktivitäten als Teil der Überlebens- und Vernichtungsstrategie in den Konzentrationslagern", in *ibid.*, pp. 983–1005, 999. Cf. Wolfgang Sofsky, *Die Ordnung des Terrors: Das Konzentrationslager* (Frankfurt/Main, 1993), esp. pp. 106 ff., translated into English as: *The Order of Terror: The Concentration Camp* (Princeton, NJ, 1997).

ˏsical survival, the last example shows that the means toward this end involve more than nutrition and escape from disease and murder. Moreover, the concept entails a variety of aspects that cannot be rigidly separated from each other. Physical survival depends very much on economic means. Historians familiar with the difficulties inherent in any attempt to calculate the subsistence needs of ordinary people in the past[31] will understand the problems encountered by economists dealing with developing countries today in assembling a basic basket of goods and services necessary for survival that relates to the realities of incomes and expenditures of the poor. As a consequence, many experts have come to define poverty, and even the means for survival, not in absolute terms but in relation to the rest of the population.[32] This is more than a problem of inadequate data and measurement techniques. It may be argued that in human society, the very notion of survival cannot be restricted to a hard core of physical subsistence, but is always shaped by perception and self-perception, i.e. socially constructed.[33] If social and cultural capital can indeed be converted into economic capital and investment in social networks regarded as a sort of insurance, social and cultural dimensions merit inclusion in the analysis of survival strategies. Taking the "native's point of view", the perceptions of historical actors seriously is important. Maintaining themselves in their social group may be a question of survival for them, as is leaving it in search of a better place, if they perceive their present situation as a state of utter deprivation.[34] Negotiations between historical actors about what is required for survival, e.g. between paupers and overseers of the poor, can be very enlightening.[35] Although overextending the concept of survival and survival strategies may ultimately compromise its explanatory power, we have avoided imposing a rigid definition as this volume's starting point. For heuristic reasons, we have welcomed individual contributors exploring a variety of approaches and aspects.

UNCERTAINTIES AND FORECASTING ABILITIES AMONG FAMILIES

Envisaging the range of opportunities and the diversity of strategies deployed by individuals and families requires considering the fundamental role of the

31. Cf. note 3 above.
32. See, e.g., J.J. Thomas, *Surviving in the City: The Urban Informal Sector in Latin America* (London [etc.], 1995), pp. 70 ff.; Rolph van der Hoeven and Richard Anker (eds), *Poverty Monitoring: An International Concern* (New York, 1994). Cf., however, Amartya Sen, *Poverty and Famines: An Essay on Entitlement and Deprivation* (Oxford, 1982), pp. 9–38; idem, "Poor, Relatively Speaking", *Oxford Economic Papers NS*, 35 (1983), pp. 153–169, reprinted in *idem, Resources, Values and Development* (Oxford, 1984), pp. 325–345.
33. Cf. *Idem*, "Poor, Relatively Speaking", pp. 158 ff.
34. See, e.g., the articles by Dennis Frey and Danyu Wang in this volume.
35. See, e.g., the article by Thomas Sokoll in this volume.

uncertainties they face. Two very different situations come to mind. The first concerns the forecasting abilities of the social actors. This capacity distinguishes those who were in a position to elaborate short-, medium-, and long-term strategies before the crisis from those who have always led a marginal existence.[36] The second situation concerns not the actors but their surroundings, and assesses the extent to which they are unforeseeable, to determine whether they help or hinder individuals in making predictions.

In this twofold selection process, based on the types of uncertainty and the ability to forecast the future, the strategies implemented by the families that ordinarily have enough income to make even the most rudimentary provisions are undoubtedly radically different from the ones implemented by those who have always lived exclusively in the present, amid insecurity, and have never felt fully integrated in society.[37] Individuals who have established a marginal existence obviously do not have the same range of survival strategies available. The other modality of uncertainty arises, not from families coping with unemployment or illness temporarily, or for more extended periods, but from the surrounding world, which undergoes economic or political crises that individuals cannot anticipate. These crises may be attributable to war or exceptional famines or epidemics. In some cases the causes are more ordinary, and reflect extreme fluctuations in prices and supply within brief periods or severe political turmoil.

Analysing these forms of uncertainty is a complex process, especially for the early modern era, as historians rarely conduct their research from the contemporary mindset of individuals into the way that relations between actions in the present, experiences with the past, and forecasts for the future have arisen historically and socially. Moreover, they are ill equipped to interpret the day-to-day economic situations affecting the poor, who engaged in a daily search for ways to subsist until the next day. Little information is available about retail pricing mechanisms or about daily price fluctuations according to the place and time of sale.[38] In addition, a detailed analysis is lacking of supply systems that would enhance our understanding of the social diversity of types and costs of supply, especially in the cities. Although these variations are difficult to take into consideration, they structure the analyses. Historians need to know the range of options available to the actors and the information they can mobilize to imagine a future. They also need to know whether the social actors had a limited scope for decision-making or had enough leeway to deploy strategies, as actions require a

36. Pierre Bourdieu, *Travail et travailleurs en Algérie* (Paris, 1964).

37. Sophie Day, Euthymios Papataxiarchis, and Michael Stewart (eds), *Lilies of the Field: Marginal People Who Live for the Moment* (Oxford, 1999).

38. The works of Valentin Groebner offer a glimpse of the vast discrepancies in food prices in fifteenth-century Nuremberg. Valentin Groebner, "Towards an Economic History of Customary Practices: Bread, Money, and the Economy of the Bazaar: Observations on Consumption and Cheating in the Late Medieval Foodstuffs Market", *German History*, 12 (1994), pp. 120–136.

modicum of anticipation and forecasting ability. Finally, they need to consider the types of conduct fostered by the instability. Contemporary experience suggests that instability promotes speculative and illegal practices.

The present studies enable assessment of the vast diversity of strategies, for dealing with all types of uncertainty, observed according to countries, residential settings (urban or rural), social origin, family configurations, and the nature of the crisis. They reveal that strategies were not merely economic: they may involve or combine different types of capital, as impoverishment entails the deterioration of economic, social and cultural capital as well. We have disregarded food strategies, which are very difficult to identify for early modern Europe. Instead, we have focused on social and professional strategies among relatives, households, and individuals. Psychological aspects are also largely missing, although it is evident that acquiring and maintaining self-esteem can be quite crucial in strategies for survival.[39]

While multiple activities are the first strategy everywhere, they are difficult to discern for lack of documentation. No traces of the common practice among men, women, and children of performing part-time or casual labour remain in the records of Europe from the past, or exist in today's world. Such work was usually off the books, and was therefore omitted from statistics and regulations. Generally, three types of activities are identifiable: the ones related to self-subsistence, the ones performed by wage earners, and the ones pertaining to nonagricultural production. Only this last type of activity – selling a few agricultural products is rarely enough to rise above the level of self-subsistence – offers entrepreneurial opportunities that might enable the replacement of the subsistence economy with an enterprise economy and survival strategies with ones of advancement.[40] Historians should examine the nature of grass-roots activities and should explore the question of whether they provide opportunities for establishing businesses (even small ones) and thereby providing access to another sphere of risk and anticipation.

Understanding where and how entrepreneurial capacities arise relates to three essential factors: geographic location, access to capital, and cultural and political taboos. Families who live near a city have more economic opportunities than those living in rural enclaves. Gathering even a modest start-up capital by borrowing or pooling resources is one of the prerequisites for running a business. This requires access to a surplus, either through wage income or through social networks conducive to such income, or reflecting successful market penetration by members of the family.

39. See, e.g., Carol B. Stack, *All Our Kin: Strategies for Survival in a Black Community* (New York [etc.], 1974), pp. 28–29.
40. See the article by Hotze Lont in this volume and, on contemporary China, Stevan Harrell, "Geography, Demography, and Family Composition in Three Southwestern Villages", in Deborah Davis and Stevan Harrell (eds), *Chinese Families in the Post-Mao Era* (Berkeley, CA [etc.], 1993), pp. 77–102.

Family strategies therefore need to be analysed according to whether they perpetuate subsistence production or help some of their members enter the market.[41]

POLITICAL ECONOMIES AND CULTURAL TABOOS

Cultural and political taboos deeply affect individual choices. Not all family members are equally capable of initiating all types of activities. In several countries, women are prevented by their legal status and prescribed roles from becoming entrepreneurs: they lack a minimum of control and power in family decision-making; they also lack the ability to manage an estate and sometimes even to own one. The conditions for access to property and the explicit and implicit contracts regulating redistribution of resources within families are therefore a frame of reference for precise questions to evaluate the leeway for initiatives of women and children, as well as certain other categories of the population, and to assess the negotiating power of everyone in their family and society. In all cases arising, legal, political, and social disregard for women limits their capacity to launch initiatives and to access information for obtaining resources, or to benefit from employment opportunities. In addition to legal regulations and social roles confining the possible strategies, the resources earned by the different family members may be monitored by outsiders. This stranglehold further narrows the options as well, as indicated by those African cultures of solidarity that impose multiple obligations on all members, or the institutional and ideological advantages granted to Chinese cities at the expense of the countryside.[42]

The accumulation of all these negative factors burdening women, exacerbated by centuries of lower wages for the same work as male counterparts, underlies their overwhelming presence among the poor. The latest report from the World Bank stigmatizes poverty's feminization: in 2000, women account for seventy per cent of the world's poor. Finally, questions arise from the fact that many families with few resources are headed by women, either officially, if these women are widows, spinsters, or divorcees, or in practice, if the husband works far away, and they are responsible for the household. Women become heads of households as a result of war and insecurity as well. At present, they head an estimated one-third of all households. In urban zones, especially in Latin America and some parts of Africa, women head fifty per cent or more of all households. In rural zones, from which men have traditionally migrated, their share is higher. These single-parent families (matrifocal families) are major sources of poverty.[43]

Penetrating the assorted social spheres that can generate employment or

41. The articles by Dennis Frey and Hotze Lont in this volume explore these issues.
42. See the articles by Alain Marie and Danyu Wang in this volume.
43. Moser, *Gender Planning and Development*, p. 17.

aid often requires using social capital. The studies also highlight cultivation of social capital as the other main group of strategies for acceding to the different social environments capable of generating resources. Though these strategies figure in all contexts and environments, the nature of this capital and its forms and modalities of action differ, depending on sites and social groups. Networks may be established in which the families habitually live. They may be horizontal or vertical, and may be based on family affiliation, friendship or clientele. Nonetheless, maintaining social capital in horizontal networks requires contributing to solidarity or conviviality expenses, and is in some cases beyond the means of the poor. Faced with these costs or the impossibility of using these conventional forms of solidarity, some families, as the African cities reveal, abandon old forms of solidarity to establish new types of social capital in other areas and with other actors or waive their traditional obligations. Joining a new religion may be one of the signs of these recompositions that always entail cultural transformation.[44]

Finally, this issue addresses the role of the political economy in which families and individuals operate, as it affects the overall conduct and choices of the most destitute: in market economies, savings strategies are privileged wherever possible, as are all forms of presenting oneself as a successful participant in the market economy. Families and individuals invest in clothing, jewels, or luxury items that denote success and can be sold or pawned as needed;[45] others prefer to invest in their children by paying for their studies or providing them with a dowry that will allow them to enter a family on which their parents will later be able to rely. The decision to activate social or cultural capital also depends on the nature of the political economy: those established in the market economy will deploy different strategies from those living through self-subsistence. In aristocratic economies of donation, charity, and assistance, however, the poor try to present themselves in a manner calculated to provide access to charitable resources, to appear as deserving poor and thus to obtain aid from various charitable institutions with which historians are now quite familiar. Absence or loss of market access transforms cultural attitudes as well: in socialist countries, when the allocation system replaced the markets from the precommunist era, citizens adapted their strategies to the new resources, and consumers became clients of the socialist state. This issue aims to convey, through examples from different political economies, the extent to which family *habitus* reflected political or economic changes.

SOCIAL ROLES AND INDIVIDUAL STRATEGIES

In addition to pursuing multiple activities and investments in social and cultural capital, poor families have limited expenses through economies of

---

44. See the article by Alain Marie in this volume.
45. See the articles by Montserrat Carbonell-Esteller, Dennis Frey, and Thomas Sokoll in this volume.

scale. In fact, poor families are caught up in a double logic. They need to pool their income as much as possible to resist the crisis. Contributions from children and parents are often complemented by individuals who do not belong to the family (neighbours or others) but share the same household.[46] These economies of scale, however, which diversify economic responsibilities in families, also broaden the scope for expressing individual strategies. In households where the men are responsible for supporting their families, work done by women and children can transform social roles and allow individuals more control over their own incomes. In the long run, these individual strategies, provided they are not channelled and repressed, lead families to break up and the better equipped to leave to earn a living.

The analyses presented raise questions as to whether the family concept applies in all cases, when we see how individuals affect their family size by abandoning children, often entrusting them to hospitals or other families, if they are expensive to feed and are not yet a useful source of labour. Migration destroys families as well, by depriving them of the departing members. If these members do not return, migration deprives families of their offspring, if the children are abandoned or run away. These changing family patterns give rise to two other questions. How do social roles and expectations evolve according to the strategies chosen or the opportunities taken by the different members of family groups, and how, in turn, do these new experiences reflect upon and transform the culture of families and individuals?

The safeguards against these centrifugal forces arise from obligations that are culturally constructed and socially imposed. Beyond the families, we need to understand how the social institutions, the social roles, and their cultural construction foster inequalities, cooperation, and conflicts, and how unequal the overall distribution of power is, especially to the disadvantage of the women. The state's role is crucial here, both in imposing new standards of conduct and in averting the disintegration of families. In the past half century, China has become a veritable laboratory for examining the state's potential to influence behaviour and impose new standards of conduct.[47] Previously, in Europe, the assistance policies fostered family and village solidarity by obstructing mobility among the poor.

With the enactment of matrimonial roles, work and values circulate throughout family life. Accordingly, analysing the cultural foundations of responsibility within the family is as important as describing the concrete conditions enabling this exercise. Studies have shown, for example, that the invisibility of women's multiple roles in the economic paradigm is one of the factors underlying their immobilization. Unlike men, they are unable to respond to market trends and economic incitement measures.[48] Likewise,

---

46. See the articles by Montserrat Carbonell-Esteller and Thomas Sokoll in this volume.
47. Davis and Harrell, *Chinese Families in the Post-Mao Era*.
48. Yvonne Preiswerk, *Les Silences pudiques de l'économie*, Cahiers de l'IUED (Geneva, 1998), p. 17.

transforming the traditional roles of fathers – or preventing them from fulfilling them, because society has rejected them and reduced them to a marginal position – may be the foundation of the disinterest they exhibit toward their children in several societies. Does the inability of fathers to anticipate their own futures prevent them from investing in their children's futures? While many studies have explored relationships between mothers and their children, a better understanding of relationships between fathers and their children is necessary as well. Other areas that merit exploration include society's acceptance of the abandonment of children by their fathers and the way labour migration facilitates these ruptures.

The unequal distribution of resources between boys and girls in the same family and expectations of them throughout different stages in the family cycle will affect the inequality of childcare in different ways. In rural China, parents make great sacrifices to send their sons to the cities,[49] while in India girls are literally sacrificed. In addition to examining the respective culturally-based expectations, the systems for helping children and the manners of state intervention merit exploration. Generally, we need to highlight the different family roles and to see how flexibly society defines them. Considered from this perspective, research on these issues is far more elaborate for contemporary society than for historical Europe: in recent years the various development organizations have measured how the gap between men and women and discrimination against women have been factors underlying universal impoverishment. In this context of helping formulate questions, the interplay between the world today, which we can observe directly, and the world of the past, for which few documents remain, is an irreplaceable confrontation for historians.

In conclusion, we will explain our choices in this comparison between historical Europe and the world today. Reflecting on the survival strategies of families in modern Europe and so-called Third World countries quickly reveals that we will never capture the diversity of the choices and actions of individuals and families in their struggle to survive, as the range of responses is infinite. We have therefore focused on the complexity of the parameters involved and have highlighted the constraints that face individuals and over which they have little control. These limitations are external, political, and geographical, as well as internal, social, and cultural. In a review issue, without even one contribution per continent, attempting to elucidate the situation in the developing countries of the world today would have been an illusory goal. We therefore felt that it would be more fruitful to highlight issues and attitudes that are revealed in contemporary analyses and are more difficult to explore for historical Europe due to the available sources and the status of debates.

The comparison's value is therefore more heuristic than descriptive.

49. See the article by Danyu Wang in this volume.

Addressing the survival strategies in a country where the market has been abolished, and the state is responsible for public assistance and imposes standards for biological reproduction, with those in a country where the market economy dominates, enables reflection on the ways that the political economy constrains family decisions. Considering the survival strategies of different types of families, according to their respective access to property and its management, conveys the role of these parameters in the entrepreneurial capacity of families in general, and of each of its members in particular. Rather than aiming to illustrate all possible strategies, this issue demonstrates definitively how tributary the solutions adopted by the families and individuals are in cultural, political, social, and economic contexts. It also encourages reflection about the realm of possibilities, the problems that the struggle for survival presents to the equilibrium of families, and the traditional structure of social values.

International Review of Social History 45 (2000), pp. 19–46
© 2000 Internationaal Instituut voor Sociale Geschiedenis

Negotiating a Living: Essex Pauper Letters from London, 1800–1834

THOMAS SOKOLL

Research undertaken over the last generation has greatly enhanced our understanding of the survival strategies of the labouring poor in early modern Europe. Under economic conditions where poverty was endemic, most families were forced to take to various forms of work and to draw on whatever forms of income were available. Whether among small peasants, proto-industrial producers, landless labourers or casual workers, their mere subsistence depended on the effort of as many family members as possible. Women's and children's work were the norm well into the nineteenth century, and their contribution to the family income greater than previously assumed. There were, nevertheless, many who could not make ends meet. The reasons for which people had to turn to others for help are legion: structural, cyclical or seasonal unemployment and underemployment; insufficient earnings and debts; illness and accidents; death within the family. A lot of assistance was informal and went through networks of kinship, neighbourhood and local community. Friendly societies provided rudimentary forms of collectively-organized support. Some state or municipal agencies supplying poor relief and charitable institutions offered assistance of various types, but most of it was meagre and combined with social control of the clients. It is no wonder, therefore, that many people took to begging, prostitution or petty crime.[1]

While there is ample evidence, then, that the labouring poor were forced to engage in a broad spectrum of activities and to draw on numerous resources in order to gain their subsistence, the strategic decisions involved in this remain less well understood. Strategic action implies choice. Ideally, it involves the rational choice between alternative opportunities and the assessment of the pros and cons of a particular course of action against other possible courses. It also involves a notion of the possible consequences of the alternative options to hand. But considerations of that kind are scarcely documented for labouring people before the middle of the nineteenth

1. Jean-Pierre Gutton, *La société et les pauvres en Europe (XIVe–XVIIIe siècles)* (Paris, 1974); Olwen Hufton, *The Poor of Eighteenth-Century France 1750–1789* (Oxford, 1974); Catharina Lis and Hugo Soly, *Poverty and Capitalism in Pre-Industrial Europe*, rev. edn (Brighton, 1982); Volker Hunecke, "Überlegungen zur Geschichte der Armut im vorindustriellen Europa", *Geschichte und Gesellschaft*, 9 (1983), pp. 480–512; Stuart Woolf, *The Poor in Western Europe in the Eighteenth and Nineteenth Centuries* (London, 1986); Marco D.H. van Leeuwen, "Logic of Charity: Poor Relief in Pre-industrial Europe", *Journal of Interdisciplinary History*, 24 (1994), pp. 589–613; Robert Jütte, *Poverty and Deviance in Early Modern Europe* (Cambridge, 1994).

century. For example, it is only from then on that working-class autobiographies survive in significant numbers. Likewise, the testimonies of the
poor, as recorded in the works of social investigators such as Henry Mayhew
or Frédéric Le Play, date only from that time. For most of the early modern
era, scholars have therefore been forced, if anything, to *infer* a strategic
rationale from the efforts of the poor towards making a living, while we
still lack research enabling the actual strategic decisions and moves behind
those actions to be substantiated empirically. It is the aim of the present
article to take a step forward in that direction, using English pauper letters
as a source which does in fact provide close insights into the strategic choices
made by the poor.[2]

The ensuing discussion is based on a particular sample of pauper letters,
namely all those surviving among the records of parochial Poor Law administration in the county of Essex (to the northeast of London). This sample
of Essex pauper letters comprises 758 pieces dated from 1731 to 1837, all of
which will shortly be available in the form of a critical edition prepared by
the present writer.[3] The letters were sent *to* places in Essex (from where they
have come down to us), but less than a third came from places within that
county. This is because pauper letters came from people who lived in
another parish than that from which they drew their assistance, and seventy
per cent of them lived in places outside Essex, mainly in London, the other
home counties and East Anglia. Particular emphasis will here be placed on
the 270 letters sent from Essex paupers residing in London (coming from
twenty-eight per cent of all senders), which survive mainly from 1800 on.
Pieces from other places will only be quoted for supplementary purposes.
Before we turn to this source, however, it is necessary to give a brief outline
of the institutional context from which they derive.

INSTITUTIONAL CONTEXT: THE ENGLISH POOR LAW BEFORE 1834

The English proletariat of the eighteenth and early nineteenth centuries
shared in the social and economic deprivations associated with the early

2. Previous advances include Louise A. Tilly, "Individual Lives and Family Strategies in the French
Proletariat", *Journal of Family History*, 4 (1979), pp. 137–152; Catharina Lis and Hugo Soly, "'Total
Institutions' and the Survival Strategies of the Labouring Poor in Antwerp, 1770–1860", in Peter
Mandler (ed.), *The Uses of Charity: The Poor on Relief in the Nineteenth-Century Metropolis*
(Philadelphia, PA, 1990), pp. 38–67; Lynn Hollen Lees, "The Survival of the Unfit: Welfare
Policies and Family Maintenance in Nineteenth-Century London", in *ibid.*, pp. 68–91; Stuart
Woolf (ed.), *Domestic Strategies: Work and Family in France and Italy 1600–1800* (Cambridge, 1991);
Catharina Lis and Hugo Soly, *Disordered Lives: Eighteenth-Century Families and Their Unruly
Relatives* (Cambridge, 1996); Tim Hitchcock *et al.* (eds), *Chronicling Poverty: The Voices and
Strategies of the English Poor, 1640–1840* (London, 1997); Lynn Hollen Lees, *The Solidarities of
Strangers: The English Poor Laws and the People, 1700–1948* (Cambridge, 1998), chs 5 and 6.
3. Thomas Sokoll (ed.), *Essex Pauper Letters, 1731–1837*, Records of Social and Economic History,
new series (Oxford, in press).

stages of industrialization throughout Europe. Typically enough, contemporaries took it for granted that manual labour and poverty went hand in hand, and hence referred to the working classes as the "labouring poor". At the height of the debate on pauperism which led to the New Poor Law, the *Poor Law Report* of 1834 declared poverty as the "natural" condition of the labourer.[4] In fact, in assessing more fully than hitherto the impact of factors like unemployment or the declining income shares derived from women's and children's work, recent research into the standard of living during the Industrial Revolution in England has again come to rather pessimistic conclusions. Scholars are now agreed that living standards stagnated between 1750 and 1820, while debate continues as to whether there was much improvement between 1820 and 1850.[5]

In their entitlement to and benefits from public welfare provision, however, English labouring people seem to have fared better than their counterparts elsewhere, at any rate before the drastic cutbacks under the New Poor Law after 1834.[6] Under the Old Poor Law, all parishes in England (or townships in the northern counties) were statutorily required to relieve their poor. In practical terms, this led to considerable income transfers. In 1802–1803, for example, total poor relief expenditure in England and Wales amounted to £4.1 million (roughly, two per cent of the national income), with just over one million people or eleven per cent of the population relieved. This was equivalent to £3.92 per recipient (or £0.45 per head of the population), a figure whose weight is readily appreciated from the estimated national income per head of £23 for the same time. The overall distributional capacity of the system must not, however, make us overlook the small compass of its actual operation in administrative and financial terms. Practically, it was a "welfare state in miniature" (Blaug), consisting of more than 15,000 parochial units, three-quarters of which had a population of

---

4. S.G. and E.O.A. Checkland (eds), *The Poor Law Report of 1834* (Harmondsworth, 1974), p. 334. The best survey of the contemporary literature remains J.R. Poynter, *Society and Pauperism: English Ideas on Poor Relief, 1795–1834* (London, 1969).

5. Maxine Berg and Pat Hudson, "Rehabilitating the Industrial Revolution", *Economic History Review*, 45 (1992), pp. 24–50; Sara Horrel and Jane Humphreys, "Old Questions, New Data, and Alternative Perspectives: Families' Living Standards in the Industrial Revolution", *Journal of Economic History*, 52 (1992), pp. 849–880; *idem et idem*, "Women's Labour Force Participation and the Transition to the Male-Breadwinner Family, 1750–1865", *Economic History Review*, 48 (1995), pp. 89–117; Charles Feinstein, "Pessimism Perpetuated: Real Wages and the Standard of Living in Britain during and after the Industrial Revolution", *Journal of Economic History*, 58 (1998), pp. 625–658. For a nuanced summary, see M.J. Daunton, *Progress and Poverty: An Economic and Social History of Britain 1700–1850* (Oxford, 1995), pp. 420–446; and for a perceptive statement of the optimistic case, Peter H. Lindert, "Unequal Living Standards", in Roderick Floud and Donald McCloskey (eds), *The Economic History of Britain since 1700*, 2nd edn, 3 vols (Cambridge, 1994), vol. 1, pp. 357–386.

6. Peter M. Solar, "Poor Relief and English Economic Development before the Industrial Revolution", *Economic History Review*, 48 (1995) p. 122; Lindert, "Unequal living standards", pp. 382–383.

less than 800 people.[7] From a comparative European perspective, it is also
important to note that the system did not involve a great deal of bureaucracy
and did not rest on professional personnel. Rather, the overseers of the poor
were unpaid parish officers, typically elected from among the leading farmers or shopkeepers within the local community, and often personally
known to the applicants. In many cases it was the same group of a dozen
people or so who served the (half-yearly) office in turn over several years. It
was only from the 1820s onwards that larger parishes increasingly came to
appoint salaried assistant overseers. But these still worked along with the
honorary officers, and what is more, to the extent that the salaried overseers
and vestry clerks stayed in office for years, their personal acquaintance with
the poor must if anything have become even more pronounced.[8]

The principle that each parish was responsible for the relief of its own
poor, but only for these and nobody else, had enormous practical consequences for people moving between parishes. People who had left "their"
parish were still legally settled in that place. Therefore, in case they became
poor and applied for relief in another parish, they had to go back (strictly
speaking, they were to be removed from the host parish) to their place of
settlement in order to be relieved there. Since the late seventeenth century
there was the alternative opportunity of obtaining a (new) settlement in
another parish, most notably by renting property above the yearly value of
£10, by working as a servant for one year, or by serving an apprenticeship
of seven years. But the settlement was thereby transferred to that parish, so
that again people could not claim poor relief anywhere else.

For ordinary labourers and their children, apprenticeship and service were
the most important ways of "earning" a settlement, the more so since in
trying to place their children with masters or mistresses in another parish,
labouring families were often supported by the overseers of their own parish.
It was a common form of assistance, for example, that the overseers paid
part of the premium for an apprenticeship indenture or that they provided
a set of decent clothes for a child going into service. In fact, this was also
often done when pauper children were placed with masters or mistresses
within their own parish. But there was a particular incentive for overseers
to arrange for children to be placed in another parish where they would

7. Mark Blaug, "The Poor Law Report Re-examined", *Journal of Economic History*, 24 (1964), pp.
229–245; *idem*, "The Myth of the Old Poor Law and the Making of the New", *Journal of Economic
History*, 23 (1963), pp. 151–184; Karel Williams, *From Pauperism to Poverty* (London, 1981), Tables
4.1 and 4.2, pp. 148–150; W.A. Cole, "Factors in Demand 1700–80", in Roderick Floud and
Donald McCloskey (eds), *The Economic History of Britain since 1700*, 1st edn, 2 vols (Cambridge,
1981), vol. 1, p. 64; Lindert, "Unequal living standards", pp. 382–383.
8. Thomas Sokoll, *Household and Family Among the Poor: The Case of Two Essex Communities in
the Late Eighteenth and Early Nineteenth Centuries* (Bochum, 1993), pp. 124–130, 221–235; David
Eastwood, *Governing Rural England: Tradition and Transformation in Local Government 1780–1840*
(Oxford, 1994), pp. 99–165.

earn a new settlement, since they could thereby "export" future claimants. By the early nineteenth century, however, these opportunities were largely exhausted, as employers had come to prefer "pure" wage labour to living-in apprentices and servants.[9]

The traditional view that the English Poor Law, by tying people to their parish of settlement, acted as a disincentive to migration has proved untenable.[10] Early modern English society was, and remained, an inherently mobile society, even though long-distance migration may have declined during the eighteenth century.[11] It is, nevertheless, obvious that the administration of the settlement laws did influence migratory behaviour, though the precise mechanisms are complex and difficult to discern. In fact, there has been a major reconsideration of this issue in recent research, with some scholars stressing the selective use of the law by parish officers and suggesting that it served as an effective instrument for the regulation and "monitoring" of people's migration. Others have been less prepared to accept this view and cast doubt on the notion of a close "surveillance" of the movements of the labouring poor by local vestries.[12] But most would probably agree that one of the chief effects of the settlement laws was "to deter the migrant poor from claiming relief – for fear that they might then be moved out".[13]

However, precisely that deterrent effect was not necessarily all that powerful, given that there was still an alternative to the removal of the claiming

9. James Stephen Taylor, "The Impact of Pauper Settlement 1691–1834", *Past and Present*, 74 (1976), pp. 42–74; Paul Slack, *The English Poor Law, 1531–1782*, 2nd edn (Cambridge, 1995), pp. 27–31. For the erosion of service and apprenticeship since the late eighteenth century, see K.D.M. Snell, *Annals of the Labouring Poor: Social Change and Agrarian England, 1660–1900* (Cambridge, 1985), pp. 67–103, 228–269.

10. The traditional view goes back to contemporary authorities such as Adam Smith and was canonized by Sidney and Beatrice Webb in their classic study of the Poor Law: *English Poor Law History. Part I: The Old Poor Law* (London, 1927), pp. 314–349.

11. Peter Clark and David Souden (eds), *Migration and Society in Early-Modern England* (London, 1987); Ann Kussmaul, "The Ambiguous Mobility of Farm Servants", *Economic History Review*, 29 (1981), pp. 222–235; Arthur Redford, *Labour Migration in England, 1800–1850* (London, 1926; repr. Manchester, 1964).

12. Norma Landau, "The Laws of Settlement and Surveillance of Immigration in Eighteenth-Century Kent", *Continuity and Change*, 3 (1988), pp. 391–420; *idem*, "The Regulation of Immigration, Economic Structures and Definitions of the Poor in Eighteenth-Century England", *Historical Journal*, 23 (1990), pp. 541–572; K.D.M. Snell, "Pauper Settlement and the Right to Poor Relief in England and Wales", *Continuity and Change*, 6 (1991), pp. 375–415; Norma Landau, "The Eighteenth-Century Context of the Laws of Settlement", *Continuity and Change*, 6 (1991), pp. 417–439; K.D.M. Snell, "Settlement, Poor Law and the Rural Historian: New Approaches and Opportunities", *Rural History*, 3 (1992), pp. 145–172; Roger Wells, "Migration, the Law, and Parochial Policy in Eighteenth and Early Nineteenth-Century Southern England", *Southern History*, 15 (1993), pp. 86–139; Byung Khun Song, "Agrarian Policies on Pauper Settlement and Migration, Oxfordshire 1750–1834", *Continuity and Change*, 13 (1998), pp. 363–389; *idem*, "Landed Interest, Local Government, and the Labour Market in England, 1750–1850", *Economic History Review*, 51 (1998), pp. 465–488.

13. Slack, *English Poor Law*, p. 30.

migrant, which was in fact of immense practical importance. This was the administration of nonresident (or outparish) relief, which meant that people who resided in another parish than that of their settlement were simply *not* removed but supported at that place, on the basis of informal arrangements between the two parishes concerned. There were basically two forms. Either the overseers of the "host" parish advanced the necessary payments, possibly at their discretion, and had them reimbursed by the "home" parish; or the home parish made the payments straight away, whether directly to the recipient or through the hands of others.

It is at this point we may now return to our major theme, for it is mainly people in receipt of such nonresident poor relief to whom we owe pauper letters. Precisely why those witnessed in our sample of Essex pauper letters had originally left their home parish is often not known. But it seems reasonable to assume that the main reason for migration was the search for better employment opportunities. With respect to people who had gone to London, it may also be assumed that on the whole their prospects in the metropolis *were* actually better, even for those who had run into trouble and turned to their home parish for relief. Under these conditions, the agreement on nonresident relief had clear advantages over removal for both parishes. Removal involved considerable expenses, which (after 1795) fell on the removing parish. For a labouring couple with children, these could easily amount to £10 or more.[14] Once removed, the homecomers were to be relieved in their parish of settlement, where they had fewer opportunities to make a living – after all, this is why they had left for London in the first place. In such cases it was simply cheaper for the home parish to provide nonresident relief, that is, to leave people where they had gone to live and arrange for their allowance to be sent there.

The suggestion that, under certain conditions, parishes may thus have ben-efited from the administration of nonresident relief is also supported by the fact that this practice of poor relief was fairly widespread. Official Poor Law statistics are notoriously defective in this respect (which is probably one reason for the long neglect of the entire issue of nonresident relief in previous research), but an overall average figure of fifteen per cent of all paupers being nonparishioners in England in 1802 is probably a good guess. The county average for Essex was about the same. By that time, Essex had lost its former cloth industry, centred in places like Colchester, Braintree and Coggeshall, and had turned into an agricultural county with high levels of seasonal unemployment and above-average poverty. Places like the ones just named had an estimated twenty to twenty-five per cent of their paupers residing elsewhere.[15] It is to people from that group of paupers or, more precisely, to those among them who addressed their overseers in writing, that we now turn.

14. Snell, *Annals of the Labouring Poor*, p. 18.
15. See Sokoll, *Essex Pauper Letters*, "Introduction", ch. 2.

PAUPER LETTERS: AN EXEMPLARY CASE AND A BRIEF OUTLINE OF SOURCE CRITICISM

Pauper letters are of major importance for the social history of poverty from below, since they provide – literally – first-hand evidence of the experiences and attitudes of the poor themselves. Despite this, however, English pauper letters are as yet virtually unknown to social historians, and research on them is still in its infancy.[16] They are also exceptionally delicate pieces of literary evidence. This poses immense problems for their historical analysis and interpretation, especially when, as in the present case, the evidence is cut into small pieces along thematic lines. Therefore, in order to introduce this unique type of record to the reader, it is appropriate to begin the discussion by presenting one letter in full.

London october 25 1827

Genteelmin I am obliged through Real distress to apply for Releaf as you Will See I dont decerve you my fits have been Such as to dissable me from Workin to keep my Family the 10 shillings you Was So kind as to leave me I Put it to the Best use I Could you are Well aware how far Such a Sum of money Will Goe I Was ordrd By this Parish to Send to you the Gentleelmin Was So kind as to Give me 2 Shillings [= 10p] I have 7 in family With my Wife Self and No house to Be in I am distresst Beyound and all I Ever met With and hope the Genteelmin Will take this in to Consideration and Releave me if Not I am Come to So much disstress I must Come Home With my Family if I Was Settled and had my few things I Would try and do all I Could Not to trouble you as I am much better in Helth if I had applid to you for my Rent this might have Been Prevented But I Was in hops I Could have done With out troublin you an answer to this Will be thankfulley Recevd by David Rivernell

Direct to Mr Howe

4 Grove S^tr
Commercial Road

This letter was sent from David Rivenall in London to the overseers of the poor of Chelmsford (231).[17] With respect to its formal characteristics, the

16. James Stephen Taylor, *Poverty, Migration and Settlement in the Industrial Revolution: Sojourners' Narratives* (Palo Alto, CA, 1989) is based on pauper letters from Cornwall, Devon and Westmoreland. The extraordinary sample from Westmoreland is also used in *idem*, "Voices in the Crowd: The Kirkby Lonsdale Township Letters, 1809–36", in Hitchcock *et al.*, *Chronicling Poverty*, pp. 109–126. For the first fruits of research on Essex pauper letters, see Thomas Sokoll, "Selbstverständliche Armut. Englische Armenbriefe, 1750–1850", in Winfried Schulze (ed.), *Ego-Dokumente. Annäherungen an den Menschen in der Geschichte* (Berlin, 1995), pp. 227–270; Pamela Sharpe, "'The Bowels of Compation': A Labouring Family and the Law, c. 1790–1834", in Hitchcock *et al.*, *Chronicling Poverty*, pp. 87–108; Thomas Sokoll, "Old Age in Poverty: The Record of Essex Pauper Letters, 1780–1834", in *ibid.*, pp. 127–154.

17. For the sake of simplicity, all references to the Essex pauper letters are given in parentheses within the main text, by quoting the number of the piece within the edition (Sokoll, *Essex Pauper Letters*). The same holds for other parish records referred to, where the details will be found in

modern reader might find the slightly phonetic spelling, the idiosyncratic capitalization, and the complete lack of punctuation a little irritating. Otherwise, however, the piece is not much different from a letter as we know it today. There is a clear, if simple, layout, and the standard epistolary elements are all given (place of sender, date, salutation of the recipient, main text, valediction, address of sender). Admittedly, the substantive message is slightly obscured by the fact that the wording and style are a little clumsy and that the narrative is somewhat poorly structured. Nevertheless, apart from a few apologetic phrases, the main points themselves are given in plain prose and leave no doubt about the sender's situation and the purpose of his writing. Illness has prevented him from work; he obtained relief from the overseers of Chelmsford (which he gratefully acknowledges) but it has proved insufficient; his goods have been (or are about to be) distrained because of his arrears in rent. He applies for further relief, apparently to enable him to redeem (or keep) his goods, and points out that if this is not granted he and his family will have to go "home" to the parish of Chelmsford.

David Rivenall lived in London, in the parish of St George in the East. But he received poor relief from Chelmsford, the administrative capital of the county of Essex (some thirty miles from London), since that was the place of his legal settlement. He was never removed to Chelmsford but stayed in London. The parish of St George in the East never even threatened to send him "home", while the overseers of Chelmsford on their part did not want him to come "back" and were actually quite happy to assist him in London as long as he stayed there. This is why he could threaten his parish to "come home" with his family in order to put more emphasis on his request for relief.

David Rivenall and his family are in evidence from Christmas 1819 till May 1829, mainly through the thirty-four letters surviving from him and his wife, but also through several other overseers' records from Chelmsford. Throughout that period, he received poor relief from there, in the form of a regular weekly allowance ranging between 4 shillings and 6 shillings (20p and 30p), with additional payments on particular occasions.[18] The money was handed out to him by people authorized from Chelmsford. There was a certain Mrs Nelson in Whitechapel, and later on Mr French, a coachman travelling between Chelmsford and London. Through these people, and through correspondence with the overseers of the parish of St George in

the critical apparatus of the edition, under the respective letter. All records are kept at the Essex Record Office (ERO) in Chelmsford and the ERO branches at Colchester and Southend-on-Sea. The precise archival references of all sources quoted in the present article are also given in the edition.

18. For readers unfamiliar with the traditional monetary units (£1 = 20 shillings (s) = 240 pence (d)), modern decimal equivalents (£1 = 100 pence (p)) have been added in brackets after quotations of specific amounts of money.

the East, the overseers of Chelmsford were kept up-to-date about Rivenall's situation. Moreover, in December 1823, at about the same time from when his first letter survives, John Sheppee, a representative of the select vestry of Chelmsford, had been sent to London to call on all Chelmsford paupers residing in the metropolis. He reported that David Rivenall was then forty-two years old. His wife Sarah was forty, and they had seven children aged between twelve years and five months. Rivenall had just had the household goods distrained for arrears in rent of 10 shillings (= 50p) "in consequence of not receiving his allowance as he formerly did". Sheppee went on:

> I gave him £1, and told him all the allowances were stopt for the present, and that he must not expect so much as 5s/ [= 25p] per Week for the future ; – The Family look in a very deplorable state; – it appears the Children are shut up in the house all day, as the Wife keeps a Stall and the Husband acts as a Porter in the day time and carries Oysters about in the Evening; – They appear to me to be both fond of Dram drinking [...] (104).

One might perhaps expect that Sheppee's final remark cast doubts among the overseers of Chelmsford as to whether the Rivenalls were truly deserving objects of charity. But this does not seem to have been the case. Occasionally, the relief payments were delayed, but this was a normal complication in the administration of relief to nonresident paupers.

It is impossible here to go through the record of the thirty-four Rivenall letters in detail. But is worth listing some "highlights" of their case, following their letters in chronological order. In May 1824, David wrote from the Clerkenwell House of Correction, where he was imprisoned for debts of £2 (116). In August of that year, one child died (130). In November 1825, the attempt failed to place the eldest son David as an apprentice with a "very respectable" master in the City (175). In April and May 1826, two further children died, Alfred and Edward (190–192). The funeral costs amounted to £2 9s (= £2.45), and Chelmsford sent an extra allowance of £1 (one letter [192] was written on the same sheet as the undertaker's bill). In August 1827 David Rivenall was in the debtors' prison at Cold Bath Fields. The letter he sent from there is also the first one mentioning that he was suffering from fits. It is worth quoting more fully.

> I have been labouring under the greatest distress for some time past being quite out of Employmt, but did not wish if possible to trouble my Parish as I was in hopes that when the oyster season would comme[n]ce that I should be able to get round and provide for my poor family by selling of oysters in which I have been always Tolerably Lucky but Just as the season began I was taken and put in prison for a the small sum of twelve shillings and Six pence [= 62.5p] which I had no mains on earth of paying so that I now remain in Confindment and Know not what will will become of my poor wife and Childrens I have also the unhappiness to State that I have been very lead in my health for a long time and are severely troubled with fits I have had several since I came to this Prison and in the Prison

chapple on sunday I had a severe one and was obliged to be taken out in the
middle of the service. (225)

The next letter, of 25 October 1827, is the one printed in full at the beginning of this section (231). That letter, as we have seen, is somewhat unclear
with respect to the distraint of his goods by his landlord for arrears in rent.
As a matter of fact, the goods were distrained two days later (232). Thereafter, David's fits occurred more and more frequently, while Sarah had
growing trouble with her stall in the street (239). In June 1828, David was
admitted to the London Hospital where he spent two weeks (249–250).
Meanwhile, at least two of the boys had been placed in service (239), and
there were prospects of finding places for the two girls as well (257). In May
1829, Sarah gave birth to male twins and David said he needed a nurse for
her (275). The last Rivenall letter came from Sarah. Apparently the two girls
had not been able to go into service because they had no decent clothes.
Otherwise, the family suffered from "the continued Severe illness with
which my Husband has been afflicted for the last 3 months, & which has
reduced us to the lowest ebb of poverty"(277).

The thirty-four letters from David and Sarah Rivenall date from
December 1823 to May 1829. Most of them are in his name, but three letters
came from her, and six were signed in the names of both. Whether they
physically wrote any of them themselves is not known. The thirty-four
letters are in sixteen different hands. Their next-door neighbour, Michael
Howe, wrote six of their letters, including the one quoted in full (231), as
is evident from a letter in the same hand in which he addressed the overseers
of Chelmsford in his own name: "Jenteelmin knowin david Rivernalls distress, I advanced him the money to Releave his things and Shall be Glad if
you Would have the Goodness to Convay it to me" (232). With thirty-four
pauper letters and further evidence, including correspondence from other
people, the case of David and Sarah Rivenall is exceptionally well documented. Otherwise, however, there is nothing special about it. The issues
brought up are also witnessed in other pauper letters. In substantive terms,
the Rivenall letters may therefore be regarded as a fair representation of the
sample of Essex pauper letters on the whole. But perhaps the most important point to note here is the particularly clear evidence of the strong negotiating position in which the Rivenalls found themselves. They knew why
they were not removed. And so, it seems, did most other pauper letter
writers. In fact, their knowledge of the disadvantages of their removal to
their home parish was the poor's best card, and it is precisely their letters
which reveal how effectively they played this card.

This brings us to the question of source criticism, though again it will be
understood that only a few remarks can be made here.[19] From our foregoing

19. For an extensive discussion of the questions involved in the source criticism of pauper letters,
with particular emphasis on their importance for the social history of literacy, see the Introduction
to Sokoll, *Essex Pauper Letters*.

discussion, it follows that pauper letters are essentially strategic pieces of writing. It would, nevertheless, be wrong to read them only with respect to the strategic interests they express. Rather, in what the letter writers felt they had to say about their condition, they often go far beyond mere strategic considerations, and open deep insights into the everyday life of the labouring poor. Moreover, in linguistic terms, pauper letters "sit" closer to the experiences and attitudes of the labouring poor than most other records. Some of them, especially those written with heavy phonetic spelling, may almost be regarded as "oral" testimonies. The fact that pauper letters were not necessarily all self-written does not invalidate this. The important point here is rather that, among the hundreds of different hands in evidence in the record, there are hardly any hands of professional scribes. Thus, when the poor arranged their letters to be written by other people, they seem to have turned primarily to members of the family and to relatives, friends and neighbours. In other words, whoever actually wrote these pieces, we can be reasonably certain that, apart from a few exceptions, pauper letters all come from within the sociocultural milieu of the labouring poor.

But would it not be naive simply to assume that pauper letters give "true" representations of their senders' circumstances? And is it legitimate to regard them as a mirror of the experiences and attitudes of the labouring poor in general? Although it is impossible to check the details of the account of the sender's case against external evidence for every individual letter, there is good reason to believe that, on the whole, pauper letters possess a high credibility. This is not to deny that there is an inbuilt "make-up" of the stories which are typically told. For example, in what people chose to say (and what not to say) they were to a certain extent guided by what they thought the overseers would want to hear. We should also expect a certain amount of exaggeration. It is even possible that individual letter writers gave false evidence and tried to deceive. But this last option must have been absolutely exceptional, given that nonresident paupers were subject to social control from two sides, with both home and host parish being alert to them. As we have seen, David Rivenall was visited at his place in London by a representative of the select vestry of Chelmsford. His money was brought by people in close contact with the overseers of his home parish. In his letter of 25 October 1827, he mentions that he also approached the overseers of St George in the East, his host parish (and that they advised him to write and send that letter). There was correspondence about his case between the overseers of the two parishes. None of this was exceptional. In fact, for many Essex pauper letter writers, the record of correspondence between the parishes concerned is particularly rich. Thus, if anything the surveillance of nonresident paupers must have been closer than that of those residing in their parishes. Otherwise, however, there is no evidence of any major differences between the two groups, which means that there is no reason why

the views expressed in pauper letters should differ from those held by the
labouring poor at large, or at least by those receiving relief.

LABOUR AND THE TIDES OF TRADE

David and Susan Rivenall made a living, or rather tried to do so, from
hawking, selling fish and oysters and whatever casual work they were able
to pick up. Most Essex paupers writing from London seem to have been
dependent on casual labour. This is not surprising. The metropolis was
notorious for its vast casual labour market, especially in the East End.[20] The
majority of the letter writers, as indeed the Rivenalls themselves, use rather
unspecific terms to describe their efforts, saying they live from "selling
things" (56, 61, 285). Occasionally, more details are given. Thus, John Spearman wrote that he had "Bought Some things for the first time and whent
all the way [from London] to Arcot [mistaken for Ascot] Races A Distance
of thirty miles to Sell them from which place I arrived last Night just
Sixpence out of pocket by the journey" (64). James Howell, who was based
in Ely, pointed to the importance of credit involved in his undertaking: "I
have six Children and the way I Get them bread is Carring a fue things to
sell about the Country I have Lived in the town a long wile and by been
nowen I have the Goods in Creadett". He was particularly concerned about
obtaining a new licence and reminded the overseer of Braintree that the
parish had always met half of the yearly fee: "Gentlman if you look in the
book you will find that two pounds is what I have per year towards the
four that is what I hav to pay for the Licences" (456). Two years later, he
wrote that he was hardly able to get on: "i have nothing to trust to for trade
but hawk the Cuntry afew Goods as i have in Credite and so i have been
on for sixteen years but Gentlman at this time i ham drove at my witsens
[wits' ends]" (487).

Some people tried to specialize in particular products. Elizabeth Goodman, in the London parish of Shoreditch, reported about her daughter
Marian, stressing the latter's "great anxiety for her Fatherless Children, &
perseverance to maintain them, her fatigue is great some days she walks
from 15-to 20 Miles to deliver her Tea, & at her return is quite exhausted
who could have thought she would have been able to get through what she
has" (663). Samuel Hearsum, in the parish of St Marylebone, also sold tea,
which brought him 6 shillings per week (110). Issac Harridge in Newington
sold quack medicines and booklets (118). John Tye in Colchester sold books
and asked the overseers of St Botolph's parish to supply him with "wrighting
paper and a Couple of Hundred of Quills that I Could Cut into pens at

---

20. Gareth Stedman Jones, *Outcast London: A Study in the Relationship between Classes in Victorian
Society* (Oxford, 1971), pt. 1; E.J. Hobsbawm, "The Nineteenth Century London Labour Market",
in Ruth Glass *et al.*, *London: Aspects of Change* (London, 1964), pp. 3–28, 12–13.

My Leasure – with a few Sweets of my own makeing To make up a Load – and to take a regular Curent round Colchester". It looks as though he not only sold books but also read them and knew how to use a pen, for he began his letter rather effectively: "It is with a Trembling hand I beg to Intrude this Letter" (364).

There are also references to tinkering and mending. Isaac Wright, in the parish of St Alfege in the City of London, said he was "fitting Tea Kettle Handles, &c which amounts to 3 or 4 shillings [15p or 20p] weekly" (256). William King in Bethnal Green, who seems to have been a shoemaker by training, was hoping to make a living from mending shoes:

> My Shoes are Nearly of My feet. I have Mended them till they are Got No foundation to work Upon – I Get a Little work ore we Should Starve But I Know Not How Long that will Last Yet as the Summer is Comeing I feel of Hope that if I was Set a Little for ward I Might Mend ore Make a few Slop womans Shoes and So hold out the Season. (38)

From his later letters, however, one gets the impression that he did not succeed in this. The only other known shoemaker in the sample, John Thurtell, does seem to have been able to work in his trade. He lived in Romford and received his leather from Mundon, the parish where he was settled (626).

Some people were in specific trades. James Albra, in the parish of St Andrew Holborn, was a bookbinder. When he fell ill early in 1829, his wife wrote to Chelmsford that he had "bin ill 3 mounth not bin able to harn a fathen" (270). George Tye, in the parish of St Anne Soho, had previously made it to Brussels where he "was Employd as a man Cook and Confectioner to verious English Famelys passing and repassing through that City – till my Return to This Countrey [...] Since which time I have lived as a wanderer by my Industrey warever I Could git Employ^d to the presant peirod" (334). William Willsher in Norwich had been a baker, but "through acomplaint I am afflicted with I cannot follow the Bakers trade nor has not for these 8 year's for I have been Weaveing but no worke of that kind is going in Norwich at this time Numbers agoing to their towns every day for want of work" (515). Norwich had long lost its former role as a centre of the woollen cloth industry. It is no wonder, therefore, that the other references to weaving, most of which also relate to that place, mainly speak about the lack of employment (285). Silk weaving in Bethnal Green was also reported to be slack (287).

Most people, however, do not name any particular occupation or trade. In fact, the usual expression is to say no more than that people "work" or "do" all they can for themselves and their families – but still are unable to obtain the "common necessaries". Given that pauper letters are strategic pieces of writing, it might perhaps be argued that tales of the daily toil involved in earning your bread were an almost compulsory rhetoric exercise.

After all, in a society which held that it was only natural that for the majority of its members labour and poverty should go hand in hand, and whose middle class was about to accentuate its work ethic ever more mercilessly under the ideological device of "self-help", people applying for poor relief would indeed have been ill advised not to point out their willingness to work and to do all they could towards gaining a living.[21] But then it is all the more surprising how little the record of pauper letters provides in this respect. For it is not so much the few passages explicitly concerned with work which are most striking: it is, rather, the general lack of detail in this respect and the overall silence about the precise nature of people's work.

There seem to be two reasons for this. The first is the semantic problem of how to talk about work without the notion of a clearly defined occupation or trade. A shoemaker might dwell on the various kinds of leather he uses, the types of shoes he makes, or the changing fashions of his customers. A hewer might refer to the heat at the coal face, or take pride in the strength of his body. But how is a casual labourer supposed to express his experience of work? The linguistic record of the pauper letters is instructive in this respect. The substantives "work", "trade", "business" and "employ" are used more or less interchangeably, and it is typical to say that work or trade is "bad" (347, 369), "slack" (26, 445), "dull" (201), "falling off" (175), "fallen short" (298, 309) or "dead" (445). Thus, the terms used in this semantic field are rather unspecific, if not to say vague. At the same time, they are mainly used from an individual perspective. People normally talk just about their own personal struggle against the vicissitudes of trade. Only very occasionally is the personal experience put into a wider context, as in the following statement by George Craddock from Westminster:

> [...] my health is very bad that I am not able to do any laborous work at all the only thing I have done Since I returned from the Country is to Sell alittle fruit or go Sometimes on an erant or any light Employment I can Get to do and there is at this time so many thousands of Strong hearty men out of work in london that it is Almost Imposable to get any thing to do at all. (522)

The second reason for the relative silence in pauper letters about work is a more general one: namely, the fact that people tend not to talk about the self-evident, the obvious, and the normal, not least because they might also think that this is not what the overseer wants to hear. For example, there

---

21. It is striking how "indigence" was distinguished from "poverty" in the *Poor Law Report* of 1834 (following Colquhoun). Indigent and hence worthy of assistance were those who were "unable to labour" or "unable to obtain, in return for his labour, the means of subsistence", whereas the "pauper" had no claim, given that poverty was the natural "state of one who, in order to obtain a mere subsistence, is forced to have recourse to labour" (*Poor Law Report*, p. 334); see Patrick Colquhoun, *A Treatise on Indigence* (London, 1806), p. 8.

is hardly ever anything said about the "family economy", because it is simply taken for granted that all members of the family work, according to their capacity, and contribute to the common income. This is also the reason why there are only very few references to the work of women or of children. It is only when the normal cause of things is disrupted that people begin to tell, and it is from these accounts of the exceptional that we can infer the rule.[22]

Perhaps the most common experience of such exceptional conditions in the field of work is the loss of bodily strength in elderly males. It is again George Craddock in Westminster who expressed this succinctly when he declared to the overseers: "would to God I was able to Labour hard as I formely have done and that it was as easily procured as then – then I should not have Trobled them for assistance but those good days are gone for ever from me" (530). Another example, in fact perhaps the most moving statement in this respect, is that made by William James in Chelmsford:

> [...] for many weeks past, sometimes work, & sometimes none, my Earnings have been but small, not more on Avarage, than six Shillings, or six, and six pence, a week, as near as I can tell – (I may say for some Months this have been my case) with which we cannot procure Necessaries, to support health nor Nature, for the want of which, I find health and strength decaying fast, so that when I have a little work to do, I find myself, through Age, and fatigue, incapable to perform it, Walking into the Country five or six Miles in a morning, working the Day, and returning home at Night, is a task that I cannot, but without great dificulty perform, several times I have thought, I could not gett home, and it have been the Occasion, of my being Ill, for two or three days, this I attribute, in a great degree, to the want, of constant Nourishment, to keep up my strength, and of Age aded there too, being now within one Year of Seventy – at this time I am Unwell, and have been several days (454).[23]

HOUSEHOLDING

Most Essex pauper letter writers must have been simple day labourers. Those writing from places in East Anglia were probably mainly landless agricultural labourers, as indicated by references to work in the fields and stables (4) or at haytime and harvest (56). Most of those residing in London, as we have

22. The silence about basic features of family life even in autobiographies (and, for the more recent past, in oral history interviews) is a well-known problem to historians. See David Vincent, "Love and Death and the Nineteenth-Century Working Class", *Social History*, 5 (1980), pp. 226–232; *idem, Bread, Knowledge and Freedom: A Study of Nineteenth-Century Working Class Autobiography* (London, 1981), pp. 40–46, and, with special reference to the family economy, pp. 62–86. For the difficulties of distilling contemporary notions of the family from literary works, see Naomi Tadmor, "The Concept of the Household-Family in Eighteenth-Century England", *Past and Present*, 151 (1996), pp. 111–140.
23. For a more detailed account of the case of William James, see Sokoll, "Old Age in Poverty", pp. 144–145.

seen, seem to have been casual workers picking up whatever "jobs" they could obtain, with some of the women doing needlework (162, 663), washing (289, 338), and mangling (133) for other people. This means that for the overall majority of the people we are concerned with here, the household was definitely not a place of production. The very few references to weaving (most of them in the negative) or other trades involving work at home are merely exceptions to prove this rule. So are the few cases where home production of clothes is referred to, as in the outcry from Mary Taylor in Hadleigh (Suffolk): "you promised me Sir to send me a peice of cloth to make my Children some shirts [...] but yet Sir you did not perform your promise" (322).

The usage of the very term "household" is instructive. Not only is it very rarely used at all, but when it turns up it refers only to reproductive or "housekeeping" functions. "Our Household is But Very Mean, My Wife is But a Poor afflicted woman", says William King in Bethnal Green (32). This is the notion of the household as a consumptive unit, based on the nuclear family of a married couple with children, where the wife is responsible for the "management" of the household. But this is not normally said explicitly, or at least not in these terms. The wife may be said to "do" for the family, but again this is not normally said explicitly because it is simply taken for granted. It is only when the normal household arrangements are disrupted that people talk about them. Thus, when the wife is ill or otherwise incapacitated, the husband might take her place, as George Rowe in Bocking did, "for the State that my Wife is in of Blindness I am forst to have me to Do for Uss" (463). More often, of course, the mother's role is given to the eldest daughter, as in the case of Samuel White in Halstead, reporting that "my eldest Daughter who is now fit for service is (much against her inclination) obliged to keep at home on account of my wives inability to Do for the Family as our Child more than a year & half old is still unable to stand alone" (252). His eldest daughter was then fourteen years old, but had already managed the household for about two years, as we know from an earlier letter (207).

In particularly critical cases the household needed extra help from outside, which had to be paid for. The case of David and Sarah Rivenall may again be quoted here. In February 1829, Sarah wrote that he was "again suffering under [h]is Old Complaint he has several severe fits of late which has left him in so low and melancholy state that requires some one constantly to mind him which prevents me entirely from endeavouring for support for my Children" (265). At that time, she was pregnant. Three months later, it was David who wrote that she had given birth to two boys but was "in a dangerous state" so that he was "Obligd to have A Nurse" (275). Thomas Hall in Bermondsey in London was in a similar situation,

[...] for i have work to do but i am not able to do it for i have bean very ill and my Wife is had a bad Brest and not able to do for her self and famley [...] my wife expcets to be Confined evry day and i cant Get a nus [nurse] or for les then 4 shilen a weak (339).[24]

William Ardley in Kelvedon wrote that "my Wife and Child have been bad with the Bad Fever for some weeks [...] I have been Obige to have a Woman to do for my Family" (100). Assistance for women during the last weeks of their pregnancy or after delivery, especially when there had been problems, was a common form of poor relief.

Predictably, the death of a parent posed particularly hard problems. Thomas Albion in Cambridge lamented the "Unfortunate situation Which I have been placed In since the Loss of my Wife, being left with Four Small children and no person to take care of them, but by Hiring a Woman, and having to Maintain her has Hadded much to my present difficulties" (89). Needless to say that widows with children were not only far more numerous than widowers, but also a lot worse off. Susan Pitt, a widow in the parish of St Giles in Colchester, "being unable to maintain the expences any longer", went so far as to say that she was "going to break up House keeping [...], by which my Daughter Sarah Baxter a Girl at the Age of 15 Years will be entirely destitute of any person to look after her conduct". This announcement to give up the household needs to be seen in the context of her attempt at having her daughter taken care of by the overseers. She urged them to provide her daughter "an ass[y]lum in the poor house of the parish of St Botolph to which parish she belongs", not forgetting to mention that the daughter had "constant employ at the Silk factory at the Weekly Wages of 5s/. per week"(382).

In other cases, however, it seems to be genuine when people express the feeling that extraordinary hardship endangered the very existence of the household. Sarah Rivenall wrote in January 1825:

> [...] my Husband Is Weary Bad And Cannot help himself No more then A young Child And Cannot go Across the house if he Could gain [A th]ousand pound Neither Can he Go to bead nor Get up without A man to help him to Bead And From Bread I Cannot shift no for Now my husband is laid Aside All is Laid Aside with me therefore I must Surmit [your] Ge[ntel]m[en] [*paper torn*] mercy For if you Gentellmen do not please to help us we must Give up housekeeping For out of nothing thear Ca[n nothing be (?)][*paper torn*] Done. (142)

The question of housekeeping also relates to the material set-up and the physical space of the household. Again, the first thing which needs to be said is that pauper letters do not normally deal with people's dwellings and their furnishings, or with people's resources in terms of elementary material goods. They do, however, allow certain basic material standards to be assessed from the way in which people talk about the lack of goods apparently regarded as absolutely essential, even for the poorest people.

---

24. The case of the entire Hall family is described in detail by Sharpe, "Bowels of Compation".

Among the basic necessaries, shoes (and perhaps, by implication, stockings) stand out most clearly. Bare feet, especially bare feet of children in winter, signify a state of absolute deprivation, which was regarded as unbearable and utterly unjustifiable (322). Sufficient clothing for summer and winter were also seen as indispensable. Underwear, however, is only very rarely mentioned. Elizabeth Goodman, who lived in the London parish of Mile End Old Town, was exceptionally explicit when she stressed "how *much*, very *much* I am distress'd for under linen, stockings (of which I have but one pair, & those mended all over) & indeed wearing apparel of all sorts" (673). By contrast, outdoor clothes and shoes are mentioned more prominently. This is, of course, not simply because they are more important in physical terms for the protection of body, but also, and perhaps most particularly so, because they show a person's condition in the open, in public. Hence the deep feelings of shame expressed in letters reporting the pawning of outdoor clothes. In the letter just quoted, Elizabeth Goodman lamented that "I was oblig'd to put my only decent Gown in pledge to make up the money & have not had it in my power to redeem it since, & by that means have not been able to go out of doors to or even to a place of worship". A similar example is that of William King in Bethnal Green. In December 1830, he wrote: "Every Little Debt is Now Looked Up for and I am ashamed to Pass the doors Where I owe the Money"(37). A year later: "I owe Menny a Shilling Round the Places and our few Cloaths a[re] Mostly all out or My wife Might apear More tidey. I Lost My Best Coat a week or two a Go wich was in for 1^s..6^d [= 7.5p]" (51). It was normal for people to pawn their clothes to raise small sums of cash to redeem their debts. Another ten months later, King's "best coat" was again (or still?) with the pawnbroker: "we have a few old Cloaths Given to Us Now and then [...] My old Great Coat wich hides the Rufull tokens of want and Poverty – will take 2/6 [= 12.5p] to Redeem" (54).

Within the physical bounds of the household, individual possession of or access to particular goods seems to have been less important. For example, George Craddock wrote from Westminster that his children had no shoes and that there was only one sheet, one coverlet and two blankets for the whole family. This, he said, was not enough any longer since "our Children are Grown to[o] Big altogether to Sleep in the Same bed with us we want to Make up another Place for them to Sleep in and Cannot do it without Alittle help" (489). Thus, he was obviously thinking of one bed for his wife and himself and another one for the children. But he did not regard individual bedlinen, let alone an individual bed, as necessary for each member of his family.

This is not to say that the poor were of necessity lacking in more precious objects altogether. In fact, recent research on the material possessions of the poor undertaken by Peter King, using pauper inventories from Essex in the eighteenth and early nineteenth centuries, has even found such items as looking-glasses, clocks, pictures, and mahogany and walnut furniture in the households of the poor.[25] To a certain extent, this picture is also confirmed by the evidence to be found in pauper letters. Some of them mention silver spoons, watches and rings (67, 288). Typically enough, however, such luxury items are only referred to when people had been forced to pawn them in order to raise cash. This means that the actual physical possession of such goods was often suspended. The "best coat" or the wife's ring were not constantly worn. They also served as small capital. After all, pawning was the most common source of credit among the working classes well into the twentieth century.[26]

While clothes and private luxury items might therefore be given away by the poor themselves, their household goods were normally taken away by others. The most frequent form of this was the seizure by the landlord of the "goods and chattels" of people who had run into arrears in rent. This is no wonder, given the substantial increases in rents during the period under discussion.[27] In numerous cases, however, people succeeded in preventing the threatened seizure of their household goods by obtaining assistance from the overseers of their home parish. The granting of a lump sum of 10 shillings (= 50p) or £1 was a common practice in such cases, and of course the accounts of threatening procedures as given in pauper letters need to be seen against that background. On the other hand, the poor did have a good point here, since their situation was indeed likely to get even worse through the loss of their goods. This was particularly true when tools or working utensils were involved, as in the case of John Spearman in London: "I am expecting Some work about a week or A fortnight time but the most of my tools are in pledge and I hope you will be so kind as to let me have A trifle as Soon as possible to redeem them" (71). But there are also cases where the creditor himself gave in. A particularly vivid account is given by George Watson in Shoreditch who reported that "when the Gent[n] & his two Men Came into my Place and saw me Ill and my Chilldren almost Naked Looking Round at they Things says he Those things are not worth my Taking" (282).

FAMILIAL ARRANGEMENTS

In the instances quoted so far, most families consisted of a married couple with children. In some cases, the family had lost a parent and been augmented by people not related to the household head, such as a paid nurse. But in the standard classification of family forms suggested by Laslett, such

25. Peter King, "Pauper Inventories and the Material Lives of the Poor in the Eighteenth and Early Nineteenth Centuries", in Hitchcock *et al.*, *Chronicling Poverty*, pp. 178–183.
26. See Paul Johnson, *Saving and Spending: The Working-Class Economy in Britain 1870–1939* (Oxford, 1985), pp. 165–188.
27. Feinstein, "Pessimism Perpetuated", pp. 638–640.

forms are also counted under the nuclear family.[28] Complex family forms, however, are also in evidence in pauper letters. In fact, as these records reveal, there were often good reasons for poorer people to form co-resident groups extending beyond the "normal" family. This suggests that the widely accepted view, again first expressed by Laslett, according to which the nuclear family was particularly prevalent among the poor, may have to be reconsidered.

Perhaps the most typical form of an extended family household encountered in pauper letters is that where an unmarried women with an illegitimate child resided with her parents. An illegitimate child had a settlement in his or her own right, on the basis of which the mother could claim relief from the parish in which the child had been born, irrespective of her own settlement or that of her husband, in case she later got married to another man than the child's father. Living in with her parents thus had a double advantage. The grandparents, or more typically the grandmother, could look after the child when the young mother went out to work. At the same time, the parochial allowance for the child could benefit the entire household. Otherwise, that is when the mother lived on her own, the allowance might have to be used for putting the child out with other people to enable the mother to work.

Interestingly enough, the possible advantages for young single mothers of living with their parents were also seen by the overseers responsible for the relief of illegitimate children. The best documented cases are those where they shared the interest in the arrangement of such extended families in order to "push" such children to other places. Thus, early in 1821, the overseers of the parish of St Botolph in Colchester sent Hannah Watson and her newborn child to Shoreditch in London, where they were taken in by her parents. Her father, George Watson, sent a long letter to Colchester in which he fiercely protested against this – not because his daughter had been sent to him, but because she had been sent without previous notice. He also said "it Surprizes me that a woman with an Infant Child only 6 Weeks old and that In the middle of Winter should take such a Journey it is a Providence she has not Suffer.d Siverely for it". With respect to the household arrangement he pointed out that "if Sir she has House room with me it is as much as I can do for her she and her Infant is Sleeping along with 2 of my Girls on a very small bed I may say all of them Crippled". Having thus made his family's precarious situation clear, he went on to bargain:

My Daughter Informs me Sir you have Propos.d allowing her 4s [= 20p] Per Week

28. Peter Laslett; "Introduction", in Peter Laslett and Richard Wall (eds), *Household and Family in Past Time* (Cambridge, 1972), pp. 23–44; E.A. Hammel and Peter Laslett, "Comparing Household Structure over Time and between Cultures", *Comparative Studies in Society and History*, 16 (1974), pp. 73–109.

with Respect I beg leave to say that she and the Child Cannot Subsist on it. she has tried it since she has been home it will Scarcely Procure her half support as she ought to have as a Woman Suckling a Child if *Sir* you will Please to allow her another Shilling she will be humbly thankfull (320).

Unfortunately, the parish records of St Botolph, Colchester, provide no clue as to whether George Watson's attempt at having the allowance for his grandchild increased was met with success. But it is clear that she did receive support during the following years. In May 1827, George Watson wrote again. His daughter and her child were still living with him, and he acknowledged that they had received 4 shillings per week. But that allowance had been reduced to 2 shillings (= 10p) and "a few Shillings Now and then" which he said was insufficient. He went on to point out that "if it was not for me she & Child Must starve", and concluded that they would have to return to St Botolph's parish in Colchester unless their allowance was increased to 2s 6d (= 12.5p):

I donot wish to send her and Child down to you without first writeing to you and haveing yr awnswer but if it is your Pleasure not to do a Little More for her they Must Come down [...] if you would Please to allow her 6d [= 2.5p] a Week more and send her a few shillings to Gett herself and Child a few Nessasaries (352).

Typically enough, the allowance was increased by 6d (= 2.5p), as is evident from his next letter of November 1827, in which he again pleaded for some additional relief "to gett a few Nessasarys such as a Pr of shoes for herself and child a bit of Linnen and and a flanell Peticoat those are the things she wants" (359). Again, the next letter, sent a month later and signed in the names of both George and Hannah Watson, reveals that the request was met favourably (360). George Watson's further letters, stretching until July 1828, leave no doubt that his daughter and grandchild received regular support from Colchester (368, 372, 373, 376, 378).

Arthur Tabrum received an allowance of 1s 6d (= 7.5p) per week for his stepson Arthur Good, the illegitimate child of his wife Ann (née Good). In this case, the self-confident tone in which he approached the overseers is particularly remarkable:

[...] whilst I Keep him I shall expect to be Paid for it, and If I do not receive any remuneration, I shall take him before the Lord Mayor, and see what is to be done, and whilst you make me keep him you are imposing upon a Man that is hardly able to support his own, it was the agreement of the Parish to allow the 1^{s}6^d [= 7.5p] if I took him therefore I have a right to it [...] if the Parish Does not Pay me I shall put it into Court, as I have had advice about it [...] when I am keeping all the expense i can of the Parish and working hard for a Living, not to be assited in a small trifle more to maintain that I have no business to Do myself (171).

Elderly people are also reported to have lived with their married children or other kin who looked after them. Elizabeth Reilly wrote from Westminster to Rayleigh:

[...] my Mother [...] is living with me and has done for sevn Years I have ben much Afflected and through that so many expenses which renders me incapable of keeping her any longer without Sum Allowance from her parish [...] She is now Eighty Years of age and very lame through one of her Legs being very bad [...] let me know what you Gentlemen will allow her or I must be under the painful necessity of sending her home to her Parish (662).

It is on similar lines that the forming of extended households was discussed, where people said they would be prepared to take in an elderly relative, but needed financial assistance. Thus, Elizabeth Philbrick wrote to Chelmsford:

I have Lived 38 years in the Parish of Wivenhoe and brought up a Famaly and paid Rates and Taxes till now I am 68 years old and am not able to do it no Longer I am now Oblight to Call on the Parish [...] I have a Daughter that will take me if you Gentlemen will be so good as to allow me something a week (269).

Similar suggestions were put to the overseers concerning the taking in or keeping of grown-up brothers and sisters (390, 409).

Without further research making fuller use of other parish records, it is impossible to say whether or not it was exceptional that parish officers gave financial support to such arrangements. However, the cases witnessed in pauper letters, which display the motives, interests and options of the various parties involved (the poor, their relatives and the parish officers), perhaps more clearly than most other records, strongly suggest that publicly-funded domestic care of elderly paupers (and of helpless people) by their relatives was probably far more widespread than has hitherto been assumed. Many parish officers seem to have agreed when suggestions of that kind were put to them, since they knew only too well that communal support of private care at home incurred far lower costs than the institutional care of old people.[29]

This contention is further supported by cases in which the parish authorities supported the care of an elderly bedridden pauper by paying someone – be he or she a relative or not – to live with and look after the old person in his or her household. Ann Thudgett, who lived in the London parish of St Giles, was looked after by her niece. She had received a weekly allowance of 3s 6d (= 17.5p) from her home parish, Steeple Bumpstead, for some time, which was handed over to her (or to her niece?) by a contact man, a certain Mr Earl. But apparently the allowance had then been reduced, because when she wrote to her parish she asked for Mr Earl to be instructed to hand her the full amount of 3s 6d (= 17.5p) as before. This, she said, was what she needed,

[...] for I canot live hear and Starve as I am a Poor Oflic[t]ed woman and Cannot

29. For a thoughtful discussion of the provision for the elderly under the Old Poor Law, see Pat Thane, "Old People and Their Families in the English Past", in Martin Daunton (ed.), *Charity, Self-Interest and Welfare in the English Past* (London, 1996), pp. 113–138.

work for my Living and likewise that my Nece has to dress and un dress me and has had for years gentelmen Mary Ann Page I am Ann Trudgett['s] Nese I have don for my poor oflic[t]ed old a[u]nt for years with your assistance I have Boarded lodg wash and Every other thing that Laid in my Pour for 6d [= 2.5p] per day (85).

This letter is also interesting with respect to the question of authorship and thus of the power of the poor to express themselves – which, as we have said, is by no means the same as the ability to write, but also includes the power to arrange for a letter to be written by someone else. Thus, the letter from Mary Ann Page begins by speaking in the person of her aunt Ann Thudgett, but then the narrative subject changes precisely at the point where the text turns to the niece. Reading it, one is tempted to imagine the situation in which it was written, with Mary Ann Page at first drawing up what Ann Thudgett told (or even dictated to?) her (or what she invoked her aunt to be saying where in fact she was writing it all by herself?), and then explicitly continuing in her own words.

All this is not to say that public assistance to the private care of elderly people was automatically given under the Old Poor Law. In fact, in the last case the issue was obviously a matter of debate between their relatives and the parish officers, since the overseers of Steeple Bumpstead were trying to withhold the allowance for the elderly lady (87). Yet even such cases sit somewhat uneasily with the notion of social isolation as a typical concomitant of poverty in old age, an idea that has become prominent in recent research on the history of poverty. Paul Slack, for instance, in his masterly survey of poverty in Tudor and Stuart England, has written to this effect: "A lonely old age was the lot of most of the labouring poor".[30] By contrast, pauper letters reveal cases in which elderly women in receipt of poor relief actually lived with their children, or conversely, that the children, as household heads, received assistance towards the keeping of their living-in relatives. And it is obvious that these cases support the suggestion long ago made by Hans Medick that the formation of complex households could be understood as a means for the labouring classes of redistributing poverty through the system of family and kinship – and, as we should add, with the assistance of the local welfare system.[31]

Middle-class observers who showed themselves shocked that the poor had their care of parents and other elderly relatives publicly funded in this way and who denounced the "deficiencies of parental and filial affection" among

30. Paul Slack, *Poverty and Policy in Tudor and Stuart England* (London, 1988), p. 85.
31. Hans Medick, "The Proto-Industrial Family Economy: The Structural Function of Household and Family during the Transition from Peasant Society to Industrial Capitalism", *Social History*, 1 (1976), pp. 308–309. For a general discussion of the demographic implications of such household arrangements, see Sokoll, *Household and Family Among the Poor*, pp. 289–293; Richard Smith, "Charity, Self-Interest and Welfare: Reflections from Demographic and Family History", in Daunton, *Charity, Self-Interest and Welfare*, pp. 23–50.

the labouring classes,[32] should, of course, have known better. The simple truth is that most elderly people in poverty could hardly expect their children to support them, given the latter's responsibilities for their own offspring. The dilemma in which they found themselves was neatly expressed in 1810 by Rachel Shoregh in a letter from Bethnal Green: "my Children are all married and got familys which these dear times they have as much as they can do to support and therefore are not able to assist me" (397).

STRATEGIC ARGUMENTS

Pauper letters were written by people who, however much they might have been suffering from destitution and been driven into despair, still found a way to express their most pressing needs. In presenting their cases, they reveal intriguing details about their living conditions, their attitudes and their expectations. Because the accounts they give often extend beyond what would seem to be necessary or appropriate for the immediate purpose, the letters provide unique insights into their daily struggle for survival and even allow occasional glimpses into their private lives. In fact, it is perhaps such unintentional details more than anything else which are particularly rewarding in analysing the substantive record of pauper letters, as we have tried to show in the previous sections, focusing on the themes of work and trade, householding and familial arrangements.

However, as the examples quoted in the last section have shown particularly clearly, in people's effort to make a living, even the organization of the family could be a matter of negotiation with the overseers. In order to round off our discussion, it is therefore appropriate to leave those thematic fields and return to the specific bargaining position from which the poor formulated their letters. Looking at the evidence from that angle, the question is not so much *what* people put forward in presenting their case, as *how* they used the account of their case to posit a claim. We want to unravel their strategic considerations in the negotiation of relief.

The letter writers use a wide range of "speech" forms, each of which corresponds to a specific social habitus. Some invest apologetic phraseology and deferential rhetoric, others prefer simple statements in plain prose. Some utter a desperate outcry, while others engage in self-conscious protest. It is tempting, of course, to assume that certain forms were more successful in obtaining relief than others. But that assumption is misleading for two reasons. First, it is typical for many letter writers not to opt for one particular form of writing but rather to combine defensive with offensive gestures. Second, even if those pieces which are more or less clear-cut are compared with respect to the response they received from the overseers, there appears

32. *Poor Law Report of 1834*, p. 115.

to be no consistent association. The modest request can be rejected, just as the most imposing demand may be granted.

What seems to be more promising here is to look once more at the strategic position in which people found themselves; or, more precisely, at the way in which that position was in itself used as an argument. As we have seen, pauper letters typically came from people who did in fact receive poor relief from their parish even though they resided in another parish. This put them in strong bargaining position. They knew that their removal was unlikely, because it would cause more trouble for their home parish (and for their host parish as well, which however need not concern us here) than the administration of nonresident relief.

The disadvantage of their "coming home" was indeed the key strategic argument in the negotiations with the overseers. It was brought forward in various forms. One form was to stress the better employment opportunities in the host parish, especially in cases where lack of work could be said to be only temporary. Thomas Cooper in Woolwich, for example, had fallen ill and asked the overseers,

> [...] to send me a Present Relief or else I shall be Oblidge'd to Apply to the Overseers of Woolwich Parish and as soon as I get better be passed home which may be Avoiead as I hope to get better for I have work to do as soon as I am Able to do it and Possable I my shortly return to it again (138).

Sarah Withnell in Bethnal Green reported that:

> [...] the Silk Weaven is So bad I can get but little Work at present I must give up My room and throw my Self upon the parrish to bring me and the Children home (which I should be greved to my hert to do for various Reasons) for as the Silk Weaven is expected to go much better In 2 or 3 months (287).

Elderly people felt that the question of employment was less important. George Rowe in Bocking pointed out that "to Leve the place will Not be No adwantage to you as I am Between 60 and 70 years of Age and I find I am Not fitt to Do Good Worke" (558). In this case, then, the argument was that it made no difference where people resided so that they might as well be left to stay in their host parish. Others took a more positive stance, stressing the psychological advantages of remaining in their familiar surroundings. William James in Chelmsford declared "I should wish to spend, the remainder of my Days, where I am, it cannot be long, E'r my head, must be laid in the dust" (484).

Another argument, which we have already encountered above in the case of David Rivenall and of other people, was not simply to point out the comparative advantages of living in the host parish over being removed but to threaten to "come home". Benjamin Brooker in Ipswich, put it succinctly: "And you May if you Please Send the ten Shillings Pr week as We Greatly Want it if you Do not think propper to Send it We Will Come home"

(506). The argument could be made more powerful by referring to the expected high cost of relief at home. Mary Taylor in Hadleigh (Suffolk), the widow who was longing for a "peice of cloth to make my Children some shirts", was particularly explicit. The payment of her weekly allowance ("the money which is my due") of 4 shillings (= 20p) had been delayed several times, and if it were not sent regularly in future, she was "determined to come home into the [Poor]House". She went on: "then instead of paying me eight shillings a week you will have to pay four or five shillings a head for us". And as if this point were still insufficient, she declared that she had sought legal advice and ended her letter by referring to a court case at the Assizes in Bury St Edmunds where a pauper had won a similar case (322).

This letter is remarkable. The tone in which Mary Taylor addressed her parish (St Botolph in Colchester) is as self-confident as her arguments appear to be well-informed and well-founded. Admittedly, the reference to the legal case is not precise. But the estimate of the amount of indoor relief her parish would have to face after her return is probably pretty accurate. Unfortunately, there is no evidence on the costs of maintaining paupers within workhouses for the time when she wrote her letter (May 1821). But if we regard the nearest figure available (for 1802) as a reasonable second-best, it appears that in the county of Essex weekly expenses for indoor relief did in fact amount to 5 shillings (=25p) per head.[33] It looks as though the overseers of St Botolph were forced to accept her point. Precisely how much the total costs for the indoor relief of her family would have been is unknown, since the number of her dependent children is not given. But we do know that two months after her letter her regular allowance was increased to 8 shillings (= 40p) per week. It was later again reduced, first to 6 shillings (= 30p) and then to 4 shillings (= 20p), but she received regular assistance at least until December 1826 (322).

Finally, there is the argument of the trouble involved in the procedure of removal itself. On 5 February 1824, Samuel Hearsum, in the London parish of St Marylebone, wrote to the overseers of Chelmsford:

According to promise I Expected a line from you before now to lit me Know Wether the Gent[n] of the Committee p[l]ease to allow me a small Trifle weekly, I think it very hard as I have pay[d] so much into the poors fund to be Forsed in to the Workhouse for the Triflon sum of 1[s]:6[d] [= 7.5p] per week, which I will Endevour to make shift with, Gentalmen If not I hope you will be so good as to let me know wether you would pay Mr French to bring me Down or to Appley to Marylebone Parish to Pass me home which will be very Expenceiv as I Am not Able to Walk

33. Parliamentary Papers, 1803–1804, XIII, *Abstract of the Returns Relative to the Expense and Maintenance of the Poor*, p. 108 (yearly workhouse expenses per inmate roughly £14). That figure, which refers to 1802, would appear to be a sound proxy, given that total poor relief expenditure in Essex (indoor plus outdoor relief) were roughly the same in both 1802 and 1821, amounting to £0.8 per head (which was relatively low in the long run). See D.A. Baugh, "The Cost of Poor Relief in South-East England, 1790–1834", *Economic History Review*, 28 (1975), p. 56 (Fig. 3).

I Almost killed my self when I Came Down last, and I never should have reached
home If I had not meet with a Good Friend I send by Coach to save Expencess
which I hope I shall have an Amswer by retrun of Coach and a few Shillings as I
Am in great Distress.

The letter needs a little explanation. Apparently the overseers of Chelmsford
had told Samuel Hearsum that they were no longer prepared to assist him
in London and that if he wished further relief he would have to enter the
workhouse in Chelmsford. In his response, he made three points. First, he
showed himself amazed that there should be so much ado about an allowance amounting to the "trifling sum" of 1s 6d. Second, he pointed out that
as a parishioner of Chelmsford he used to pay poor rates when he had been
better off, so that he now felt entitled to relief. Third, he made it clear that
he was not prepared to "come home" voluntarily, which meant that his
conveyance or removal was going to be a troublesome and expensive affair.

This case is particularly interesting when compared to those encountered
so far. Unlike Susan Pitt or Mary Taylor, Samuel Hearsum did not even
insinuate that he could ever make positive use of the workhouse. He simply
loathed it, and was shocked that he might be subjected to what came to be
known as the "workhouse test" under the New Poor Law. Next, Mr French,
the man mentioned in the middle of the letter, was that coachman travelling
between Chelmsford and London who handed out the allowances to the
Rivenalls and several other Chelmsford paupers living in London. And
finally, on his journey to London in December 1823, on behalf of the select
vestry of Chelmsford, John Sheppee had not only visited the Rivenalls, but
also called on Samuel Hearsum. According to Sheppee's report, Hearsum
was then aged 71 and sold tea on commission which brought him 6 shillings
(= 30p) per week. But his rent alone was 2s 6d (= 15p) per week, and he
was indebted with £11 to his former master. He used the allowance he
received from Chelmsford to repay his debt. Sheppee gives a vivid account
of their conversation: "I told him that as I did not consider that the Parish
of Chelmsford were bound to pay his debts, no further allowance would be
given him. – his answer was 'Then I must come down'". As a matter of
fact, Samuel Hearsum does not seem ever to have turned up in Chelmsford.
He did not have to, since his relief was continued. However, this was not –
or rather, not only – the result of his threat to "come down" as expressed
in that conversation and then again in his letter sent two months later. For
what he did not know is that Sheppee, on his part, had closed his report to
the select vestry with the telling remark: "from appearances I think 1s/
[= 5p] pr week would prevent him from coming home" (110).

This assessment is exceptionally explicit. But otherwise there is nothing
special about it. For the irony that Hearsum must have thought that *he* had
got his own way against the parish officers of Chelmsford, where in fact he
had only kicked at an open door, does not mean that *they* had won the day.
On the contrary, it underlines the point on which our entire discussion has

been based, namely that pauper letters have emerged from cases in which the host parish and the home parish basically shared the pauper's interest in not being removed. Pauper letters need not only to be seen in that context – they are in themselves part of that particular situation. In particular cases, it might even be said that this peculiar convergence of interests led to a balance of forces between the overseers on the one hand and the pauper on the other.

Whether or not one wants to go as far as this, the conclusion seems plausible that the poor had considerable room for strategic manoeuvring. The Old Poor Law was not only a measure of social control. It also provided an institutional platform on which the labouring poor could effectively express their needs, pursue their interests and establish their claims.[34] This was not least the understanding of the Poor Law by the poor themselves, of which pauper letters probably provide the richest record of all. These letters remind us that poverty is not a condition but a social relationship. The poor are always forced to extreme efforts to make a living. But there are historical situations where they possess the opportunity, at least to some extent, to negotiate a living.

34. For similar conclusions with respect to the actual practice of relief in London even under the New Poor Law, see Lees, "Survival of the Unfit", pp. 69–71, 87–88.

International Review of Social History 45 (2000), pp. 47–69
© 2000 Internationaal Instituut voor Sociale Geschiedenis

"It Is Extreme Necessity That Makes Me Do This":[1] Some "Survival Strategies" of Pauper Households in London's West End During the Early Eighteenth Century*

JEREMY BOULTON

INTRODUCTION

Although research on survival strategies is still at a relatively early stage, there are clearly some areas where there is considerable difference in emphasis placed by historians on the relative importance of particular "expedients" deployed by the poor *in extremis*.[2] There is, for example, uncertainty regarding the amount of support given by neighbours as opposed to relatives. There is some historical contention, too, over the importance to the elderly of care by their children, as opposed to alternative sources of maintenance such as earnings, charity and especially the formal institutions of poor relief. After all, in the early modern period the principle source for a study of the survival strategies of poor people is always likely to be the records of poor

---

* I would like to thank Tim Hitchcock and Leonard Schwarz for their comments on earlier versions of this paper.
1. This quotation, the spelling of which has been modernized, comes from a letter "found with a Child at Mr Defountain's door in Blew Cross Street on Wednesday night June 29 1709 between 12 & one a clock & taken up by me Robert Mason, Overseer", Westminster Archives Centre [hereafter, WAC] , F5002/fos 165aʳ–165aᵛ.
2. Robert Jütte, *Poverty and Deviance in Early Modern Europe* (Cambridge, 1994), especially pp. 83–99. As always, much of the literature is summarized expertly, or anticipated, in Paul Slack's seminal *Poverty and Policy in Tudor and Stuart England* (Harlow, 1988), esp. pp. 73–85. See also the contributions in the special issue of *Social History*, 18 (1993); and Marco H.D. van Leeuwen, "Logic of Charity: Poor Relief in Pre-industrial Europe", *Journal of Interdisciplinary History*, 24 (1994), pp. 589–613; Catharina Lis and Hugo Soly, "Neighbourhood Social Change in West European Cities: Sixteenth to Nineteenth Centuries", *International Review of Social History*, 38 (1993), pp. 1–30. Another particularly insightful contribution relating to the nineteenth-century city is that by Peter Mandler, "Introduction", in Peter Mandler (ed.), *The Uses of Charity: The Poor on Relief in the Nineteenth-Century Metropolis* (Philadelphia, PA, 1990), pp. 1–37; Catharina Lis, *Social Change and the Labouring Poor: Antwerp, 1770–1860* (New Haven, CT, 1986), pp. 150–162. For another comprehensive and insightful discussion see, Peregrine Horden, "Household Care and Informal Networks: Comparison and Continuities from Antiquity to the Present", in Peregrine Horden and Richard Smith (eds), *The Locus Of Care: Families, Communities, Institutions, and the Provision of Welfare Since Antiquity* (London, 1998), pp. 21–67. For a modern study see, Donald W. Foster, *Survival Strategies of Low-Income Households in a Colombian City* (Urbana, IL, 1975), a published Ph.D. thesis, a work of urban anthropology which uncovers a range of survival strategies very familiar to early modern historians.

relief or charitable agencies and institutions.[3] The obvious danger here is that historians of poor relief consistently overestimate the importance of such relief to the poor.[4] Both Richard Wall and Pat Thane, using evidence from nineteenth- and twentieth-century England, for example, have demonstrated that the elderly received far more support from relatives than has been realized. Professor Thane has argued that this situation is unlikely to have been new.[5] Other historians, however, are much more sceptical over the value of intergenerational flows of wealth from children to elderly parents.[6]

This essay is avowedly experimental in character in that its main aim is to reconstruct with as much detail as possible some of the *alternative* survival strategies of the pre-industrial metropolitan poor. This is not intended, then, merely to be an essay on the running of the poor relief system or on how that system impacted on the lives of the poor, a subject which is being treated in depth elsewhere.[7] The article must begin by assessing briefly the

3. Valuable work can also be done using exceptionally detailed household listings of the poor, although survival strategies have usually to be inferred from patterns of co-residence. See, Margaret Pelling, *The Common Lot: Sickness, Medical Occupations and the Urban Poor in Early Modern England* (Harlow, 1998), pp. 145–148, 152. Pelling prefers "expedient" to "strategy" to "reduce the connotation of deliberate (and free) choice"; Thomas Sokoll, *Household and Family Among the Poor: The Case of Two Essex Communities in the Late Eighteenth and Early Nineteenth Centuries* (Bochum, 1992). Sokoll published some preliminary observations in his, "The Pauper Household Small and Simple? The Evidence from Listings of Inhabitants and Pauper Lists of Early Modern England Reassessed", *Ethnologia Europaea*, 17 (1987), pp. 25–42.

4. For similar sentiments see Tim Hitchcock, "Habits of Industry: The Eighteenth-Century English Workhouse Movement", (unpublished typescript, 1993).

5. Pat Thane, "Old People and Their Families in the English Past", in M. Daunton (ed.), *Charity, Self-Interest and Welfare in the English Past* (London, 1996), pp. 113–138; Pat Thane, "The Family Lives of Old People", in Paul Johnson and Pat Thane (eds), *Old Age from Antiquity to Post-Modernity* (London, 1998), pp. 180–210, the quotations are from p. 206; Richard Wall, "Relationships Between the Generations in British Families Past and Present", in Catherine Marsh and Sara Arber (eds), *Families and Households: Divisions and Change* (London, 1992), pp. 63–85. See also Richard Wall, "Beyond the Household: Marriage, Household Formation and the Role of Kin and Neighbours", *International Review of Social History*, 44 (1999), pp. 55–67.

6. Richard M. Smith, "The Structured Dependence of the Elderly as a Recent Development: Some Sceptical Historical Thoughts", *Ageing and Society*, 4 (1984), pp. 409–428. Richard Wall's work suggests that much of the help received by the elderly in the nineteenth century was not in a financial form.

7. This paper derives from the author's long-term reconstruction of the lives of the poor in London's West End, based on a biographical reconstruction of all those who received pensions from the parish. This will appear as *The Making of the London Poor* (Manchester, forthcoming). For preliminary forays see, Jeremy Boulton, "Going on the Parish: The Parish Pension and its Meaning in the London Suburbs, 1640–1724", in Tim Hitchcock, Peter King and Pamela Sharpe (eds), *Chronicling Poverty: The Voices and Strategies of the English Poor, 1640–1840* (Basingstoke, 1997), pp. 19–46; *idem*, "The Poor Among the Rich", in Paul Griffiths and Mark Jenner (eds), *Londinopolis* (Manchester, 2000, forthcoming); *idem*, "The Most Visible Poor in England? Constructing Pauper Biographies in Early Modern Westminster", *Westminster Historical Review*, 1 (1997), pp. 13–18.

role of institutional poor relief, but it then attempts to uncover the alternative survival strategies used by paupers in the parish.

THE LOCAL CONTEXT: LONDON'S WEST END IN THE EARLY EIGHTEENTH CENTURY

It is necessary to begin with a brief description of the parish of St Martin's as it had developed by the early eighteenth century. By 1700 the parish had been completely developed as part of the massive growth in London's West End that occurred after the Restoration. Its population had mushroomed from about 18,000 people in 1660 to something like 45,000 by 1715, a figure which does not include those inhabitants of parishes split off from St Martin's parish in 1686. About one-quarter of the parish's population was lost in 1724 on the formation of the new parish of St George, Hanover Square. St Martin's contained the royal palaces of Whitehall and St James's, and many government offices and departments. Proximity to the courts and government offices meant that the social structure of the parish was unusual, to say the least, with a significant, if declining, number of titled residents, living in purpose-built streets and squares in the parish. Otherwise, its occupational structure was dominated by the provision of a range of services (from domestic service and carriage to medical and legal advice) to courtiers and officials, some luxury manufactures and a significant military presence. The focus on the early eighteenth century is a further complicating factor since there can be little doubt that the large-scale wars against France (1689–1714) in this period had a direct impact on the lives of the poor. What is not known at this stage is whether the damage done to pauper household economies by the recruitment of married men into the armed forces was outweighed by the greater employment opportunities, for both men and women, provided by the consequent reduction in the pool of surplus labour in the metropolitan economy.

The parish of St Martin's operated what might be called a "classic" English poor relief system from 1601, based on the collection and distribution of the proceeds of a compulsory parish rate by the overseers of the poor. Smaller sums of money were distributed by the churchwardens, who kept separate accounts. From the late seventeenth century, local justices became much more directly involved on a daily basis in the administration of this relief. Their greater involvement stemmed from the powers given to them by the English laws of settlement and from other Poor Law legislation designed to tighten up the granting of public relief.[8] Until 1724, most of

8. For this legislation, see Paul Slack, *The English Poor Law, 1531–1782* (Basingstoke, 1990). It seems likely that the examination books were initiated by a statute of 1692, which ordered that no names were to be added to parish pension lists unless authorized by a Justice of the Peace. A list of paupers drawn up in 1707 (which omits orphans) contains a number of entries which suggest that pensioners lacking age information had entered the lists "before 1692"; WAC F4509.

the relief granted in the parish was so-called "outdoor" relief, with cash being paid to recipients in their own homes. The bulk of funds spent by the overseers was spent on regular payments to the parish pensioners and orphans, although over time increasing amounts of money were channelled to the so-called casual or "extraordinary" poor. Indoor relief was restricted to a short-lived attempt to erect a parish workhouse shortly after the Restoration and to the maintenance of around thirty parish almswomen who lived in purpose-built almshouses. All this changed in 1724 when the parish, in common with the neighbouring parish of St James and many others throughout England, took advantage of the so-called Workhouse Test Act of the previous year to try out a policy of *indoor* relief and built a large workhouse to house their poor. The erection of this parish workhouse went hand in hand with a dramatic curtailment of the payment of cash pensions to the parish poor living in their own homes.[9]

PAUPER SURVIVAL STRATEGIES: THE LIMITS OF PAROCHIAL RELIEF

Before considering the informal means deployed to survive in this urban environment, it is clearly necessary to arrive at some estimate of the degree to which paupers in need might be relieved by the parish. Too much space will not be spent on this, since the focus of this essay is intended to be on less formal sources of support. But clearly poor relief was valued. One finds, for example, paupers distorting the truth of their circumstances to the poor relief authorities in order to achieve a legal "settlement", and paupers petitioning the parish authorities for relief, deploying the expected conventions as to their personal probity, worth and reputation.[10] How *necessary*, then, were alternative sources of support? Surviving listings of the parish pensioners suggest that amongst the urban poor, severe "relievable" hardship was thought to have occurred only when individuals reached their sixties and seventies. The average age of those on regular parish pensions in 1707 was sixty-eight, in 1716 it was sixty-six.[11] Even then, parish pensions were granted to perhaps eight per cent or so of those in their sixties in the parish,

It seems likely that the two earlier examination books have been lost, since the second surviving book is entitled "This is the fourth Book"; WAC F5002/1.

9. Slack, *English Poor Law*, pp. 40–48. The best survey of the rise of indoor relief in early eighteenth-century England is Tim Hitchcock, "Paupers and Preachers: the SPCK and the Parochial Workhouse Movement", in Lee Davison, Tim Hitchcock, Tim Keirn and Robert B. Shoemaker (eds), *Stilling the Grumbling Hive: The Response to Social and Economic Problems in England, 1689–1750* (Stroud, 1992), pp. 145–166.

10. For this strategy, see Pamela Sharpe, "'The Bowels of Compation': A Labouring Family and the Law, c. 1790–1834", in Hitchcock, King, and Sharpe, *Chronicling Poverty*, pp. 87–108.

11. Calculated from WAC F4509, F4539.

and to perhaps fifteen per cent of those aged seventy or over.[12] Many of the elderly, of course, would have been comfortably off in this relatively wealthy parish but such figures do demonstrate that many elderly persons must have had to fend for themselves. This would have been especially true of elderly males since there was, as was usual in this period, a large surplus of women in the pensioned population.

Even those who received parish pensions, too, would, as is commonly recognized in the literature, probably have needed supplemental sources of support.[13] The average pension received in the early eighteenth century in this parish was between 1 shilling(s) and 6 pence(d) and 1s 8d a week, at a time when a building labourer would have earned about 2s a day or 12s in a six-day week. Unsurprisingly, therefore, we know that some pensioners were still working, even one Alice Evans, a woman said to be 107 years old, who was receiving one of the highest rates of pension, 10s a month, or 2s 6d a week, was in 1707 said to supplement that income by selling "fruit at Savoy Gate".[14] She only seems to have received that pension for just over a year, presumably near the end of her long life, between 1707 and 1708.[15]

Further evidence that alternative strategies were deployed even when poor relief was available derives from the fact that some paupers *preferred* to maintain themselves in their own dwellings rather than endure institutionalized relief. Diana Lothlane, for example, stayed for just one month in the parish workhouse and then "went out again to try to maintain herself" in 1725. We know a lot about her situation, for Diana had come to the notice of the local justices as early as 1708:

> Diana Lathlane says she knows not whether she is a Widow of Andrew Lathlane a fringe & lacemaker who was a housekeeper in Rose Street about 20 years ago in King James time [1685–1688], she says she or her husband never was housekeepers since, nor never lived out of the parish since but kept shop in Bedford Street in this parish & paid Taxes. She has no children to be provided for; she lives at

12. This has been estimated by inflating the number of pensioners in 1716 to take account of those whose ages were missing, and applying to a total population of 45,000 the age structure for eighteenth-century London estimated in John Landers, *Death and the Metropolis: Studies in the Demographic History of London, 1670–1830* (Cambridge, 1993), p. 180. The figures are minimum ones, since they take no account of any aged spouses, who were not usually listed, and the twenty-seven to thirty parish almswomen, who were also not listed.

13. Ian W. Archer, *The Pursuit of Stability: Social Relations in Elizabethan London* (Cambridge, 1991), p. 195, for example, after an exhaustive reconstruction of pauper budgets, concludes that the parish pension "was no more than an income supplement".

14. WAC F4509/9.

15. Peter Laslett's comment that "only a small proportion of persons in need, therefore, could have been completely and permanently dependent upon the community" seems amply borne out in this parish; Peter Laslett, "Family, Kinship and Collectivity as Systems of Support in Pre-industrial Europe: A Consideration of the 'Nuclear Hardship' Hypothesis", *Continuity and Change*, 3 (1988), pp. 153–175, 164.

Burdett's in Feather Ally, her husband went away about 7 year ago to the East Indias. He has been 10 year in the East Indias at the Fort of St George & is a merchant. She was married at Marylebone to Andrew Lothlain above 30 year ago. She has a Daughter Charlotte Lathlane – about 20 year old.[16]

Diana, then, claimed to have been married to a respectable housekeeper, paying taxes and keeping a shop. Her circumstances clearly declined after her husband left for the East Indies. From occupying a shop on a thorough-fare, Bedford Street, she was now lodging in Feather Ally. At the time of her examination she would have been in her very late fifties. Diana began receiving a pension from St Martin's ten years before her admittance into the workhouse. Her pension began at 1s 1d a week in 1714 and had risen to 2s before her admittance into the workhouse in 1725 at the advanced age of seventy-six.[17] Her case is valuable, since it demonstrates explicitly that there must have been a range of alternative survival strategies even to an aged pauperized widow, who had been receiving a regular parish pension. Diana must have perceived sources of income and support outside the parochial relief system with relatives, friends and/or from local employment oppor-tunities. That this was commonplace can be deduced from the fact that many pensioners chose to give up their pensions and attempted an indepen-dent existence rather than enter workhouses following a move to indoor relief in early eighteenth-century England.[18]

Even entering a parish workhouse, of course, did not mean permanent and utter dependence. Workhouses like that of St Martin's were usually "revolving doors": only about one-third of those admitted in St Martin's seem to have died in the institution. It is clear that this workhouse, like others in early modern Europe, played a part in local household survival strategies, being used as a temporary source of childcare and shelter by the local pauper population.[19] Most who left either departed voluntarily or were

16. WAC F5001/44.
17. WAC F4002/11 and the following overseers accounts: WAC F444/154, F445/148, F446/140, F447/153, F449/167, F451/180, F452/167, F454/159, F459a/220. Diana was listed in 1716 as a sixty-seven-year-old pensioner, F4539/43.
18. Tim Hitchcock has described how "at St. Margaret's, Westminster, 108 people were listed as receiving collection from the parish in 1726, all of whom were offered the house when it opened. Only forty-one people eventually entered, the rest giving up their weekly doles. At Tavistock in Devon, thirty-one people were listed on the poor books in 1747. When the parish opened a workhouse, seventeen of these refused to enter and lost their pensions", Hitchcock, "Habits of Industry".
19. For the notion that workhouses might play a central role in paupers' survival strategies, see Catharina Lis and Hugo Soly, "'Total Institutions' and the Survival Strategies of the Labouring Poor in Antwerp, 1770–1860", in Mandler, *Uses of Charity*, pp. 38–91. For an Italian example, see Giovanni Gozzini, "The Poor and the Life-Cycle in Nineteenth-Century Florence, 1813–59", *Social History*, 18 (1993), pp. 300–316. His Pia Casa took in "above all those expelled temporarily or definitively from their original nuclear families which were no longer able or willing to provide for their support"; *ibid.*, p. 313.

"taken out" by a surviving parent after a relatively short stay, which in a few cases was the same day, an indicator that some found the calculation between sentimental attachment and material hardship a desperately difficult one to resolve. It is noticeable that only six residents, out of 270 whose departure was described, were taken out by "friends". These might have been neighbours, although contemporary use of the word "friends" might include a degree of kinship.[20] Residence in an institution does *not*, of course, anyway preclude regular contact, help and support from the nearby family of those incarcerated, as is sometimes implied by the literature.[21] A century earlier, in Southwark, for example, the son-in-law and daughter of a deceased almshouse resident, Roger Cotton, petitioned the parish authorities for his effects, claiming that they had "been at great charges and expenses with him, by reason of providing things necessary for him, in time of his sickness and likewise for burying of him, which he desired might be by her mother in the church yard".[22] Just as kinship does "not stop at the front door", so kin ties are not shut out by the workhouse gate.[23]

Few households headed by young and middle-aged married couples, too, could expect *regular* relief from the parish. Single parents, usually single mothers, might be given childcare. When a child lost one or both of its parents, it might qualify for an orphan's pension, the money being paid to the orphan's carer. Orphans supported by the parish, however, formed a minuscule proportion of children in the appropriate age groups in the parish, in 1716, no more than one to two per cent of those aged ten and below. As Table 1 makes reasonably clear, most parish orphans in the early eighteenth century seem to have been cared for by family members, most often by the surviving mother or father. Only one-third of the parish orphans (which included surviving foundlings dropped in the parish) seem to have been cared for by professional parish nurses. Some orphans cared for by such nurses were probably returned to parents, or occasionally relatives, in the same way that children left in the workhouse were. Evidence that this latter practice was widespread in London comes from the "Returns from the Register of Parish Infant Poor" in 1778. The returns provide convincing confirmation that one widespread survival strategy amongst the poor was to jettison children, for a temporary period. Nearly half of all children

20. See, Diana O'Hara, "'Ruled by My Friends': Aspects of Marriage in the Diocese of Canterbury, c.1540–1570", *Continuity and Change*, 6 (1991), pp. 9–41; *idem, Courtship and Constraint: Rethinking the Making of Marriage in Tudor England* (Manchester, 2000), pp. 30–56.
21. Laslett, "Family, Kinship and Collectivity", p. 166. This assumption surely informs the famous English example cited in Peter Laslett, *Family Life and Illicit Love in Earlier Generations* (Cambridge, 1977), p. 60.
22. Jeremy Boulton, *Neighbourhood and Society: A London Suburb in the Seventeenth Century*, (Cambridge, 1987), p. 260.
23. The quotation is from Michael Anderson, *Family Structure in Nineteenth-Century Lancashire*, (Cambridge, 1971), p. 56.

Table 1. *Specified carers of parish orphans 1716*

Relationship to orphan	Number	Percentage
Sister	1	1.1
Grandmother	2	2.2
Uncle	3	3.3
Father and mother	4	4.3
Father	17	18.5
Nurse	31	33.7
Mother	34	37.0
Total	92	100.1

Source: WAC Pensioner listing, F4539

left on the parish aged six years and under, were ultimately returned to their parents.[24] The extent to which the parish paid for the maintenance of orphans cared for by the surviving parent marks the extent to which significant resources were directed at the early stages of married life.[25] It is noticeable that orphans' pensions were paid to only a handful of married couples (perhaps following a remarriage).

A proportion of parish orphans were foundlings, abandoned in the parish when parents were desperate. These were not necessarily illegitimate. Dorothy Shepheard, widow, who claimed that her late husband had sired *nineteen* children, for example, admitted that "being in great necessity soon after her said husbands death was forced to leave one of the said George Shepheard's Children upon the said [London] parish who received the same".[26] Nor is it necessarily the case that children were abandoned shortly after their birth. Ann Clark, recounted how she had borne a bastard child and,

> [...] that she kept the Child about 2 year *as long as she could* [my italics] & she being a Lodger against Cross Lane in Long Acre now the Sign of the Star & from thence [she was] carried to the prison, she left the said child at her lodging & so the same came to the parish".[27]

Many of those parents who abandoned young children on the parish intended to recover them, when their circumstances improved. As one mother wrote, "if ever God makes me able I will repair the charge & redeem

24. M. Dorothy George, *London Life in the Eighteenth Century* (Harmondsworth, 1966), p. 405.
25. This is a typical finding for the period before 1750. A large family was the smallest percentage "cause" of poverty in Norwich in 1570, and Salisbury in 1635; Slack, *Poverty and Policy*, p. 79.
26. To "leave a child on the parish" means to abandon a child as a foundling. This is not to be confused with applying for, or being granted, an orphan's pension. Parish orphans usually stayed with the surviving parent, if any. All foundlings, but only a minority of orphans, were cared for by professional parish nurses. In the accounts, foundlings and orphans are lumped together as the "parish orphans". Some foundlings can be identified from their surnames, which were often the names of the streets in which they were abandoned.
27. WAC F5001/35, 51, F5002/125.

the child with thanks to you for the Care".[28] Many of the children left with the London Foundling Hospital (founded 1739) carried identifying items to facilitate their later collection. Some of these foundlings, like those left on the parish, were not unwanted bastard children, but were legitimate "surplus" children left by destitute parents.[29] The point of all this is that the abandonment on a temporary or permanent basis of children by pauper households was the strategy, but the parish was, of course, by no means the only possible destination for such children.[30]

Couples, as opposed to single parents, "overburdened with young children", although a traditionally recognized object of charity and frequently listed as a separate category of pauper by writers on the subject, were *not* considered as deserving of regular pensions in this part of early eighteenth-century London.[31] There are a number of reasons why this may have been so. One is that relatively few pauper households in early eighteenth-century London would have contained large numbers of young children, given the lethal rates of infant and childhood mortality then prevailing. Another possibility may be that many couples, like many single parents, placed small children on relatives as a survival strategy.[32] We must clearly now look, as most paupers may have done, to sources of support outside the usual poor relief agencies.

SURVIVAL STRATEGIES: THE INFORMAL SECTORS

Individual examples of a range of household survival strategy cases can be found in St Martin's. A few paupers were recorded as getting a living as

28. WAC F5002/fo. 165aʳ. These letters left with foundlings in St Martin's are discussed, and reproduced in full, in the useful survey by Valerie Fildes, "Maternal Feelings Reassessed: Child Abandonment and Neglect in London and Westminster, 1550–1800", in Valerie Fildes (ed.), *Women as Mothers in Pre-industrial England: Essays in Memory of Dorothy McLaren* (London, 1990), pp. 139–178, (letters on pp. 153–155).

29. Between 1768 and 1772, some 15.5 per cent of successful petitioners to the London Foundling Hospital were married or widowed women; R.B. Outhwaite, "'Objects of Charity': Petitions to the London Foundling Hospital, 1768–72", *Eighteenth-Century Studies*, 32 (1999), pp. 497–510, 505.

30. For the hospital, see the important article by Adrian Wilson, "Illegitimacy and Its Implications in Mid-Eighteenth-Century London: The Evidence of the Foundling Hospital", *Continuity and Change*, 4 (1989), pp. 103–164. Wilson argues that "neither marital poverty nor orphaning led parents to take their children to the Foundling Hospital" (p. 135) and that most foundlings were illegitimate. Valerie Fildes has argued, conversely, that many foundlings of London and Westminster were "legitimate children whose parent(s) could not afford to feed another mouth"; Fildes, "Child Abandonment and Neglect", p. 157.

31. Smith, "Structured Dependence", p. 426, argued that this category, together with the elderly, "overwhelmingly dominate the bulk of recipients of relief in the Poor Law account books and censuses of the poor which survive from the sixteenth century".

32. Adrian Wilson suggests that in the event of a woman losing her partner whilst pregnant, or shortly after the birth, either the woman remarried or "a parent's own family rallied in support"; Wilson, "Illegitimacy and Its Implications", p. 136.

prostitutes or in "bawdry".[33] The poor can be found begging in the streets, crowding around the church for handouts from the collection money, accosting coaches, or pleading on the doorsteps of parish officials and other local worthies.[34] Many pauper household economies were clearly joint efforts, since women as well as men clearly worked, and worked in the range of occupations mostly familiar to early modern historians.[35] Poor women in St Martin's in the early eighteenth century are recorded selling newspapers, hawking fruit, eggs and oysters, teaching school, nursing children and the sick, keeping shops and drinking establishments, singing, washing gloves, lining clogs, sewing, making gloves (at which she was said to "work for her living"), cooking, cleaning chimneys and carrying water.[36] It is also clear that paupers might sacrifice living space to make ends meet. Some poor people took in lodgers, an important income supplement in the early modern city.[37] Others made considerable savings in rent by moving frequently to cheaper accommodation. A particularly common response to hard times was to leave a "house" where one might be an accredited respectable "housekeeper", liable to rates and probably with a lease, paying a sum of money to a nonresident landlord, by the year or at least by the quarter, and move in to cheaper "lodgings" with little or no security of tenure, which might be no more than a single room or even a cellar. As I argued some time ago, the high rates of residential mobility found in the early modern city are partly due to this further "survival strategy" of poor households.[38] It is rare to find this strategy articulated, but Francis Place, the "radical tailor of Charing Cross" did record, during the 1790s, the reasons for his local residential mobility within the area. In particular, he recalled taking "an unfurnished back room up two pairs of stairs at a chandlers shop in Wych Street". He remembered that "we paid four shillings a week for the room we quitted and two shillings for that we removed to. This was a savings of some importance to us".[39]

What happened when this economy of "makeshift and mend" failed? How useful were relatives and neighbours in the survival strategies of the poor? Can we uncover any evidence about the range of kin that paupers might draw on when destitution threatened? We can assume that the population of this West End suburb consisted mostly of first-generation migrants

33. WAC F5002/47.
34. Boulton, "Going on the Parish", pp. 26–33; *idem*, "The Poor Among the Rich".
35. Peter Earle, "The Female Labour Market in London in the Late Seventeenth and Early Eighteenth Centuries", *Economic History Review*, 42 (1989), pp. 328–353.
36. For the occupations listed here, see WAC F5001/38, 92, 100, 103, 115, 123, 131, 151, 160; F5002/28, 37, 42, 43, 59, 60, 74, 95, 101, 153.
37. Outhwaite, "'Objects of Charity'", p. 506.
38. Boulton, *Neighbourhood and Society*, p. 221. For the mobility of Londoners see also Wall, "Beyond the Household", pp. 62–64.
39. Mary Thale (ed.), *The Autobiography of Francis Place 1771–1854* (Cambridge, 1972), p. 111.

and contained a large shifting population of servants and lodgers. The circumstances of migration, we can further assume, must have distanced households and individuals from families of origin and produced lower levels of kin density than might be found in rural areas. Such kin networks as did exist, moreover, would be relatively transient.[40] Some aged paupers had no surviving children anyway.[41] None of this means that kin were not important sources of help and aid for the urban migrant. In the early seventeenth century approximately thirty-seven per cent of migrant women had kin present in London and just over one-fifth co-resided with them.[42] Studies of English kinship argue that *in extremis*, effective kin recognition might be extended beyond the "nuclear core", and succour might be provided and assistance sought within a system of "situational flexibility".[43]

In order to make some investigation of this difficult topic, the sources of help mentioned by paupers in two examination books of St Martins were analysed. This source cannot, unfortunately, give any sort of guide as to the *volume* of help received by paupers, because information on pauper support was mentioned only in passing and was not always relevant to one's settlement or request for poor relief. It is probable, too, that references to kin in the books were driven partly by the famous clause in the 1601 Poor Law statute which placed a clear obligation on parents, grandparents and children to maintain each other, if they were of "sufficient ability".[44] That such help was valued can be deduced from those comments made by paupers who explicitly said that they lacked support or relatives or "friends". Abigail Rumbold for example, left a letter for the grandmother of her abandoned one-year-old son, asking her to provide for him (Abigail had kept his older sister):

> I am not able to support myself, having neither money, any calling, or friends, much less am I able to support them, and I cannot see them starve, and I thank God that He has given me his grace to overcome the temptation I lay under to make away with them.

Abigail had made an unfortunate marriage. Her fascinating letter (dated May 1709) veers from plaintive appeals to thinly veiled threats, including an accusation that the grandmother had embezzled money from her first husband's estate. It ends with the comment that,

40. Boulton, *Neighbourhood and Society*, pp. 247–261.
41. Pamela Sharpe, "Survival Strategies and Stories: Poor Widows and Widowers in Early Industrial England", in Sandra Cavallo and Lyndan Warner (eds), *Widowhood in Medieval and Early Modern Europe* (Harlow, 1999), pp. 220–239, 225–226.
42. Vivien Brodsky Elliott, "Single Women in the London Marriage Market: Age, Status and Mobility, 1598–1619", in R.B. Outhwaite (ed.), *Marriage and Society: Studies in the Social History of Marriage* (London, 1981), pp. 81–100, 93.
43. David Cressy, "Kinship and Kin Interaction in Early Modern England", *Past and Present*, 113 (1986), pp. 38–69.
44. Thane, "Old People and their Families", p. 117.

> I think it is but highly reasonable that you should either keep your grandson (this present child Charles Rumbold) or some way or other provide for him; and if it be consistent with your natural affection (which you ought to have) and your present manner of living to send him to the parish you are the best judge of that.

There is no trace of any Charles Rumbold amongst the parish orphans, so perhaps the grandmother took in her grandson as requested.[45]

Justices also sometimes recorded those unfortunates who lacked such means of assistance. The unfortunate "Margaret Holemaid says she is the wife of John Holemaid a Taylor who was pressed into the foot service in my Lord Orkney's Regiment, she does not know any of his relations or kindred & never heard where any of them lived".[46] Joan Groom, a sixty-year-old widow had "3 children, but not in capacity to keep her", although a daughter was providing her with lodgings.[47] A poor crippled twenty-year-old woman, Ann Mann, "has no relations".[48] The seventy-year-old widow, Mary Inger, was granted a parish pension after testifying that "She has no Child nor friend, her husband Richard Inger was a Groom to King Charles".[49] There was sometimes an air of disapproval when local relatives were neglecting their responsibility to care for elderly parents, such as when Jane Heap a widow deposed that "she lodges near John Owen's in Moors yard – she has a son a musician who lives plentifully, Anthony Heap at the Red Lyon in Princes Street".[50] A few of the elderly, too, were unsure even about the whereabouts or even continued existence of their own children.[51]

Tables 2–4 represent an attempt to explore pauper sources of support beyond that of the parish. It should be stressed that the figures must be read as the absolute minimum level of support, given that one cannot assume that failure to mention support from family or friends means that

---

45. WAC F5002/169. One Charles Rumbold married an Abigail Gouch at St James's Duke Place, once a notorious centre of clandestine marriage, in 1706. Charles, their son, was baptized in St Andrew's Holborn on 30 April 1708.

46. WAC F5001/161. Margaret (earlier known as Meade, Holemead might have been a scurrilous nickname) gave a somewhat different account of her circumstances in an earlier examination; WAC F5001/149.

47. WAC F5001/4. Following her examination Joan was granted a pension by the parish, which began at 1s 6d per week in 1708 rising to 2s a week in the last recorded year of her pension in 1721; WAC F438/183, F440/229, F441/155, F442/167, F444/151, F445/146, F446/138, F447/150, F449/164, F451/177, F452/163, F454/156.

48. WAC F5001/101.

49. WAC F5002/24. Her pension started at 1s 6d a week and rose to 2s by the year of her last recorded payment in 1719. WAC F440/231, F441/156, F442/168, F444/152, F445/147, F446/139, F447/152, F449/166, F451/179.

50. WAC F5001/14. A neighbour later stood security for 40s (£2) to enable her to go back to Ireland, WAC F5001/15.

51. Frances Taton, a seventy-year-old widow, for example, "believes she has one Child in the Army", WAC F5001/21. She was granted a pension of 1s 3d a week in 1708 and continued receiving it until 1715, by which time it was worth 2s; WAC F438/191, F440/239, F441/161, F442/175, F444/158, F445/152.

Table 2. *Types of support mentioned in examination books, 1708–1709*

Help provided	Count
Childcare	35
Lodging	33
Unspecified help	9
Employment	8
Maintenance	6
Healthcare	4
Security for loan	1
Education of child	1
Total	97

Source: WAC Examination books, F5001–F5002

such help was not being received. In addition to the ninety-seven cases where a pauper narrative mentioned some type of support, there were a further thirty-seven or so where relatives of some sort were reported as being available, most of them locally or scattered across London. Some of these kin were clearly not involved directly in the care of relatives, which had devolved thereby on to the parish. Thus, for example, two aunts reported that their orphaned two-year-old niece, was "now at the Widow Battin's in Hedge Lane".[52] It must further be noted that what is being analysed here is *any* period of support mentioned as being given at any time during the period of the narrative. It is hoped that this method is sufficiently robust to give, firstly, some sort of notion of the type of help provided, and, secondly, some idea of the relative importance of particular family members in providing it. It would have been sensible to break down such information by age, but at present there is insufficient data to make this a useful exercise.

Table 2 suggests that childcare, as expected, and lodgings were the most common type of help mentioned by the poor. We do not know, of course, the extent to which, if at all, relatives and friends were paid for providing this help. The direction in which help flowed, too, could also clearly be misleading. As Margaret Pelling has pointed out, there were possible reciprocal benefits which might accrue from the elderly keeping a poor child. Again, widows living with married children might provide childcare or domestic labour in return for such shelter. To begin with, only six paupers referred explicitly or implicitly to some form of maintenance, transfer payments that are usually unrecoverable in the early modern historical record. Thus "Margaret Blanford in Mercers Street says she has been a widow [near] 20 years, and her Daughter Catharine Crookchank has maintained her", or take William Naylor and his wife Alice, of whom it was noted, "William Nayler their son is a painter, & he did support them".[53]

52. WAC F5001/139.
53. WAC F5001/8, 155.

Table 3 lists the categories of relatives and unrelated who were mentioned
as providing any type of support and Table 4 (on p. 62) provides an analysis
of this in terms of the direction in which such support apparently flowed.
It should be noted that Table 3 quantifies the relationship between carer
and the person assisted. A grandparent caring for a grandchild, however,
might be doing so to help her widowed (or deserted) daughter or widowed
son. Take, for example,

> Parker Taylor lodging at the Castle alehouse by Great Moor Gate, St Stephen
> Coleman Street, kept house in Russell Court [in St Martin's] about a year & half
> ago at £28 per annum, & never kept house since, has 3 Children: Elizabeth 9 year
> old, Sarah a year *dead*, Thomas 15 months *with his Grandmother*: his wife Mary
> sold old Clothes, he does some Toys or Turners work.[54]

Here then is a pauper family in dire straits. They were lodgers, having once
been substantial housekeepers. The youngest child had been farmed out
with his grandmother, presumably to reduce the financial burden of care.
Both husband and wife (the implication is that she was no longer employed)
worked in unrelated occupations. Following his examination Taylor was,
relatively unusually, given short-term relief at 1s 6d per week as one of the
"extraordinary" or casual poor. He never seems to have received a parish
pension from St Martin's. This is another example, too, of how survival
strategies could be mixed, and how help from relatives might be only a
temporary solution. It is possible, too, that relatives might care for the
children of previous partners. Given the frequency of remarriage in early
modern London, some female paupers had children by previous husbands.
It seems at least possible that relatives might take care of these, rather than
a new partner, perhaps, we may surmise, to facilitate remarriage. Thus one
Hester Sorycole, reported that she was the widow of one George Sorycole,
a soldier and "out pensioner" but had a son, John Allen, by a previous
husband, a deceased guardsman. She also admitted that she "has one more
[daughter] Elizabeth Allen 8 years old now with her Grandmother Elianor
Morgan at Marlborough".[55]
    As the previous example demonstrates, the help given to local paupers by
relatives was by no means bounded by the parish. Anne Lane, a widow
living in Hyde Park Road, had one child living with her mother in Shrews-
bury.[56] Sarah Parrett, another single parent, lodging in Hungerford Market,
deposed that her father, living in Kingston, Surrey, "keeps one of her Children Sarah about 4 year old – but he is a very poor man".[57] Such ties as
existed, then, were often, perhaps surprisingly, maintained over considerable
distances. A number of paupers were intent on travelling long distances to

54. WAC F5002/28.
55. WAC F5002/134. Hester falsely claimed to be married to another soldier as well.
56. WAC F5002/53.
57. WAC F5002/38.

Table 3. *Stated relationships between the poor and their helpers, 1708–1709*

Nature and direction of relationship	Number
Aunt helps nephew	3
Aunt helps niece	2
Aunt helps step-nephew	1
Brother helps brother	2
Brother helps sister	11
Brother-in-law helps sister-in-law	2
Brothers help sister	1
Cousin helps cousin	1
Daughter helps mother	9
Father helps daughter	2
Father helps son	1
Father-in-law helps daughter-in-law	2
Grandfather helps granddaughter	1
Grandfather helps grandson	2
Grandmother helps granddaughter	3
Grandmother helps grandchild	4
Grandmother helps grandson	1
Grandparents help granddaughter	1
Great-aunt helps grandniece	1
Great-grandmother helps great-grandchild	1
Mother helps daughter	7
Mother helps son	2
Mother-in-law helps daughter-in-law	1
Neighbour helps bastard child	1
Neighbour helps child	2
Neighbour helps lunatic	1
Neighbour helps widow	1
Neighbour helps couple	1
Neighbours help child	1
Niece helps aunt	1
Parents help daughter	3
Patron helps child	1
Relation helps orphan child	1
Relation helps relation	1
Relations help child	3
Relations help children	1
Relations help kin	1
Sister helps brother	1
Sister helps sister	4
Son helps mother	1
Son helps parents	1
Stepfather helps stepson	1
Stepmother helps stepchildren	1
Uncle helps bastard niece	1
Uncle helps nephew	3
Uncle helps nephew-in-law	1
Uncle helps niece	3
Total	97

Source: WAC F5001–F5002

Table 4. *Direction of help given by kin*

Category	Number
Unknown direction	2
No relation	8
Vertical-up	12
Horizontal	22
Vertical-down	53
Total	97

Source: Table 3

be cared for by relatives, or like Anne Lane, sent their children out of London to be looked after by their kin. One Scottish women, for example, Catherine Steward, wife of an army sergeant lodging at the Hole-in-the-Wall, Panton Street, "desires to have something to carry her & her Children to Scotland, her relations there will keep her".[58] Mary, the widow of Daniel Ellis, was given 50s (£2 10s) after security was found "to carry her to her brother Somerton a Blacksmith at Shipton-upon-Bower beyond Oxford".[59] Occasionally even physically remote relatives seem to have taken the initiative in providing assistance at times of difficulty. Elizabeth Baker, for example, the wife of one Morgan Baker, a glover, agreed with an informant who told the authorities that Elizabeth Morgan the mother of the said "Elizabeth Baker lives at Usk in Monmouthshire & is a very able woman & has sent for her said Daughter & 3 children".[60]

It is also apparent from Table 4 that those grandparents or parents, like Margaret Blanford or William Naylor, who received maintenance or other forms of assistance from their children were relatively unusual. Most assistance mentioned by paupers in their examinations seems to have flowed *down* or across family relationships rather than *upwards*, within a fairly narrow circle of close kin. Of the twelve relationships that can be categorized as being vertical, and in which the help apparently flowed upwards, nine were daughters helping their mothers, usually by providing lodging (which might have been reciprocated with domestic help or childcare). Parents seem to have been more likely to be providing assistance to grandchildren or their children than to be in receipt of such help. The range of kin that provided help were very similar to those providing lodgings to single women in London a century earlier. Brodsky Elliott likewise found that it was the

58. WAC F5002/124. The passage to Scotland cost 20s (£1), on security from a Mr Lindsey, who "promises to return it if she does not go".
59. WAC F5001/9. Another relative, one Edward Somerton, was amongst those standing surety for this money.
60. WAC F5002/89. It was noted that the daughter "had something to carry them thither". Morgan (and his family) seems to have been lodging in the Strand, after being a housekeeper at two previous addresses in the parish.

immediate family, grandparents, parents, together with uncles, aunts, sisters and brothers who provided the bulk of this help.[61] Cousins seems to have provided little help in either period. It is significant, nonetheless, that this range of kin providing help to paupers was significantly wider than envisaged in the original 1601 Act. Of the eighty-nine relatives recorded as helping paupers, about half of them, forty-five, lay outside the narrow range of grandparent, parent and children specified in that statute.

One has the impression, too, that as one would expect, paupers lacking such kin were seen as particularly deserving of help from the parish, and this was presumably why the presence or absence of relatives was sometimes noted. It is also possible to show that help and support given by relatives was, as in later periods, not unlimited and that it did not necessarily preclude seeking help from the parish. Arguably, the very reason that paupers were examined at all as "likely to become chargeable", a burden on the parish and its ratepayers, was because other means of support were proving inadequate. Particularly revealing is the case of Anne Wherrett, a nineteen-year-old servant, who after being discharged from service "went to Westminster [ie. St Margaret's, Westminster] where she had some Relations, vizt Mr England a Brewer her mother's brother & others". Sadly for Anne, she fell sick, and turned to the parish (rather than these relations) perhaps to facilitate a hospital admission, which promptly sent her back to St Martin's, her parish of settlement. In her words,

> [...] going to the Overseers there for relief they and the Churchwardens Mr Eales a Goldsmith ordered Caudle a Beadle to put her in a Coach and set her at Mr Pashly's door one of the Overseers of St Martins, but he not being at home, the Coachman set her at Mr William's door in Hedge Lane.[62]

Again, Ann Howes, a pensioner of St James, a neighbouring West End parish, seems to have been keeping her grandchild for her son, whilst he was at sea. Following her examination, however, the grandchild was placed on the orphan's book, "until her father comes home".[63] Kin then, in this urban environment, were only part of a larger "package" of survival strategies. Such expedients only come to the historian's attention when they fail, and provoke an application for poor relief or detection by local officials as "likely" to fall on the parish.

The evidence from St Martin's is suggestive about household strategies, although hardly definitive. Its poor represent a sample of the population whose survival strategies, or expedients, were proving inadequate. Those adults in need, who had not yet reached sixty years of age, the age at which

---

61. Brodsky Elliott, "Single Women", p. 93 (column showing kin providing lodgings).
62. WAC F5001/66. See also, 77, 80 for the same case. A William Naylor received a pension for four months in 1712, WAC F442/171.
63. WAC F5002/135. In the event Ann was on the orphans' book at a pension of 1s a week until she was bound apprentice in 1712, F440/211, F441/170, F442/154.

their chances of a parish pension were better, must have had even greater recourse to more family and social networks to survive. The poor were using a range of kin to help them survive in the city, more widely defined than the very immediate family. The findings here suggest, however, that few paupers received direct help from their children, the one exception was that daughters might, if able, provide help to mothers. Elderly men seem usually to have done without the support of their children, perhaps by seeking a "remarriage of mutual convenience".

Assistance from neighbours has left few traces in the records analysed here. This is probably because there was a hidden hierarchy of the types of care that kin and neighbours might provide.[64] Few of the poor, for example, seem to have expected their neighbours to provide childcare. The few occasions when that was specified, there often seems to have been money changing hands. So that the private care of a bastard child was recorded in the testimony of Jane Henry:

> Jane Henry wife of Thomas Henry lodging at the lower end of Hartshorne Lane says that Mary (Ann Catherine) Hill aged about 18 months was born on Catharine Wetherell & is a bastard: & was born (at a Leathercutter's in Dyet Street) in St Giles parish & she says she was paid 2s a week for about 5 months last past for keeping the child by the father's brother.[65]

When such a significant need occurred, the poor seem to have looked to their family of origin, or to other reasonably close relatives, or to the parish, rather than seek to burden neighbours. It is highly unlikely, especially in an urban area experiencing a lucrative demand for housing, that lodgings would be provided free to those in need. True, it is sometimes possible to find genuine examples of friendship between apparently unrelated individuals, usually based on periods of relatively long acquaintance, which are associated with the provision of shelter. Thus one Anne Ludlow was providing lodgings for her long time friend Robert Finly and his wife, but she may have been merely a friendly landlady, not an altruistic neighbour.[66] Neighbours may well have provided less onerous or short-term financial help, particularly credit.[67] Outhwaite's recent study of foundling petitions

64. Wall, "Beyond the Household", pp. 64–66, notes the qualitative differences revealed between support from neighbours and kin in his sensitive analysis of Flora Thompson's *Lark Rise to Candleford*. Of neighbours he notes that "relationships were not always harmonious, and that the nature of the contacts although frequent avoided the creation of burdensome and expensive ties of obligation in that meals were never provided nor would neighbours undertake the personal care of the ill and elderly", *ibid.*, p. 66.

65. WAC F5001/95. For the case of a female newspaper-seller, Ann Crook, the examining justice recorded that she "did lodge in at Mrs Wyatt's in Shugg Lane, who nursed her Child & her Child is there now & she says she pays 2s 6d per week for keeping her Child"; WAC F5002/37.

66. WAC F5002/106. Anne stated that "she has known him 18 years".

67. Craig Muldrew, *The Economy of Obligation: The Culture of Credit and Social Relations in Early Modern England* (Basingstoke, 1998), p. 82, points out the immense financial value to the poor of the extent of debt forgiveness. The amount of unpaid debts was "in fact many times larger than

found that "there are numerous examples [...] of humane actions performed by employers, neighbours, and kin", and his examples reveal much interim support for the parents of foundlings, particularly from ex-employers. Such support, however, was often supplemental to earnings and only helped delay rather than prevent a slide into helpless destitution. Paupers were aware that there were very real limits to the generosity of neighbours and friends. One widow hoping that the Foundling Hospital would take her youngest child claimed that,

> I am left in the greatest trouble that tongue can express, having to [two] helpless infants and no way of providing for them at present, but through the goodness of few friends who kept me and mine from starving for some time. But I cannot rely on there favours for ever, as I have been burthensome to them for so long.[68]

Perhaps we should not assume that, in the relatively harsh environment of a pre-industrial city, neighbours were always anxious to help the less fortunate. For every example of generosity, there might be indifference or suspicion. Historians are well aware that neighbours were perfectly capable of expressing considerable hostility to poor immigrants, expressed via informing parish officers of the arrival of paupers in the parish, or heartlessly evicting them. Evictions were experienced not only by single women, such at Margaret Hughes, an Irish migrant evicted from her lodgings whilst actually in labour, but were also directed at poor women such as one Susannah Wilcox, a seaman's widow, who "was turned out of [her] lodgings in a little Ally turning into the 2 Brewhouses in Tyburn Road, & for a month last she lay in a cellar under the Playhouse".[69] The current literature may sometimes paint too rosy a picture of the supporting networks of neighbours enjoyed by the poor. The pressure on pauper household economies and the consequent desire to curry favour with those in authority responsible for awarding pensions and doles could, for example, have produced a culture of suspicion and informing amongst the poor, rather than neighbourly reciprocal aid. Jane Price, a soldier's wife, living in Hartshorne Lane, for example, was examined by the justices in 1708. At the end of her examination the clerk recorded that Jane Price had volunteered the information that "Margaret Crurley [*Crutchley?*] in Hartshorne Lane over against the two Brewers with one Child has 12s a month on the Pension & [from the] Extraordinary". Since Jane was probably hoping for childcare support from the parish, her information may have been a tactic designed to pressurize the parish to grant her a greater sum, since she had four rather than one

charitable bequests and poor rates", and was an important income supplement which would have raised the income of "poor labourers'" families to a much higher level than that indicated by wage rates.

68. Outhwaite, "'Objects of Charity'", p. 508.
69. WAC F5002/91, 155.

child to provide for.[70] The effect of Jane's information, however, may well have been to get Margaret's regular pension stopped.[71]

CONCLUSION: THE SIGNIFICANCE OF "HOUSEHOLD SURVIVAL STRATEGIES"

It could be argued from some of the foregoing that the very phrase "household survival strategies" is something of a misnomer. Many pauper households, actually, did not really survive at all. What strikes one is the relative lack of family sentiment. *In extremis*, poor households deliberately fragmented.[72] The desertion of wives and children by hard-pressed husbands could even be said to be an extreme example of rational and calculating behaviour on the part of poor families which is revealed time and time again. Single mothers, poor widows and hard-pressed married couples were perfectly capable of sending their children to live with relatives, sometimes many miles away, as well as leaving them on the parish. Reduced levels of family sentiment was, in itself, a survival strategy.

> I am not able to subsist any Longer by reason of my Husband being Dead & the times is so very hard & having had much sickness this half year, that I cannot keep the Child any Longer by reason of Infirmities of Body & Limbs, being Lame & Cannot go without help, so [...] your Speedy care is desired herein, either to find a Careful nurse to your own liking or [...] to find a Good nurse for the Child [...].[73]

Such strategies, however, were probably mostly short-term. Evidence from the St Martin's pauper biographies,[74] as well as the observed tendency to stay for a relatively short time in the parish workhouse, demonstrate that periods of hardship were often relatively short-term. When circumstances improved, families or households might be reconstructed.

The strategy of abandoning children, usually the youngest, on the parish or at the door of an institution, or sending them to live with relatives, was, moreover, a strategy far from being unique to England. It is well known throughout early modern Europe that many illegitimate children were abandoned by their mothers shortly after their births.[75] What is less well known

70. WAC F5001/63. Jane had one bastard child, a stepson, and two children from her current marriage. One child was placed on the orphans' book.
71. WAC F4509/5. A Margaret Crutchley living in Hartshorn Lane, receiving, however, just 4s a month from her pension, was crossed out of a list of pensioners made the year before this examination.
72. For this see also, D.A. Kent, "'Gone for a Soldier': Family Breakdown and the Demography of Desertion in a London Parish, 1750–91", *Local Population Studies*, 45 (1990), pp. 27–42.
73. WAC F5002/167. From a letter attached to a foundling dropped in Durham Yard, 1709.
74. Boulton, "Poor Among the Rich".
75. For foundlings in Europe see, for example, Isabel Dos Guimarães Sá, "Child Abandonment in Portugal: Legislation and Institutional Care", *Continuity and Change*, 9 (1994), pp. 69–89;

is that a significant proportion of foundlings were deposited by poor families, often headed by widows, but sometimes by married couples.[76] That this
was a genuine problem was recognized, for example, in Paris by the found-
ing in 1788 of the Society for Maternal Charity, explicitly designed to care
for the "legitimate infants of the poor". Those running the charity concentrated their efforts on the two most vulnerable groups of poor families,
namely those where pregnant women had lost their husbands or where their
spouse was sick; and those families where pregnant mothers already had
large numbers of young children. In 1788 it was estimated that between
eleven and fifteen per cent of the foundlings left at the Paris Hôpital Gén-
éral, the largest foundling hospital in Europe, were legitimate.[77] How many
other poor families in Europe sent children to relatives, rather than the
(frequently lethal) available institutions when times were hard? To what
extent did the poor rely on kin, rather than charitable handouts and institutional relief for support?

This essay has attempted to reinforce the obvious point that there is
always an, albeit largely invisible, balance between informal support networks and the all too visible activities of Poor Law administrators.[78] Historians have noted that the poor might seek help from family and relatives,
but they have been slower to appreciate the fundamental importance of
such strategies to our understanding of the structure and nature of poverty
in the past. McIntosh, in her fine survey of poverty in fifteenth and six-
teenth-century England, noted that economic and demographic patterns
impacted not merely on vulnerable families, but also on the "ability of other
lesser members of the community – relatives and neighbours of similar
status – to give informal assistance".[79] Speculation this may be, but this
notion goes some way to undermine those histories of poverty which assume
a simplistic equation between, say, larger numbers of poor relieved and
macro-economic changes such as industrialization, falls in living standards
and so on. Historians who seek to measure the extent of destitution by
comparing the proportion of formally relieved with the total population are

David I. Kertzer and Michael J. White, "Cheating the Angel-Makers: Surviving Infant Abandonment in Nineteenth-Century Italy", *Continuity and Change*, 9 (1994), pp. 451–480.

76. See above, note 30.

77. Stuart Woolf, "The Societé de Charité Maternelle, 1788–1815", in Jonathan Barry and Colin
Jones (eds), *Medicine and Charity before the Welfare State* (London, 1991), pp. 99–103. The estimate
was of some 800 legitimates, out of between 5,500 and 7,500 total foundlings. The proportion of
legitimate foundling children is remarkably similar to the estimate for London at the same period;
see above note 29.

78. For this point see also Steve King, "Reconstructing Lives: The Poor, the Poor Law and Welfare
in Calverley, 1650–1820", *Social History*, 22 (1997), pp. 318–338. One can only agree with one of
Dr King's concluding comments that "there is scope for a renewed focus on the role of kinship
in the welfare patchwork deployed by individuals and families", *ibid.*, p. 338.

79. Marjorie K. McIntosh, "Local Responses to the Poor in Late Medieval and Tudor England",
Continuity and Change, 3 (1988), pp. 209–245, 219–220.

certain to be underestimating levels of need, since those poor who were maintained or relieved by their kin rather than the parish will be omitted. Again, changes in the proportions of the population applying to public relief might also partly reflect the changing ability and inclination of relatives and friends to support needy relatives rather than an absolute increase in the numbers of the destitute. At the very least, historians of European poverty, as the work of Thane and Wall surely implies, need to pay still more attention to the alternatives to institutional poor relief and charitable institutions, in the struggle for survival of the poor.

APPENDIX: SOURCES TO RECONSTRUCT PAUPER "SURVIVAL STRATEGIES"

The parish of St Martin's has a rich set of poor relief records which, unusually, can shed valuable light on less formal survival strategies. Firstly, most of the overseers and churchwardens accounts have survived for the entire period, and these form the basis of the "pauper biographies" constructed as part of the ongoing larger study. For the late seventeenth and early eighteenth centuries, these are supplemented by a number of detailed listings of the parish pensioners, including two listings which supply age information and residence. The first workhouse admissions book survives, and contains details on the age, duration and condition of many of those paupers admitted between 1725 and 1726.[80] The most useful and voluminous of the records, however, are a nearly complete set of "examination books" recording the activities of local justices. These examination books record short settlement examinations, notes and comments on individual cases, records of decisions as to the granting of pensions, the care of parish orphans, foundlings, illegitimate children and the sick. The bulk of the material relates to attempts to establish a given person's settlement, although some of it records decisions on granting pensions or putting parish orphans out to apprenticeship.[81] The detail they give varies enormously in quality and quantity, ranging from a few words or a couple of lines to a full page of testimony. The books appear to have been written on the spot, contain many corrections, further information gathered from local informants and occasional marginal comments on the veracity or otherwise of pauper testimony. Because of the size of the parish and the regular inflow of pauper immigrants "likely to become chargeable" the number of persons examined by the justices was considerable. The first two surviving books, which cover

80. WAC F4002. The exact period covered by this first admissions book is a seven-month period from 29 July 1725 to 26 February 1726.
81. The examinations are very far from the more familiar, relatively formulaic and formally written-up settlement examinations. For a splendid example and a guide to the English law of settlement, see Tim Hitchcock and John Black (eds), *Chelsea Settlement and Bastardy Examinations 1733–1766*, London Record Society 33, (London, 1999).

only a couple of years, contain records relating to over 600 cases, and name many thousands of persons therein. This essay represents a preliminary attempt to mine these books, more properly "notebooks", for the minutiae of pauper lives and to uncover some of the survival strategies buried within them.

International Review of Social History 45 (2000), pp. 71–92
© 2000 Internationaal Instituut voor Sociale Geschiedenis

Using Microcredit and Restructuring Households: Two Complementary Survival Strategies in Late Eighteenth-Century Barcelona*

MONTSERRAT CARBONELL-ESTELLER

INTRODUCTION

In the last third of the 1700s Barcelona was a city undergoing a major transformation. The regional specialization process that took place in Catalonia, and the intensification of exchange, generated spectacular economic growth and an unprecedented increase in population. The city of Barcelona tripled its population in just over seventy years; in 1787 it already had around 100,000 inhabitants. Immigration, both from the Pyrenean areas and from the proto-industrial areas of central Catalonia, the natural growth of the population, the intense process of urbanization, and the dynamism of the labour market explain the densification of the city and the rise in the price of rents.

At the end of the eighteenth century Barcelona had an expanding labour market and a welfare system which facilitated immigration and helped people to settle in the city. The changes in occupation, the progressive transformation of apprentices into wage earners, the appearance of the first calico factories (cotton textiles printed with motifs and colours characteristic of the precious Indian cotton fabrics), as well as the growth of the service sector, allowed the influx of numerous people in search of work. Barcelona also had an important and dynamic network of public welfare services. These allowed the new arrivals to join the urban fabric, as they helped young people of both sexes to find apprenticeships and to enter the labour and marriage market. They also allowed young children to be temporarily left in specialized centres and, at the same time, they guaranteed survival in periods of separation or definitive expulsion from the labour market for reasons of illness or old age.[1] The following were the key institutions of this

* This research forms part of a current project entitled "Crédit, consum i gènere als orígens de la Catalunya Contemporània", covered by a Collaboration Agreement between the Institut Català de la Dona (Generalitat de Catalunya) and the Departament d'Història i Institucions Econòmiques of the Universitat de Barcelona. Part of this research was presented in session C59 "Les femmes et le crédit dans les sociétés européennes (XVIe–XIXe siècles)", Twelfth International Economic History Congress, Madrid, August 1998; and in the seminar on "Urban Credit and Consumption In Pre-industrial Europe (1650–1850)", Barcelona, December 1998. I would like to express my most sincere gratitude to Teresa Cubí for her work on the database as research assistant. I would also like to express my gratitude to the late Manuel García Arribas and Manuel García Gascóns for their comments.
1. See Montserrat Carbonell, *Sobreviure a Barcelona. Dones, pobresa i assistència al segle* XVIII (Barcelona, 1997).

welfare system: the *Casa de Infants Orfes*, which took in children under thirteen years old; the *Casa de Misericòrdia*, which took in poor people from both sexes and all age groups, and which also acted as both a workhouse and hospice; the *Hospital de la Santa Creu*, which took in the sick and needy; and, lastly, the *Casa de Penedides*, which took in women and was linked to the *Mont de Pietat de Barcelona*.[2] These public institutions, together with the parish charity (*Borsa de Pobres Vergonyants*)[3] and the public soup kitchen, organized at times of crisis by the local authorities, made up the dynamic welfare system of Barcelona at the end of the eighteenth century, offering the population a wide range of social benefits.

Working families and individuals had to find a way to adapt to the profound changes that were taking place in Catalan and Barcelona society at that time. This adaptive capacity of family and individual economies generated a series of survival strategies,[4] of which there was a number of different complementary kinds. Apart from work, there was a wide range of strategies which could be carried out simultaneously, or alternated, and which could offset the irregularity and fragility of employment. These included emigration, variations in household size and nature, the use of microcredits, the use of public assistance, the use of mutual help networks (relations, neighbours, trade), begging, and crime. This article deals almost exclusively with two of these: the use of microcredit institutions, and variations in household size and composition. Some references are, however, made to the use of welfare institutions.

Two principal sources were used. Firstly, the *Llibres de Comptaduria del Mont de Pietat* (pawn shop) *de Nostra Senyora de la Esperança de Barcelona*, which recorded the name, civil status, trade and address of the borrower, the object pawned, the valuation of the object, the credit obtained, whether or not the credit was repaid and therefore whether the pledge was recovered or definitively lost.[5] The second source studied was the *Llibres de Matrícula dels alcaldes de barri* corresponding to the Sant Pere neighbourhood. These recorded the people living in each household in the year 1770, giving the first name and surname, civil status, trade, relationship or other kind of

2. The same *Congregació de Nostra Senyora de l'Esperança* governed the *Mont de Pietat de Barcelona* and the *Casa de Penedides*. The profits of the *Mont de Pietat* were used to finance the *Casa de Penedides*.

3. Poor people not daring to beg openly.

4. At the end of the 1970s Louise Tilly raised the issue of the development of family strategies. See Louise Tilly, "Individual Lives and Family Strategies in the French Proletariat", *Journal of Family History*, 4 (1979), pp. 137–152; Stuart Woolf, *The Poor in Western Europe in the Eighteenth and Nineteenth Centuries* (London, 1986); and Tamara K. Hareven, *Family Time and Industrial Time* (Cambridge, 1982). Richard Wall, in the mid-1980s, formulated a key concept for the study of family economies and strategies; see Richard Wall, "Work, Welfare and the Family: An Illustration of the Adaptive Family Economy", in Lloyd Blonfield and Richard M. Smith, *The World We Have Gained* (Oxford, 1986), pp. 261–294.

5. Arxiu Històric de "la Caixa" (hereafter, AHC), Llibres de Comptaduria, 1770.

link, as well as the changes recorded in each household, and the movements of the men and women who made them up between 1770 and 1777. This source does not, however, allow us to quantify these movements, as it is not sure that they represent comprehensive records, and it was therefore only used to locate the households in 1770,[6] and to show changes in some households between January 1770 and December 1777. The Sant Pere neighbourhood was chosen because it is the area where most of the new calico factories were located, the vast majority of which concentrated the weaving and printing in the same building until the end of the 1780s. This neighbourhood took in a large proportion of the working families of the eighteenth century, as shown by the population density of the area. Other complementary sources were also used, such as applications for help from parish and state welfare institutions.

The aim of this article is firstly to show the use of institutionalized micro-credit by part of the lower class, taking as a documentary base 1,015 pledges corresponding to the months of January and February 1770. Secondly, it presents the structure of the households of the Sant Pere neighbourhood for the same period, starting from a sample of the first hundred households which appear in the *Llibres de Matrícula dels alcaldes de barri*, corresponding to a total of 504 people. The results show us the extent of co-residence and the proportion of complex households (whether extended family households, those including some relatives, or multiple family households, those having more than one conjugal unit). Thirdly and lastly, crossing the two sources mentioned makes it possible to establish a sample composed of those eighteen, of the one hundred households studied, which used the *Mont de Pietat* between January and February of 1770.[7] A qualitative approach to these eighteen households suggests tentative answers to the following questions. Did different types of households prefer specific strategies? Were using credit, relying on welfare institutions and transforming households through co-residence alternative or complementary strategies? Did different individual and family strategies coexist at the heart of the same household?

MAKING ENDS MEET: THE USE OF PAWNING FOR CREDIT IN BARCELONA, 1770

The use of credit was a common practice for the family economies of the lower classes, thus ensuring continual access to consumption in a context

---

6. The registers preserved do not cover all the neighbourhoods of Barcelona. We have used the volume corresponding to "Libro de Matrícula o Descripción de las Iglesias, Familias e Individuos de ambos sexos con las casas que componen el B de San Francisco de Paula del Quartel 2 nombrado de San Pedro [...]", Arxiu Històric de la Ciutat de Barcelona (hereafter, AHCB), Cadastre I-5, 1770. For criticism of this source see Pilar López, "Evolució demogràfica", in Jaume Sobrequés (ed.), *Història de Barcelona*, vol. 5, *El desplegament de la ciutat manufacturera (1714–1833)* (Barcelona, 1993), pp. 111–166.
7. The crosscheck is carried out starting from coinciding first name, surname, job and address.

characterized by irregular income. The discontinuity of individual and family income led to consecutive debts and, in many cases, made it necessary to enter the informal credit market, informal credit being that which is not subject to any kind of document and which is established orally.[8] The appearance of an institution such as the *Mont de Pietat* in the Barcelona of the mid-1700s represented the first attempt to formalize and institutionalize microcredits in the city, allowing the mass influx of families who turned to this institution in search of credit in exchange for the pawning of objects.

The credit and welfare functions were intertwined in the origins of this kind of institution. Throughout the long history of the *Mont de Pietat de Barcelona*, the predominance of one aspect or the other, either the purely welfare or the strictly credit, would mark its evolution. The movement between the two was determined by the capacity of the *Mont de Pietat* to act as a genuine credit entity. This, in turn, depended absolutely on the *Mont de Pietat* being able to attract the depositing of funds in exchange for offering interest, to thus be able to lend to the families in need. Graph 1 shows how, from the 1770s, the ban on interest that the king imposed on the Mont de Pietat in 1767 dealt a severe blow to the credit side of the institution.[9] Indeed, the institutional, political and ideological ideas on interest and usury led to a modification of the market and the offer of credit in the city.

Graph 1 shows how the culminating moment for the number of pawns, that is for the number of families obtaining credit, is the mid-1760s. If we take into account that in the 1760s the city had approximately 80,000 inhabitants,[10] the figure of 10,000 families helped by the *Mont* in the year 1764 shows the tremendous dynamism of the institution, which saw between one-third and one-half of the city's family units pass through its office, in a year marked by the appearance of an old-style subsistence crisis. There was an evident demand for credit. In 1770, the year from which our sample comes, the *Mont de Pietat* still acted as a genuine popular credit institution.

Who were the users of the *Mont de Pietat* in this period? Firstly, it is the

---

8. See Manuela Rocha, "Credito privado enm Lisboa; numa perspectiva comparada (séculos XVII–XIX)", *Análise Social. Revista do Instituto de Ciências Sociais da Universidade de Lisboa*, 33, No. 145 (1998), pp. 91–115, and Laurence Fontaine, Gilles Postel-Vinay, Jean-Laurent Rosenthal, and Paul Servais (eds), *Des personnes aux institutions. Réseaux et culture du crédit du XVIe au XXe siècle en Europe* (Louvain-la-Neuve, 1997).
9. In 1767 a royal decree settled the controversy in the *Mont de Pietat* between the clergy and laymen concerning interest. The king intervened, suspending the acceptance of funds in exchange for interest and obliging the existing funds to be repaid with the interest due. In practice the deposits began to be returned in 1770; Llibre d'Acords, AHC.
10. Considering the figures offered by the Floridablanca census for 1786 and the estimates of the rate of growth of the population of Barcelona in the second half of the seventeen hundreds offered by P. Vilar. See Pierre Vilar, *Catalunya dins l'Espanya moderna*, vol. 3 (Barcelona, 1966), and Josep Iglesias, *El cens del comte Floridablanca*, 1787 (Barcelona, 1970).

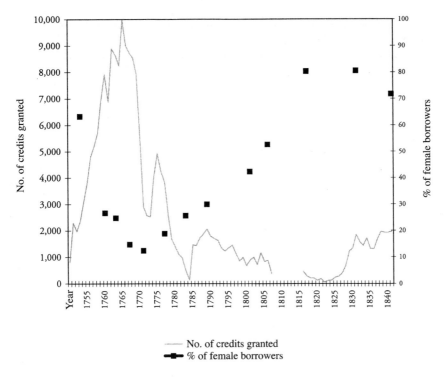

Figure 1. *Number of credits granted and percentage of female borrowers: Mont de Pietat de Nostra Senyora Esperança de Barcelona, 1751–1842*
Source: Own elaboration from the *Llibres de Comptaduria*, AHC

families from the lower-class neighbourhoods, those with the highest density and those nearest to the new calico factories. As regards the profile of the borrowers, we shall first indicate their sex and occupation. In 1770, only fifteen per cent of the borrowers were women, the majority of whom were widows.[11] This was not always the case. In the long run, the rate of female borrowers of the *Mont* was inversely proportional to the intensity of the number of credits granted (see Graph 1). When the *Mont* acted as a genuine credit institution with sufficient resources to meet the enormous demand for credit in the city, the clients were mainly married men, whereas when the number of loans granted plummeted and the *Mont de Pietat* became entrenched in a welfare rather than credit function, the clients *par excellence* were married women, single women and widows. This phenomenon – which will not be developed in this article – suggests that there were different gender strategies at the heart of the families and households. These gender-specific strategies were in response to the policy of the *Mont*, which

11. Of the 159 women who appeared as borrowers the majority (78 per cent) were widows.

Table 1. *Occupation of the borrowers of the Mont de Pietat de Nostra Senyora de l'Esperança, Barcelona, 1770*

Sector	Subsector	No.	%
	Agriculture	78	9.5
	Fishing and Sailing	64	7.8
Total agriculture & fishing		142	17.4
	Wax and soap	3	0.3
	Building	50	6.1
	Leather and shoes	57	6.9
	Esparto	13	1.5
	Wood	35	4.2
	Metals	56	6.8
	Glass and ceramics	2	0.2
	Textile and clothing	268	32.8
	Workers	22	2.6
Total manufacturing		506	62.1
	Food sector and derivatives	20	2.4
	Artists	5	0.6
	Trade	22	2.6
	Teaching	4	0.4
	Liberal professions and officials	9	1.1
	Services	37	4.5
	Transport	44	5.3
Total services		141	17.3
	Clergy	6	0.7
	Army	8	0.9
Total clergy, army and inactive		14	1.7
	Various	12	
Total various		12	1.5
Grand total		815	100.0

Source: Own elaboration, *Llibres de Comptaduria*, 1770, AHC

sometimes gave a different valuation to an object depending on whether it was pawned by a man or by a woman.[12]

The occupation of the borrowers using the *Mont de Pietat* reveals the characteristic profile of a strongly manufacturing port city (see Table 1). This is shown by the high representation of the manufacturing sector –

12. An initial approach can be found in Montserrat Carbonell, "Crédito al consumo y economias familiares. Barcelona, 1750–1850", in Albert Carreras, Pere Pascual, David Reher, and Carles Sudrià (eds), *Doctor Jordi Nadal. La industrialización y el desarrollo económico de España* (Barcelona, 1999), vol. I, pp. 304–320.

Table 2. *Distribution of the credits granted according to their value, Mont de Pietat, Barcelona, 1770*

Type loan	Borrowers		Amounts borrowed	
	No.	%	No.	%
From 0–24 reales	709	69.9	9,112	28.6
From 25–49 reales	163	16.1	5,412	17.0
From 50–99 reales	86	8.5	5,204	16.4
From 100–149 reales	30	3.0	3,204	10.1
<150 reales	27	2.7	8,878	27.9
Total	1,015	100.0	31,810	100.0

Source: Own elaboration, *Llibres de Comptaduria*, 1770, AHC

especially textiles and clothing – as well as the fishing and marine subsector and the service sector. However, at the end of the 1700s the city was already beginning to generate a series of transformations within the sphere of occupation. This is demonstrated by the difficulty for many apprentices of gaining promotion within the guilds, and the appearance of an important contingent of salary earners outside the guilds.[13]

What was the value of the credits granted and what objects were pawned? The distribution according to the value of the credits granted (see Table 2) shows that the pawning of objects was a short-term survival strategy, aimed at day-to-day survival. Most of the loans (seventy per cent) were for an extremely small amount, equivalent to payment for between two and six day's work for a construction labourer, according to the wages indicated by P.Vilar for the year 1764.[14] The articles pawned could not be land, furniture, cessions, bills of exchange or state bonds. Only jewellery, or gold or silver objects (cutlery, buttons, small boxes, rosaries, candelabra, pieces of necklace, etc.), articles of clothing, unmade-up fabrics or raw materials (wool, silk, cotton, flax or hemp), and household appliances (copper pots, etc.) could be pawned (Table 3).

What adaptive skills did the family economies and the households develop in order to make the best use of the credit offered by the *Mont*? The success or failure of the return of the loan and the recovery of the pledge, as well as the frequency with which this operation was repeated, is a good indicator of the type of strategy implemented. The payment of the debt demonstrated the capacity of the family economy to overcome

13. In Table 1 the workers' subsector includes the categories of day labourer, wage earner, worker, labourer and journeyman. With these occupations, usually no specific trade was indicated. Cf. Manel Arranz and Ramon Grau, "Problemas de inmigración y asimilación en la Barcelona del siglo XVIII", in *Revista de Geografía*, 4 (1970), pp. 71–80.
14. See Pierre Vilar, "Transformaciones económicas, impulso urbano y movimiento de los salarios: la Barcelona del siglo XVIII", in Pierre Vilar, *Crecimiento y desarrollo* (Barcelona, 1974), pp. 209–210.

Table 3. *Value of the loans by type of pledge, Mont de Pietat, Barcelona, 1770*

Type loan	Jewellery No.	%	Clothes No.	%	Various No.	%	No. of loans Total = 100
From 0–24 rals	235	33.1	463	65.3	11	1.6	709
From 25–49 rals	119	73.0	43	26.4	1	0.6	163
From 50–99 rals	72	83.7	14	16.3	0	0.0	86
From 100–149 rals	28	93.3	2	6.7	0	0.0	30
<150	25	92.6	2	7.4	0	0.0	27
Total	479	47.2	524	51.6	12	1.2	1,015

Source: Own elaboration, *Llibres de Comptaduria,* 1770, AHC

successfully the deficit in its budget, without having to abandon the pledges. This constituted a form of precaution, as it allowed the operation to be repeated as often as necessary. On the other hand, the inability to pay the debt and to recover the pledge was not necessarily synonymous with failure, as some people might decide to sell off cheaply certain dispensable objects. However, for the immense majority, the inability to recover the pledges represented the beginning of a course of successive material losses and therefore of progressive impoverishment. In 1788 A. Capmany i Montpalau illustrated that described above: When the craftsman "resorts to the shelter of the hospital [...] we must suppose that all of his household furnishings, his best jewellery and maybe the tools of his trade have already been sold off cheap, because in the pride of an artisan this humble recourse should be seen as the saddest extremity".[15]

The sample studied reveals that, in the winter of 1770, there was a fairly similar proportion of those who did and those who did not pay off the credit, although there was a slight predominance of those who did not manage to repay the credit and recover the pledge (Table 4). Therefore, the

Table 4. *Repayment of credit by its value, Mont de Pietat, Barcelona 1770*

Type loan	Total repaid No.	%	Total not repaid No.	%	Total = 100 No.
From 0–24 rals	318	44.9	391	55.1	709
From 25–49 rals	82	50.3	81	49.7	163
From 50–99 rals	38	44.2	48	55.8	86
From 100–149 rals	9	30.0	21	70.0	30
<150 rals	12	44.4	15	55.6	27
Total	459	45.2	556	54.8	1,015

Source: Own elaboration, *Llibres de Comptaduria,* 1770, AHC

15. See A. Capmany i Montpalau, *Discurso económico-político en defensa del trabajo mecánico de los menestrales* (Madrid, 1788).

percentage of success in the adaptive strategies of the family economies and of the households was considerably high, as it was around fifty per cent. The microcredits and small credits are those which showed the greatest degree of success in their repayment, and therefore they bear witness to a greater precision in the credit operations among people who administer scarce resources. The presence of a high percentage of repayment of the bigger loans is partly explained by the institution's policy for granting credit. The loans for jewellery represented a lower percentage of credit in relation to the valuation, inciting the borrowers to repay these loans.[16] When not recovered, the jewellery was sold in public auctions, ensuring important profits for the institution. The occupational subsectors whose success in repaying was above average were fishing and sailing, the army, services, building and textile and clothing (Table 5 overleaf). This seems to suggest that some of the groups with the most irregular incomes, like soldiers, fishermen and sailors, succeeded best in using credit without losing their pawns. In any case, the craft and wage-earning classes of the city used the possibility of obtaining microcredit offered by the institutions of the city with considerable success.

FAMILIES AND HOUSEHOLDS IN BARCELONA IN 1770: THE PREDOMINANCE OF CO-RESIDENCE

With the growing number of inhabitants and domestic units, late eighteenth-century Barcelona witnessed a progressive subdivision of flats into smaller units and a systematic increase in the size of the buildings through the addition of new floors.[17] Economic differences within the lower classes, whether or not new immigrants, grew larger. The vigour and change of the labour market under construction is demonstrated by the distance between the craftsmen belonging to guilds and those not belonging to guilds, and by the progressive proletarianization of the apprentices who found it difficult to become masters.[18] This is also seen by the increasing appearance of salary or wage earners, the flow of young people – especially women – in search of a position in domestic service, multiple employment, underemployment and unemployment. The increase in rents[19] encouraged an increase in residential

16. From among the 1,015 pawns carried out between January and February 1770, a credit of 78.2 per cent of the valuation was obtained for jewellery, 81.2 per cent for clothes and 82.2 per cent for objects such as copper pots or others.

17. See Pilar López Guallar, "Les transformacións de l'habitat: la casa i la vivenda a Barcelona entre 1693 i el 1859", in *Actes del Primer Congrés d'Història de Catalunya*, vol. I (Barcelona, 1985), pp. 111–117; and *idem*, "La densificación barcelonesa: el territorio de la parroquia de Santa Maria del Pi, 1693–1859", in *El Pla de Barcelona y la seva historia. Actes del I Congrés d'Història del Pla de Barcelona* (Barcelona, 1984), pp. 275–298.

18. See Manel Arranz and Ramon Grau, "Problemas de inmigración", pp. 71–80.

19. See Elisa Badosa, "Els lloguers de cases a la ciutat de Barcelona (1780–1834)", *Recerques*, 10 (1980), pp. 139–157.

Table 5. *Repayment of the credit by occupation, Mont de Pietat, Barcelona 1770*

Sector	Subsector	Repaid No.	Repaid %	Not repaid No.	Not repaid %	Total No.
	Agriculture	22	28.2	56	71.8	78
	Fishing and sailing	37	57.8	27	42.2	64
Total agriculture and fishing		59	41.5	83	58.5	142
	Wax and soap	2		1		3
	Building	26	52.0	24	48.0	50
	Leather and shoes	29	50.9	28	49.1	57
	Esparto	3		10		13
	Wood	15	42.8	20	57.1	35
	Metals	20	35.7	36	64.3	56
	Glass and ceramics	0		2		2
	Textile and clothing	137	51.1	131	48.9	268
	Workers	9	40.9	13	59.0	22
Total manufacturing		241	47.6	265	52.4	506
	Food and derivatives	7		13		20
	Artists	1		4		5
	Trade	7	31.8	15	68.1	22
	Teaching	1		3		4
	Liberal professions and administration	4		5		9
	Services	21	56.8	16	43.2	37
	Transports	23	52.3	21	47.7	44
Total services		64	45.4	77	54.6	141
	Clergy	3		3		6
	Army	6		2		8
Total clergy, army and inactive		9		5		14
Various		5		7		12
Not recorded		81	40.5	119	59.5	200
Grand Total		459	45.2	556	54.7	1,015

Source: Own elaboration, *Llibres de Comptaduria*, 1770, AHC

Table 6. *100 Households of Sant Pere neighbourhood by household type, Barcelona 1770*

Type household	With co-residents No.	Without co-residents No.	Total = 100 No.
Solitaries*	4	4	8
Without family structure	8	2	10
Simple family household	19	31	50
Extended family household	11	11	22
Multiple family household	10	0	10
Total	52	48	100

Source: Own elaboration, *Llibres de Matrícula dels alcaldes de barri*, 1770 AHCB
*Single people, widows, widowers and married people with absent partners.

mobility. The rise in the price of accommodation must have stimulated different forms of co-residence and the appearance of complex households with several nuclei. The documentation consulted shows how numerous household forms were improvised, such as households of apprentices and labourers, of journeymen and wage earners, of artisans or hawkers. There were co-residences of single people, both men and women, of siblings, of maids, of apprentices and lodgers. In short the adoption of a certain profile of household constituted in itself a strategy for survival.

There are many questions in relation to the survival strategies of the households consisting of artisans and workers in late eighteenth-century Barcelona which are just beginning to be answered. We still know little about the artisans, apprentices, wage earners, maids, sellers or salary earners. We do not know about their marriage patterns, how and when an independent household was created, how the accommodation was transferred, the information and solidarity networks and how the cycle of the domestic group developed. As a first approach, we have analysed 100 households of one of the poorest neighbourhoods of Barcelona – the Sant Pere neighbourhood in the year 1770 – which registered the highest population density, and which took in a large part of the workers who had just arrived in the city. The profile of occupations of all household members studied demonstrates the predominance of the manufacturing sector, followed by the service sector.[20] We analyse the composition of these 100 households using Peter Laslett' s typology (Table 6).[21] Only nineteen of them had a woman as the head of the household, mainly widows or women whose husbands was absent.

20. Manufacturing (60 per cent), services (24 per cent), clergy, army and inactive (14 per cent), agriculture and fishing (2 per cent).
21. See Peter Laslett, "Introduction: the history of the family", in Peter Laslett and Richard Wall (eds), *Household and Family in Past Time* (Cambridge, reprinted 1978), pp. 1–90.

Table 7. *Condition of solitary co-residents, Barcelona (Sant Pere neighbourhood) 1770*

Solitary* Co-residents	Men No.	Women No.	Total No.	%
Guest	5	2	7	5.1
Undetermined	36	8	44	31.9
Apprentice	28	0	28	20.3
Servant/maid	9	36	45	32.6
Boy	1	0	1	0.7
Widow	0	9	9	6.5
Widow/maid	0	4	4	2.9
Total	79	59	138	100.0

Source: Own elaboration, *Llibres de Matrícula dels alcaldes de barri*, AHCB
*Single people, widows, widowers and married people with absent partners.

Two interrelated facts emerge strikingly from this exercise: more than half of the households had nonrelated co-residents, and only a minority consisted of just a nuclear family, i.e. of parents with or without unmarried child(ren), or of a single parent with child(ren) (Table 6). The importance of co-residence converted the head of the household into a key figure, as he or she distributed and controlled access to it. In the same way the condition of a co-resident – who does not have family links with the household – shows the central importance of individual life courses, and shows how individual strategies act in a transverse manner, merging at certain times with those of the household, while at other times they run parallel or apart. For example, the fact that there are co-residents who use the *Mont* as borrowers, instead of the head of the household doing so, shows an individual strategy which overlaps with the option of co-residence in a household. Moreover, in many of the households studied the co-residents change but their number and their category remain the same: servants were replaced by servants, apprentices by apprentices, lodgers by lodgers. This corroborates both the fact that there is indeed a domestic group dynamic, which is fuelled by both the family and the individual strategies, and the fact that there are individual strategies which demand the integration and/or separation of successive households.

Among the co-residents whose status could be determined, male apprentices and female servants stand out (Table 7). Generally speaking, co-residence involved contractual links between the head of the household and the co-resident – either formalized, such as, for example, some apprenticeship or domestic service contracts, or of an informal and oral nature. These contractual links could move resources in either direction. The head of the household – or the family or families which defined it – could obtain work in exchange for money and payments in kind (this would be the case of apprentices and maids), or else receive money in exchange for allowing access to the roof in the case of lodgers and tenants. The group whose condition is not defined in the sources would probably form part of the lodgers and tenants group, as the apprentices and maids are always defined as such in the documentation. Co-residence does not, however, only affect single men and women, but can also affect married couples, many households thus becoming multiple. In this respect, in most of the multiple family households studied, the families were not related but were probably linked by a contractual relationship. It was not just their own interest, but also the practice of reciprocity and solidarity which allowed many homes to open up to different forms of co-residence. Indeed, co-residence was decisive for immigrants, allowing the newly arrived to obtain a roof and an essential network. For the households who already lived in Barcelona, it was a key supplementary source of income to balance the family budget, as demonstrated by the incorporation of tenants, lodgers or relatives.[22] Lastly, it was one of the formulae used in the drawn-out process of expulsion from the labour market in old age, as demonstrated by the temporary or permanent co-residence of the elderly. In short, co-residence was fundamental in the survival strategies of individuals, families and households in late eighteenth-century Barcelona, and was used systematically in a complementary manner together with other strategies, such as applying to welfare institutions.

The second result is that only a minority of the households (31 out of 100) coincided with a nuclear family (Table 6). It makes a significant difference whether or not simple family households take in co-residents. For example, Jayme Abriart, a tailor, is the head of the household, is married, lives with his wife, his daughter and other co-residents (an apprentice, a maid, a widower and a baker).[23] The presence of the widower and baker without explicit relationship links suggests that they were probably lodgers. The solitaries' households were not just households formed by a widow/widower or a single person, but rather these households could include other members, thus becoming a household without family structure, or perhaps a household led by a widow who took in lodgers, maids or other undetermined people .

From among the extended family households, i.e. those made up of a conjugal unit with relatives, only half incorporated nonrelated co-residents. On average, the number of household members was larger than in the simple family households, but smaller than in the multiple family house-

22. See the essential role of co-residence in relation to family budgets and the labour market for Catalonia in subsequent periods in Enriqueta Camps Cura, "Transitions in Women's and Children's Work Patterns and Implications for the Study of Family Income and Household Structure: A Case Study from the Catalan Textile Sector (1850–1925)", in *The History of the Family: an International Quarterly*, 3 (1998), pp. 137–153; and David S. Reher, *Perspectives on the Family in Spain, Past and Present* (Oxford, 1997).
23. AHCB. Cadastre, 1–5.

Table 8. *100 households of Sant Pere neighbourhood, Barcelona, 1770: household type by household size*

Household size	Solitaries* No.	Without family structure No.	Simple family household No.	Extended family household No.	Multiple family household No.	Total No.
1 member	3	0	0	0	0	3
2–4 members	2	8	29	8	0	47
5–7 members	2	1	18	10	6	37
More than 7 members	1	1	3	4	4	13
Total	8	10	50	22	10	100

Source: Own elaboration, *Llibres de Matrícula dels alcaldes de barri*, 1770, AHCB.
*We consider solitary households those whose head is a widower, an unmarried person or an undetermined person, with or without co-residents.

holds (Table 8). The relatives incorporated by the conjugal unit tended to be nieces, parents-in-law, sisters-in-law, or simply appear in the documentation as a relative. Mobility was infrequent among these related members, and they appear fairly well integrated in the family structure, compared to the much more mobile unrelated co-residents. Solidarity, reciprocity, but also mutual interest were what led many simple family households to incorporate more or less distant relatives. This is demonstrated by the large number of requests from those who went to the city poorhouse to recover nieces, or other relatives, so that they might help in the home.[24] On the other hand, in adverse circumstances, extended family households were prepared to relinquish these close relatives. The applications for admission to the poorhouse are full of the testimonies of women who (temporarily or permanently) were leaving their nieces or other relatives, and children leaving their elderly mothers. This shows the complementary nature and simultaneity of strategies: changes in household size and composition, and the use of social institutions.

All the ten multiple family households had nonrelated co-residents (Table 6). These households – those made up of more than one conjugal unit – were the largest in the sample analysed up to now: six had between five and seven members, and the remaining four over seven members. It would therefore appear that, despite the multiplicity of conjugal nuclei, the presence of apprentices, maids, or tenants was still required, depending on the circumstances of each household and on the status of the families making it up. It is interesting to underline that most multiple-family households were made up of conjugal units not related to each other – as one might expect them to be – but rather linked by contractual relations, often of an informal nature. The juxtaposition of artisan and wage-earner families, gardeners and veil-weavers, day labourers and streetsellers, galloon-makers and stocking-weavers, among others, was common. The formation of multiple-family households was probably due to different reasons, either need, interest and/or reciprocity. These households often originated from the sum of fragile conjugal units of two or three members. This, for example, would be the case of the household formed – according to Laslett's terminology – by two "incomplete" conjugal nuclei and one single person, distributed as follows: (a) Francisca Martí, a widow, the head of the household with a day labourer son and his wife; (b) Josepha Mas, whose husband is absent, being in exile, and a son who appears as a trader and who must have been a street seller; (c) Mariangela Guitart, a widow who after a short while moved to another household in a nearby street.[25] In other cases the multiple or

---

24. Regarding the role welfare institutions had in migration and in entering the labour market, see Carbonell, *Sobreviure*, pp. 125–169. Regarding the role of the state, see Carmen Sarasúa, "The Role of the State in Shaping Women's and Men's Entrance into the Labour Market: Spain in the Eighteenth and Nineteenth Centuries", *Continuity and Change*, 12 (1997), pp. 347–371.

25. AHCB, Cadastre I–5.

plurinuclear households are conceived as a temporary alliance to lessen the cost of the rent, or to help the integration of those who have recently arrived in the city. This would be the case of Juan Solé, a velvet-weaver who shared his home, together with his wife, Madalena Solé, their two sons and one daughter, with Joseph Campdesunyer, a veil-weaver and his wife, Manuela Campdesunyer, and three boys.[26] One year later they no longer live at the same address, once again demonstrating the enormous residential mobility and dynamism of the households in the lower-class neighbourhoods of Barcelona at the end of the 1700s.

Lastly, a significant percentage of households without a family structure and of solitaries' households with co-residents is observed. The line between the two types is very delicate. Using Laslett's terminology, those households made up of brothers and/or sisters and those made up of unrelated men and women were considered to be households without a family structure. In general, the households of this type are made up of people whose links are due to relations of craft and opportunity. This is the case of the household whose head was Antonio Cervera, a regimental cadet, made up of a further two cadets and a sub-lieutenant,[27] or the case of Pablo Vilarubias, an incumbent of the church of Sant Pere, who shared a household with a legal practitioner, a lawyer and a servant.[28] On the other hand, the solitaries' households included both those which consisted just of one person, mainly widows, and those where a single person had taken in a servant, lodger or even tenant. For example, Pedro Bayon, a guard lieutenant, with a servant and his wife, or Miguel Soler, a priest of Las Junqueres monastery, with a servant and a student.[29]

COMPLEMENTARY SURVIVAL STRATEGIES: THE USE OF CREDIT AND WELFARE INSTITUTIONS, AND CHANGES IN HOUSEHOLD COMPOSITION

On crossing the sources relating to household composition and to the men and women who used the *Mont de Pietat de Barcelona* between January and February 1770 as borrowers, we can observe that eighteen per cent of the households studied used pawning as a means of obtaining credit. Generally speaking, the behaviour of these households in relation to credit comes within the outline described in the first section of this article.[30] Which

26. *Ibid.*
27. *Ibid.*
28. *Ibid.*
29. *Ibid.*
30. Out of eighteen pawnings, three were done by women, one of whom had an absent husband. Two of the male pawners were widowers. Concerning the household heads' occupations, the most represented sector is manufacturing (twelve cases), especially textiles and clothing, followed by services (three cases). The articles most frequently pawned were clothes, and the value of the loans was extremely small. About half of the pawners recovered their pledge, as in the large sample.

Table 9. *Borrowers of the Mont de Pietat by household type, Barcelona 1770*

Household type	With co-residents	Without co-residents	Total = 100
Solitaries	2	0	2
Without family structure	0	0	0
Simple family household	5	7	12
Extended family household	2	0	2
Multiple family household	2	0	2
Total = 100	11	7	18

Source: Own elaboration, *Llibres de Matrícula dels alcaldes de barri*, AHCB

were the households that demonstrated the greatest tendency to use this institution? Table 9 shows that the simple family households, and especially those without co-residents, are overrepresented. This finding suggests that these households are more vulnerable and at greater risk of depending on credit institutions. The complexity of the households, and co-residence, was probably a strategy which allowed families and individuals a greater degree of independence from both the joint credit and welfare institutions, such as the *Mont*, and the purely welfare institutions.

This is not necessarily contradicted by the fact that many households with co-residents also resorted to pawning. The borrower was often not the head of the household but rather a co-resident – and not necessarily a maid or a servant, who could be pawning on the orders of their masters. Here we have a clear demonstration of individual strategies which overlap or run parallel to those of the household, an aspect which will be tackled later. This would be the case of Jayme Matheu, a shoemaker, who was a co-resident paying for his lodgings. He lived in a simple family household consisting of the head of the household, Jayme Blanch, another shoemaker, with the latter's wife, two apprentices and a married man, whose trade and the whereabouts of whose wife are not known.[31] Jayme Matheu, in his capacity as a lodger, used the *Mont de Pietat* on two occasions. On the first he obtained an important credit for which he eventually abandoned the pledge, earrings and a gold ring. On the second occasion, he just pawned some woollen skirts and obtained a microcredit that he would manage to repay. This constitutes an example of an individual strategy at the heart of a simple family household with apprentice and lodger co-residents.

The most revealing result of Table 9, however, is the predominance of simple family households without co-residents which coincide fully with the nuclear family. Seven out of the eighteen households which used the *Mont* belong to this group. These include those with a woman as the head of the

From January to December 1770, most clients (fifteen out of eighteen) used the *Mont* several (up to seven) times.
31. AHCB, Cadastre 1–5.

household, and those formed by a couple with several small children. An illustration of the first of these two types is the household of Catarina Martí, with an absent husband, her son, Francisco Martí, a sailor, who used the *Mont* on three occasions to pawn a woollen cloak which he recovered and again pawned, representing an example of successful management of the microcredit.[32] This case shows how not only a lodger, but even a son had his own property and strategy. Another case of a simple family household without co-residents was that of Magin Pares, a tailor, his partner Madalena Pares and their four under-age children, three boys and a girl, who used the *Mont de Pietat* on two occasions in the winter of 1770.[33] On the first occasion they lost the pledge and on the second occasion they recovered it. After one year the simple family household still had the same composition but they moved house. In this case, access to credit allowed them to over-come their difficulties without varying the composition of their household. Despite this, the percentage of failure in the repayment of loans among simple family households was the highest of the sample.

The simple family households, without co-residents, are also those which appear most frequently in the requests for admission to the public or parish welfare institutions of the time in the city of Barcelona.[34] Illness or the death of one of the spouses could make it impossible for all the members of the household to survive in the same house. Rosa Vidal, a young widow resident in Barcelona, requested admission to the *Borsa de Pobres Vergonyants*[35] of the parish of El Pi of this city, arguing that her husband had died a year earlier and that the little she earned was not enough to maintain her young daughter. She related all the difficulties that she had to go through during the illness of her husband and complained that she "had to abandon and sell everything she had to relieve the illness of her husband".[36] The term "abandon" undoubtedly refers to the pawning of belongings that she never recovered. Obtaining credit by pawning did not succeed in detaining the process of progressive impoverishment which led this nuclear family, struck down by the demographic lottery, to dependence on assistance and charity. The response of this nuclear family to these adversities begins with the pawning and loss of belongings, and ends with admission to the *Borsa de Pobres Vergonyants* of the parish of Santa Maria del Pi. We do not know all the successive steps that this woman and her young daughter followed, but they most probably had to resort at some time to temporarily leaving the daughter in the *Casa de Misericòrdia* and the woman joining another house-hold as a servant or close relative. The complementary nature of the survival

32. *Ibid.*
33. *Ibid.*
34. See Carbonell, *Sobreviure a Barcelona*, pp. 119–161.
35. See note 3 above.
36. Arxiu Parroquial de Santa Maria del Pi, Pobres Vergonyants, 1798.

strategies undertaken – access to social institutions, co-residence and net-works of relations – are clear in this example.

The vulnerability of the nuclear family emerges as an irrefutable fact in the welfare archives of the eighteenth century. Given the fragility of the critical phases of the family cycle (infancy, the raising of children and old age), the survival of the nuclear family inescapably depended both on the existence of a network of social benefits arising from public and/or parish assistance, and on networks of relations, neighbours, trade or co-residence with which to establish relationships of reciprocity. These options were not dichotomous in the Barcelona of the late 1700s, but rather complementary. To be sure, the welfare institutions in the period studied were insufficient for the needs of the city. Evidence of this is that between 1772 and 1775 a Royal Commission was created to plan a new hospice in the city and King Charles III increased the funds that the public treasury regularly provided for the existing institutions. Nevertheless, many simple family households resorted to public assistance. In addition, they activated their networks of relations or neighbours, and at the same time many transformed the compo-sition of their households in their fight for survival. Co-residence of an institutional (hospitals, hospices, shelters, poorhouses, etc.) or civil (common households) nature were options taken simultaneously by some family units. For example Paula Martí, whose soldier husband was absent, had her daughter admitted to the *Misericòrdia* and went to serve in the house of a relative.[37] The different forms of co-residence, whether civil or institutional, could therefore offset the vulnerability of the nuclear family. Simple family households without co-residents, that is those corresponding to the nuclear family, were those which were at a greater disadvantage when faced with the difficulties raised by the situation of the times or the demo-graphic lottery.

The analysis carried out so far suggests that the extended family house-holds – those which include close relatives – had a greater degree of flexi-bility when faced with adverse situations. Their composition allows the number of members to be modified without altering the family nucleus. This is the case of a household whose head was Raymundo Mullet, a veil-weaver, who, after losing and abandoning the objects pawned in the *Mont de Pietat*, chose to have a relative admitted to the *Casa de Misericòrdia*. Raymundo Mullet lived with his wife Paronilla Argemí, their journeyman son, a niece, his wife's stepmother and an apprentice called Joseph Masso. It was the latter who went to the *Mont de Pietat* on seven occasions in 1770 (from January to December), almost always abandoning the pledge. He only recovered it on two occasions when he had pawned gold earrings, in contrast losing hemp sheets, napkins, pieces of cotton, doublets, breeches

---

37. Arxiu Històric de la Casa de Misericòrdia de Barcelona (AHCMB), Assistencial, Expedients d'ingrés d'acollides, any 1777.

and woollen skirts. This apprentice probably went to the pawnshop on behalf of the family who took him in, like a maid would have done for her master, as it is unlikely that an apprentice would have had items of household furnishing such as napkins and sheets. What is certain is that this extended household of a veil-weaver systematically used the credit institution throughout 1770, could not repay its debts and abandoned a good part of its belongings. A few months later, during 1771, Mullet's wife died. On 14 January 1772 Maria Busquets, his wife's stepmother, was taken to the hospice (*Casa de Misericòrdia*) by her son-in-law, where she died two years later. In 1777 the former extended household of Raymundo Mullet had already parted with – or been abandoned by – the apprentice and the niece, and had thus been reduced to two members: the veil-weaver and his son.[38] Indeed, extended family households played a key role in shaping the interest and reciprocity networks which governed blood relationships. The welfare archives are full of examples of households who part with and/or recover, temporarily or permanently, elderly parents or other close relatives, often youths of both sexes who work as apprentices or servants. For example Joan Barnius, a wage earner from Badalona, married with two children, asked for his mother, Maria Foxart, to be admitted to the *Misericòrdia* in June 1777, as he could no longer maintain her, and undertook to pay the institution a daily sum to support her thanks to "the mercy of some relatives [who] helped me to pay".[39] This is an example of an extended family household which simultaneously used the institutions, the relationship networks and modification of the household composition in its survival strategy.

Lastly, the analysis of the households of the Sant Pere neighbourhood who resorted to pawning between January and February 1770 has demonstrated the coexistence of different individual and family strategies which arose at the heart of some households, especially in complex households with a high degree of co-residence. We confirmed this phenomenon on observing that, in seven out of eighteen cases, the borrower who went to the *Mont de Pietat* in search of credit was not the head of the household but rather another member, acting in accordance with their own needs and strategies, which were sometimes individual and sometimes family. This is the case of the multiple household made up of two conjugal units and two single people, in which the heads of the families were a velvet-weaver journeyman and a galloon-maker journeyman, together with two co-residents, one of them a stocking-weaver journeyman and the other an unspecified apprentice.[40] This household presented a great homogeneity of trade, silk appearing to be the element which brought them together. The

38. AHCB, Cadastre 1–5. This household is one of those for which the documentary evidence is particularly rich.
39. AHCB. Assistencial, Expedients d'ingrés d'acollides, any 1777.
40. AHCB, Cadastre, 1–5.

appearance, in the sample analysed, of plurinuclear households of journeymen and apprentices was a recurrent phenomenon. We do not know what contractual and/or reciprocal relations were established between these conjugal units and these single people, but the surname of all the male members of the domestic unit was Ribó, and therefore, although the documentation exceptionally does not specify this, they were probably related, if only distantly. The head of the household was Juan Ribó, the velvet-weaver journeyman, married with four young children. It was Gaspar Ribó, the galloon-maker journeyman, married with one son, who went to the *Mont* in search of credit on three occasions. On all three occasions he pawned and recovered the same article, a pair of gold earrings. The fact that it was not the head of the household who went to the *Mont* suggests the coexistence of different strategies at the heart of the domestic unit. Decision-making could come from different coexisting decision centres, depending on the type of relations linking the members of the domestic unit, and on the different degrees of autonomy and complementariness of the individual, family and household strategies. Therefore, household survival strategies should not necessarily be seen as singular and homogeneous. They are often supported by the confluence or simultaneity of individual and family strategies which can coexist under the same roof. This multiplicity of strategies at the heart of the domestic unit is also observed in the case of households whose head is a single person who takes in co-residents. A good example of this is Joseph Casals, a stocking-weaver journeyman, head of the household, who lived with Pedro Curulla, a baker journeyman, his family – made up of wife, two sons and one daughter, and another suckling that the wife was wet-nursing in exchange for a regular income – and a surgeon journeyman.[41] The head of the household, who in this case was single, probably controlled access to the house, but it was the baker whose family circumstances obliged him to use the pawnshop. This example therefore constitutes a further indication of the diversity and complementary nature of the strategies taken within a household, in which complex forms of co-residence and the use of credit institutions occurred in a parallel manner.

CONCLUSION

This study on microcredit and household composition in one of the densely-populated lowest-class neighbourhoods (Sant Pere) of Barcelona in the late eighteenth century, has shown how common all forms of co-residence were. Complex households were frequent, whereas simple family households, especially those without co-residents, were relatively few. Crossing the sources on households and on microcredit revealed the complementary nature of the survival strategies, which went from the option

41. *Ibid.*

of co-residence, with the consequent modification in household size and composition, to the option of access to credit and welfare institutions. In Barcelona at the end of the 1700s these two options were not mutually exclusive but rather occurred simultaneously at the heart of many households. The households most dependent on these institutions were probably the simple family households without co-residents, whose viability required the use of the social benefits available. Finally, this study also shows the need to understand the household as a space where different individual and family strategies can come together or be developed in a parallel way. Household survival strategies did not therefore always have a single, homogenous character, but rather they could be the result of the confluence of various different strategies, and they were thus plural.

Translated by Richard Pike

International Review of Social History 45 (2000), pp. 93–113
© 2000 Internationaal Instituut voor Sociale Geschiedenis

Poor Jewish Families in Early Modern Rural Swabia

SABINE ULLMANN

I

"Jewish protection rights" (*Judenschutzrechte*) – the legal category according to which Jews were tolerated in a few territories of the old German Empire during the early modern period – made it difficult for Jewish subjects to establish a secure existence. There were, above all, two reasons for this. First, the personalized nature of protection rights enabled the respective authorities to develop selective settlement policies oriented consistently towards the fiscal interests of the state. The direct results of this were increased tributary payments and the withdrawal of one's "protection document" (*Schutzbrief*) if taxes were not paid. Second, legislators for the territories developed a multiplicity of restrictive decrees concerning the gainful employment of Jews.[1] Consequently, there were only a few economic niches in which "privileged Jews" (*Schutzjuden*) were permitted to earn a living. In the countryside – which is where such settlements were mainly situated in the early modern period[2] – Jews were thus dependent upon peddling foods, textiles and cattle as well as upon lending money. The specific methods of business which developed from this were reflected in the anti-Jewish legend of the deceptive travelling salesman who, by awakening ever new consumer needs, brought his Christian customers into increasing debt.[3] If one confronts this legend with reality, one finds two characteristic methods of business which arose out of necessity: the cultivation of a varied palette of goods offered, and the development of a differentiated system of payment by instalments. At the same time, these business methods accorded with the

1. On the status of protected Jews (*Schutzjuden*), see in particular the work of Friedrich J. Battenburg (with references to older articles): Friedrich J. Battenberg, "Rechtliche Rahmenbedingungen jüdischer Existenz in der Frühneuzeit zwischen Reich und Territorium", in Rolf Kießling (ed.), *Judengemeinden in Schwaben im Kontext des Alten Reiches*, Colloquia Augustana 2 (Berlin, 1995), pp. 53–79.
2. On this phenomenon in general, see Monika Richarz, "Die Entdeckung der Landjuden. Stand und Probleme ihrer Erforschung am Beispiel Südwestdeutschlands", in Karl Heinz Burmeister (ed.), *Landjudentum im süddeutschen und Bodenseeraum. Wissenschaftliche Tagung zur Eröffnung des Jüdischen Museums Hohenems 1991*, Forschungen zur Geschichte Vorarlbergs 11 (Dornbirn, 1992), pp. 11–22; Monika Richarz and Reinhard Rürup (eds), *Jüdisches Leben auf dem Lande. Studien zur deutsch-jüdischen Geschichte*, Schriftenreihe wissenschaftlicher Abhandlungen des Leo Baeck Instituts 56 (Tübingen, 1997).
3. On the formation of stereotypes, see Stefan Rohrbacher and Michael Schmidt, *Judenbilder. Kulturgeschichte antijüdischer Mythen und antisemitischer Vorurteile* (Reinbek, 1991).

model of an "economy of makeshift".[4] In the sense of such "makeshift trade",[5] Jewish peddlers were prepared to travel for days in order to make even the most insignificant profits.

Since both the permission to engage in a trade, and residency rights, depended upon the possession of a "protection document", acquiring such a document assumed a key position in the life plans of Jews. At the same time, the loss of this privilege, or refusal to permit it to be passed on to the next generation, implied the danger of slipping into the status of vagabonding "begging Jews",[6] not only for the male head of the family, but for the other members of the household as well.

Thus, the basic situation of Jewish families struggling for subsistence differed fundamentally from that of their Christian neighbours. Securing an existence under these difficult conditions – limited settlement possibilities, greater tributary payments and trade restrictions – required a broad repertoire of survival strategies. In this article, I will use the example of Simon and Merle Ulman, a married Jewish couple from Pfersee, to illustrate some of the characteristic risks to which Jewish families were exposed (section III), as well as how these families coped with such risks (section IV). In order to highlight the behavioural patterns, I have consciously chosen a "borderline case", that is, a family which was threatened with the loss of its privileges, but which was able ultimately to avoid a life on the streets – a life which had its own forms of existence, such as vagabonding, begging and petty crime. Thus, my focus is not on members of the so-called "beggar Jewry", who lived on the margins of Jewish society, but rather on a family from the poorest class of those rural Jews who were settled and privileged with a "protection document". My investigation begins with a depiction of the Ulmans' work situation and their financial circumstances, as well as their marital work organization (section II). In a final section, I will discuss

---

4. On the concept of an "economy of makeshift", see Olwen H. Hufton, *The Poor of Eighteenth-Century France 1750–1789* (Oxford, 1974), pp. 69–127. See also Jürgen Schlumbohm, *Lebensläufe, Familien, Höfe. Die Bauern und Heuerleute des Osnabrückischen Kirchspiels Belm in proto-industrieller Zeit, 1650–1860*, Veröffentlichungen des Max-Planck-Instituts für Geschichte 110 (Göttingen, 1994), pp. 293f.
5. On the radius of activity of Jewish peddlers, see Sabine Ullmann, *Nachbarschaft und Konkurrenz: Juden und Christen in Dörfern der Markgrafschaft Burgau*, Veröffentlichungen des Max-Planck-Instituts für Geschichte 151 (Göttingen, 1999), pp. 255–265.
6. Rudolf Glanz, *Geschichte des niederen jüdischen Volkes in Deutschland. Eine Studie über historisches Gaunertum, Bettelwesen und Vagantentum*, (New York, 1968), pp. 60–128; Uwe Danker, *Räuberbanden im Alten Reich um 1700. Ein Beitrag zur Geschichte von Herrschaft und Kriminalität in der frühen Neuzeit* (Frankfurt/M., 1988), pp. 318–326; Ernst Schubert, *Arme Leute, Bettler und Gauner im Franken des 18. Jahrhunderts*, Veröffentlichungen der Gesellschaft für fränkische Geschichte Reihe IX, 26 (Neustadt/Aisch, 1983), pp. 169–178; Jacov Guggenheim, "Meeting on the Road: Encounters between German Jews and Christians on the Margins of Society", in Ronnie Po-chia Hsia and Hartmut Lehmann (eds), *In and Out of the Ghetto: Jewish–Gentile Relations in Late Medieval and Early Modern Germany* (Cambridge, 1995), pp. 125–137.

several possible consequences which these specific patterns of behaviour had on the structure of Jewish households (section V).

In order to support my interpretation of the case study selected here, I will also draw upon supplementary references to other families throughout the article. However, due to the limitations of existing sources regarding Jewish history, we will have to content ourselves with relatively limited insights into the details of Jewish life at this time. There are several reasons for this. Before the legislation concerning the emancipation of Jews, Jewish legal autonomy dictated that private legal contracts as well as intrafamilial disputes were negotiated before a rabbi. Since the Jewish communal archives in Swabia have been almost completely destroyed,[7] we are dependent to a great extent upon sources which are Christian in origin. During the course of the eighteenth century, the recording of such documents did increase, as many protected Jews also began to provide evidence of their marital contracts or testaments before Christian courts. However, the use of Christian authorities was by no means generally adopted among Jews, and, even when it was used, Hebrew contracts were often kept by Christian authorities only in summarized translation. Thus, the insights into the intra-Jewish world offered by such sources is often selective. The gainful employment of protected Jews, on the contrary, has been documented much more substantially. We owe the existence of these documents to the legal requirement that Jewish–Christian trade contracts, even for the most insignificant business transactions, be recorded – a measure supposed to protect the Christian population from what was held to be Jewish "profiteering". Although the authoritarian measures in the Swabian territories investigated here by no means provide us with a complete record of documents, they do offer us a significant amount of material about Jewish businesses. In this way, we are able to follow the business dealings of the Ulman family, albeit with interruptions, for the time period between December 1700 and October 1723, with selective references for the years 1686 and 1725.

II

Simon and Merle Ulman earned a living in Pfersee primarily as pawnbrokers and merchants, engaging in business with the inhabitants of the imperial city of Augsburg located nearby – a specialization which was typical for this suburban community.[8] Due to the great concentration of Jewish settlements in this region, the merchants in the Swabian Jewish villages – for whom we are able to make the following observations[9] – were faced with intra-Jewish

7. Doris Pfister, "Quellen zur Geschichte der Juden in Schwaben", in Peter Fassl (ed.), *Geschichte und Kultur der Juden in Schwaben*, Irseer Schriften 2 (Sigmaringen, 1994), pp. 9–19.
8. Ullmann, *Nachbarschaft und Konkurrenz*, pp. 265–268.
9. Rolf Kießling, "Zwischen Vertreibung und Emanzipation – Judendörfer in Ostschwaben während der Frühen Neuzeit", in Kießling, *Judengemeinden in Schwaben*, pp. 154–183.

competition, which led to a spatial and functional specialization. While Jews
in the so-called suburban communities, such as Pfersee, supplied urban residents with rural goods and money loans, communities located in the provinces, away from urban centres, concentrated above all on doing business with
peasants in the surrounding villages. The village Pfersee, situated directly
before the gates of the imperial city of Augsburg, was one of the typical "Jewish
villages" in Swabia. Around 1700, approximately sixteen per cent of its inhabitants were Jewish. All of them can be characterized as "protected Jews", i.e.,
they had been granted residential and business privileges.

Judging from the magnitude of the Ulmans' business contracts in the
years between 1686 and 1725, as well as from descriptions of the items
pawned with them, we can classify their business unambiguously as the
most minor retail trade. These documents also reflect the explicitly poor
economic situation of the family. The textiles recorded are without exception of inferior quality, the designs so simple that they required no further
description. They are usually described tersely as "1 coat or 1 piece gray
cloth".[10] In those cases in which there is a more detailed entry, the comments suggest an inferior design, indicated by the predominance of the
colours black and brown, and of cotton flannel and wool as materials, as
well as the lack of silk and velvet. Pieces of jewellery or more valuable
household items were not among the objects pawned with them.[11] A dispute
with a customer, the craftsman Mathias Mennhofer from Augsburg, reveals
that Simon did not always have the necessary capital for his loan business.
On 2 January 1772, Mennhofer accused him of not being able to return
pawned items – a belt and two bedspreads – which Mennhofer had wanted
to redeem for 6 florins. During the course of the court proceedings, we
learn that Simon had himself sold the objects to a Jewish man from Kriegshaber before the prescribed expiration date, as he desperately needed the
money. The authorities refrained from punishing Simon, but ordered him
to buy back the pawned items and to give them to Mennhofer.[12] In addition
to this business, Simon Ulman engaged in a goods trade which is not more
precisely described in the records – references to this trade can be found
above all in his outstanding debts to businessmen in Augsburg.[13] The con-
nection between the pawn business and the small goods trade is obvious and
has been demonstrated often. Numerous items were pawned with Jewish
merchants and then were never bought back. After the expiration of a certain amount of time, these unredeemed items became the property of the

10. Staatsarchiv Augsburg [hereafter StaatsAA], Reichsstadt Augsburg, Literalien, St. Jakobs
Pfründe no. 202, fos 90, 98, entries from the year 1686.
11. StaatsAA, Reichsstadt Augsburg, Literalien, St. Jakobs Pfründe no. 207, fo. 47, entry from the
year 1722.
12. *Ibid.*
13. See section IV of this article.

Jewish merchants, who could then resell them. From the loans for deposits, a small goods trade developed with these unredeemed items.

Given the conditions described above, it is clear that a Jewish family could not earn a subsistence living through the male head of the household alone. His wife had to work in the family business as well. On numerous occasions, the pawn contracts of Simon's wife were recorded with the bailiff (*Dorfvogt*). For example, the student Philipp Anton Schmidt pawned "upper and lower beddings" with her for 6 florins and 15 kreuzer.[14] In concluding the deal, Merle had the authorities confirm that after the expiration of a four-week period the bedclothes would become her property. In 1725, she reported the purchase of a "poor and completely worn out red coat for the sum of 2 fl".[15] Merle was not an isolated case in this respect. In the first two decades of the eighteenth century alone, there are ten Jewish businesswomen in the Pfersee community who appear in the official protocols. For the most part, these cases dealt with business transactions which had led to disputes as the result of lost pawn tickets or unredeemed items. In February 1702, for example, a Jewish woman named Vögelin brought a complaint against a gold-beater from Augsburg, because the latter was more than a year over-due in paying her interest. Vögelin received permission from the bailiff to resell the pawned objects – several pieces of jewellery – in order to compen-sate for her losses.[16] In the same year, a Jewish woman named Schenlin reported a pawn deal in which "1 green woman's jacket and 1 black shirt" had been left with her – the deal had been concluded several months ago and the ticket had subsequently been lost. She, too, received permission to resell the articles of clothing.[17] Although evidence of women's business activities can also be found sporadically in trade with rural goods and cattle,[18] the pawn business appears to have played a particularly important role for women. Being a widow was not a precondition for such business activity. Jewish wives also engaged in such transactions.

Michael Toch has repeatedly emphasized the special economic position of women in all social classes in late medieval urban Jewish communities.[19]

14. StaatsAA, Reichsstadt Augsburg, Literalien, St. Jakobs Pfründe no. 207, fo. 47, entry from the year 1722.

15. StaatsAA, Reichsstadt Augsburg, Literalien, St. Jakobs Pfründe no. 207, fo. 360, entry from the year 1725.

16. StaatsAA, Adel, Literalien, von Langenmantel no. 34, fo. 69v.

17. StaatsAA, Adel, Literalien, von Langenmantel no. 34, fo. 91v. See in addition to this, the following entries regarding Jewish business women: StaatsAA, Reichsstadt Augsburg, Literalien, St. Jakobs Pfründe no. 204, fo. 56; no. 207, fos 37, 46, 223, 254, 486; StaatsAA, Adel, Literalien, von Langenmantel no. 34, fos 20v, 46v, 92v, 131v, 169r.

18. On 16 April 1706, the Jewish woman Köhlin from Pfersee had the courts record a cattle contract which she had made with the peasant Jakob Mayer. See StaatsAA, Adel, Literalien, von Langenmantel no. 34, fo. 162v.

19. Michael Toch, *Die Juden im mittelalterlichen Reich*, Enzyklopädie deutscher Geschichte 44 (München, 1998), p. 15; *idem*, "Die jüdische Frau im Erwerbsleben des Spätmittelalters", in Julius Carlebach (ed.), *Zur Geschichte der jüdischen Frau in Deutschland* (Berlin, 1993), pp. 37–48. For

Evidently this was also true for Jews in village communities in the early modern period. This economic position accords with the image – almost a *topos* – of the independent Jewish businesswomen in the pre-Assimilation era, an image which we have come to know, for example, through the memoirs of Glückel von Hameln.[20] Merle's business activities were thus typical for the life conditions of rural Jewish women in the early modern period. They also seem to have been a plausible necessity for a family engaged in the pawn business. Since making rounds through the trade district required extended travel by the husband, local business was probably carried out to a large extent by their wives. The entries in the official protocols of such communities and the regular business contracts with Christian village neighbours demonstrate, in addition to this, that a portion of business life was actually carried out within Jewish villages, and that there were also business deals which were not concluded during such travel on the road.

In spite of their familial cooperation, the Ulmans were able to make only very small profits from their businesses. This is indicated by their position within the social structure of the Jewish village. According to the Pfersee tax list from 1689, Simon Ulman had assets of 700 florins, which placed him among the poorest in his community – only three other protected Jew households had less than this (600 fl., 500 fl., and 200 fl.). Lazarus Günzburger had the greatest assets in the community with 18,500 fl., and a different Ulman family,[21] who where "court Jews", had assets of 5,000 fl. Simon and Merle's modest living conditions were also reflected in the house they owned. Like most of the Jewish households in Pfersee – only five of which are listed in the records as renters (*Beisasse*) – the Ulmans owned real estate.[22] According to the Pfersee property register from 1701, Simon possessed a so-called *Selde*, a house without agricultural acreage, which was valued at 500 fl.[23] We find similarly low valuations for a series of other Jewish houses

the early modern period, see Monika Richarz, "In Familien, Handel und Salon. Jüdische Frauen vor und nach der Emanzipation der deutschen Juden", in Karin Hausen and Heide Wunder (eds), *Frauengeschichte – Geschlechtergeschichte*, Reihe Geschichte und Geschlechter 1 (Frankfurt/ M. [etc.], 1992), pp. 57–66, 60, and Julius Carlebach, "Family Structure and the Position of Jewish Women", in Werner E. Mosse *et al.* (eds), *Revolution and Evolution: 1848 in German-Jewish History*, Schriftenreihe wissenschaftlicher Abhandlungen des Leo-Baeck-Instituts 39 (Tübingen, 1981), pp. 157–187. See also the critique of Carlebach by Marion Kaplan, "Family Structure and the Position of Jewish Women: A Comment", in *ibid.*, pp. 189–203.

20. Glückel von Hameln, *Die Memoiren, aus dem Jüdisch-Deutschen von Bertha Pappenheim* (1910, new edition Weinheim, 1994). Most recently, Natalie Zemon Davis, *Women on the Margins: Three Seventeenth-Century Lives Glikl, Marie de l'Incarnation, Maria Sibylla Merian* (Cambridge, 1995).

21. Sabine Ullmann, "Zwischen Fürstenhöfen und Gemeinde. Die jüdische Hoffaktorenfamilie Ulman in Pfersee während des 18. Jahrhunderts", *Zeitschrift des Historischen Vereins für Schwaben*, 90 (1998), pp. 159–187.

22. Ullmann, *Nachbarschaft und Konkurrenz*, appendix no. 11.

23. *Ibid.*, p. 533 and appendix no. 14 (Kartenbeilage).

in the community, several of which were even valued significantly lower than the Ulmans' house. However, the wealthy Löw Simon Ulman had property valued at 1,800 fl., again illustrating the significant differences in assets within the community, and placing Simon and Merle's household among the poorer in the community. In 1723, Simon's house was described as being in a "completely ruinous" condition.[24] Significantly, Simon also used the epithet "the Small", which allowed him to be distinguished unambiguously from the court Jews of the same name in the village.

III

Initially the Ulman couple was able make a living and to pay the authorities' tax demands. Only in the winter of 1718 did Merle Ulman decide to disclose their economic crisis. She had the local authorities declare her husband legally incapacitated, and pressed to have the residency rights of his two sons in the village withdrawn. The official village protocol stated that in the future "on directions of his wife, no one should loan him any items or lend him money, and that he should also be requested by officials to remove his two sons from his house so that they earn a living elsewhere".[25] With this, Merle had violated basic norms of traditional Jewish society. She not only provided the Christian authorities with an opportunity to intervene in intra-Jewish affairs — an occurrence which the leaders of the Jewish community complained about repeatedly[26] — but demanded, at the same time, the use of an anti-Jewish legal instrument, i.e., the withdrawal of residency privileges. Turning to Christian authorities appears to have had little success initially, as Simon Ulman's business activities are recorded even after this, for example, in January 1722.[27] Only following the summer of 1723 do his traces disappear from official documents. Whether the sons were actually expelled from the village cannot be determined from the records. On the tax lists from 1722, there are three children listed in the Ulman household,[28] but since the sex of these children is not recorded, it is not clear whether these were daughters of the couple or whether they included the two sons.

References to Simon Ulman's business dealings in the Pfersee judicial protocols make Merle's decision perhaps understandable and also indicate that this crisis had a long history. Her husband's first debt contract for over 75 fl. dates from 12 December 1700. In 1702, he had to appear before the village administrator's office twice to answer the demands of a creditor, the businessman Andreas Wagner from Kaufbeuren. After Simon was not able to make his payments on time, he was finally forced to take out a mortgage

24. StaatsAA, Reichsstadt Augsburg, Literalien, St. Jakobs Pfründe no. 207, fo. 119.
25. Stadtarchiv Augsburg [hereafter StadtAA], St Jakobs Pfründe, Fach 112 Lit. A, fo. 191.
26. Ullmann, *Nachbarschaft und Konkurrenz*, pp. 192f.
27. StaatsAA, Reichsstadt Augsburg, Literalien, St. Jakobs Pfründe no. 207, fo. 3. See also above.
28. Ullmann, *Nachbarschaft und Konkurrenz*, pp. 535f.

on his house.[29] Although he did not pay back the mortgage, he was subsequently able to borrow 160 fl. on his property again in July 1705, and on 17 September 1706, Johann Jakob Goldschlager even raised the mortgage another 24 fl.[30] By February 1711, Simon's situation had worsened to such an extent that there was supposed to "be a public auction by the authorities due to his many debts", i.e. Simon was threatened with a forced sale of his house. Since another Augsburger merchant, Philipp Heggenauer, was prepared to assume Simon's debts to Goldschlager, the compulsory auction, however, was again delayed.[31] In spite of this, Simon could not in the end prevent financial ruin. In the following year, the couple was summoned before the bailiff by Andreas Wagner from Kaufbeuren due to an unpaid bill of 50 fl. Merle now used her dowry to assume liability for this debt. She signed the contract under the express waiver of her "female privilege", i.e. the right that her own capital remain untouched.[32] When, in the summer of 1718, her husband finally pawned their two synagogue seats, Merle filed charges and the conflict between the couple was settled in court. She requested that the bailiff "look into the matter, to find out why the two men and women's school seats had been sold".[33] The pawning of synagogue seats, admittedly, was not an unusual solution for poor Jewish families.[34] However, the possession of such seats not only identified the owner as a full member of the Jewish community and provided him with a place in the village hierarchy analogous to the seating arrangement. It was also tied to the enjoyment of honorary functions in the synagogue. For this reason, seats were pawned usually only as a last resort.[35] In selling the synagogue seats, Simon had crossed a boundary, and provoked Merle to take the respective countermeasure of turning to the Christian authorities. Caught in a spiral of increasing debt, Simon had lost not only his house and a portion of his wife's dowry, but the family's synagogue seats as well, which – in addition to their material value – were understood as symbolic capital.

29. StaatsAA, Adel, Literalien, von Langenmantel no. 34, fos 32r, 68, 87v, 97v.
30. *Ibid.*, fos 144r, 178r.
31. StaatsAA, Reichsstadt Augsburg, Literalien, St. Jakobs Pfründe no. 204, fo. 42.
32. StaatsAA, Reichsstadt Augsburg, Literalien, St. Jakobs Pfründe no. 204, fo. 111. This procedure accords with the Christian practice. On this, see David Warren Sabean, "Allianzen und Listen: Die Geschlechtsvormundschaft im 18. und 19. Jahrhundert", in Ute Gerhard (ed.), *Frauen in der Geschichte des Rechts: Von der Frühen Neuzeit bis zur Gegenwart* (Munich, 1997), pp. 460–479. I owe the reference on the conceptual explanation of "female privilege" (*weibliche Freiheit*) to Christine Werkstetter. See also her investigation of the legal practice in Augsburg: Christine Werkstetter, "Frauen im Augsburger Zunfthandwerk. Eine Studie zu Arbeit, Arbeitsbeziehungen und Geschlechterverhältnissen im 18. Jahrhundert", (Ph.D. dissertation, Universität Augsburg, 1999).
33. StadtAA, St. Jakobs Pfründe, Fach 112 Lit. A, fo. 181.
34. Ullmann, *Nachbarschaft und Konkurrenz*, p. 181.
35. Ismar Elbogen, *Der jüdische Gottesdienst in seiner geschichtlichen Entwicklung* (Hildesheim, 1995), p. 475.

According to Merle, Simon was also no longer in a condition "to continue to support his sons due to his poor health".[36]

This dire financial situation, however, did not develop solely through the couple's own mismanagement. Initially, the crisis was rather an expression of their poverty, as is evident from the economic relations described at the beginning of the article. Yet in addition to this, there is repeated evidence that Simon Ulman's behaviour also caused significant conflict. Twice in the second half of 1718, the couple's disputes escalated to such a degree that they had to be settled before the Christian court. When, in 1723, proceedings began for the compulsory sale of their house, Simon – who could not appear at a number of court dates due to illness – was accused of having repeatedly led a "bad household" (*ein böses Hauswesen*). In the course of the proceedings, Merle obtained the assurance that in the future she "was responsible for providing him [Simon] with no more than the necessary food and drink for as long as she lived".[37] It is not clear whether the dispute was ultimately aimed at divorce – which was possible according to Jewish law[38] – or whether Merle only wanted to secure the revenue of her own business deals from her husband. In any case, illness and family disputes were among the most frequent problems in the Ulman household. At the same time, these problems also reflect – in addition to the structural–causal complex described – the concrete, individual risks which the family faced. Poorer protected Jewish households were not always able to compensate for marital conflicts which prevented a smooth cooperation between the couple in their business, or for the extended loss of work hours of a family member due to illness. As the Jewish peddling trade was organized as a "family business", any disruption which reduced earning possibilities – be it dispute or illness – potentially posed an existential threat to maintaining the family's protection document. At the same time, family disputes were not only the cause of such crises, but could be the consequence of them as well, for example, when no agreement could be reached about the necessary strategies of action or when different interests existed – as in the case of the Ulmans.

Among those events which most frequently threatened a family with the loss of their protection privileges were the death of a spouse and misfortune in the family business. I mention several examples here. Widow households were usually confronted directly with the "necessity of replacing role functions",[39] in order to maintain the basis of the family income. The economic situation for such households could become very difficult. Since it was impossible to combine business transactions while travelling with caring for

36. StadtAA, St. Jakobs Pfründe, Fach 112 Lit. A, fo. 191.
37. StaatsAA, Reichsstadt Augsburg, Literalien, St. Jakobs Pfründe no. 207, fo. 141.
38. On Jewish marital law, see Rachel Monika Herweg, *Die jüdische Mutter. Das verborgene Matriarchat* (Darmstadt, 1994), pp. 53–65.
39. Michael Mitterauer, *Familie und Arbeitsteilung. Historischvergleichende Studien*, Bibliothek der Kulturgeschichte 26 (Wien [etc.], 1992), pp. 171–176.

the household and raising children, it was usually the husband who undertook the necessary business travels within the trade district. Consequently, a merchant household could fall into a sustained crisis following the husband's death – as it could following the wife's death as well. The widow, for example, would now have to make the necessary protection payments as well as earn a living herself without the assistance of her husband.[40] One possible initial solution was to attempt to have the tax payments reduced. Thus, many women in Pfersee sought to receive a reduction in payments through a petition – often with success. On 10 February 1723, the widow of Henle Ulman, for example, was granted permission by the bailiff to pay a reduced tax of only 12 fl. in the future, instead of the original 25 fl.[41] In the same way, the Jewish woman Rifga was also granted a reduced residency payment (*Sitzgeld*) of only 12 fl. in February 1727.[42] Although we cannot draw any direct conclusions about the actual situations of the households from the descriptions in these petitions, as the rhetorical strategies employed by the women here may have played an important role, their economic plight remains understandable.

Many widows were thus forced to transfer their protection rights as quickly as possible, either to a son or a son-in-law, and then to acquire residency rights in the newly founded household. In June 1728, for example, the Pfersee protections rights of Lev Ulman's widow were transferred to her son, who established his own household following his marriage to the daughter of the Jewish leader Samuel Liebermann from Höchstadt.[43] Reduced taxes frequently provided the possibility of maintaining protection privileges until a widow was able to remarry. In several of such tax exemptions, it was stated explicitly that the waiver would only be granted up to the point of "remarriage".[44] Here, the authorities' interest in having subjects who were as stable and solvent as possible, and who could provide secure revenue, was of central importance. Within the framework of such protection policies, it was entirely possible for authorities to tide over individual households during a financial crisis by allowing for reduced tax and tributary demands. The unambiguous boundaries of such assistance, however, can be seen in those cases in which local authorities no longer recognized any prospects of the household regenerating in the future and thus decided that

40. On this subject, see also Rainer Sabelleck, "Soziale Versorgung von Angehörigen jüdischer Familien in norddeutschen Städten des späten 18. und frühen 19. Jahrhunderts", in Jürgen Schlumbohm (ed.), *Familie und Familienlosigkeit. Fallstudien aus Niedersachsen und Bremen vom 15. bis 20. Jahrhundert*, Quellen und Untersuchungen zur Wirtschafts- und Sozialgeschichte Niedersachsens in der Neuzeit 17 (Hannover, 1993), pp. 127–130; Rainer Sabelleck, *Jüdisches Leben in einer nordwestdeutschen Stadt: Nienburg*, Veröffentlichungen des Max-Planck-Instituts für Geschichte 99, (Göttingen, 1991), pp. 83f.
41. StadtAA, St. Jakobs Pfründe, Fach 118 Fasz. A, fo. 120.
42. *Ibid.*, fo. 158.
43. *Ibid.*, fo. 161.
44. See for example, StadtAA, St. Jakobs Pfründe, Fach 112 Lit A, fo. 239.

a valuable source of revenue had been lost. The widow of Simon Weil, for example, was initially granted reduced widow protection money. However, when she was not able to remarry or to improve her financial situation in another way, she was finally forced to leave Pfersee in March 1719.[45] In October 1743, the widow Marium appeared before the bailiff of the same locality, and unsuccessfully requested a waiver of her protection money "because her husband David has been dead for six years and left her nothing other than [the possibility of] begging". Because of her poor health, she continued, she was not even able to beg daily and now "had to suffer the greatest misery in her old age". A note in the margins of the document records that she was expelled from the community.[46] The fate of these two women indicates that the death of a husband could lead to the loss of protection privileges. Regardless of their economic position, widows thus belonged to a group which was particularly at risk.

A final example from Binswangen – a Jewish settlement in Swabia removed from urban centres – illustrates the direct consequences of illness and accident for families in lower-income groups. The business dealings of a protected Jew named Mayer can be followed in the Binswangen village protocols from 1662 to 1681. Mayer concentrated initially on the cattle trade; in addition to this, he provided loans for various items and sold grain, vegetables, fruit and wood as well as iron and leather goods.[47] None of his business dealings were of great value: a head of cattle was sold or bought for a small sum of money, 18 fl., 15 fl. or sometimes only 9 fl.[48] This impression of extremely meagre earnings is also reinforced by the mode of payment employed. As a rule, Mayer received the purchase price in an extremely complex instalment system which followed a specific temporal rhythm. The peasants agreed to pay off their debts "by autumn", i.e. the contracts were tied to the seasonal work and earning cycle of the agrarian economy.[49] In the spring, before the approaching field work, older cows or horses were exchanged for newer animals, but payments were only made after the harvest. Thus extended periods of time for payments were often set in the contracts: for example, Magdalena Spitzer testified that she had already owed Mayer 14 fl. for years, as the result of a horse deal, and that she now had agreed to repay him in several instalments ending on the "next *fastnacht*".[50] Although the protected Jew, Meyer, attempted to increase his

45. *Ibid.*, fo. 210.
46. *Ibid.*, fo. 221.
47. StaatsAA, Adel, Literalien, von Knöringen Herrschaft Binswangen no. 9, fos 22, 24, 28; no. 8, entries from 25.2.1669, 27.2.1669, 22.3.1671, 11.3.1671, 21.12.1672; no. 9, entry from 17.3.1677.
48. StaatsAA, Adel, Literalien, von Knöringen Herrschaft Binswangen no. 9, fo. 28, entries from 9.8.1680, 6.10.1680.
49. StaatsAA, Adel, Literalien, von Knöringen Herrschaft Binswangen no. 9, entry from 29.7.1678; fo. 28, entry from 31.12.1680; no. 8, entry from 27.2.1669.
50. StaatsAA, Adel, Literalien, von Knöringen Herrschaft Binswangen no. 9, fo. 29.

revenues as much as possible through the enormous selection of goods he offered and through his continual readiness to allow long-term payments on instalment, the protocol entries document his acute financial straits, which are reminiscent of those of the Ulmans in Pfersee. Between 1664 and 1681, he was summoned before the village court fourteen times by his creditors, each time because he had outstanding debts with them.[51] In spite of this, Meyer continued to be able to pay his taxes and to maintain his protected status for many years. As it was apparently impossible for him to accumulate even the smallest reserves for an emergency, several events lead to a dramatic worsening of his situation. In the winter of 1671, he was forced to apologize in court to creditors for the fact that he had not been able make the instalment payments he had agreed to. He explained he had not been able to tend to business over the past weeks due to illness in his family: "His wife is said to have been deathly ill, as were the children, so that he was not able to leave his house".[52] When, in 1672, he was accused of breaches of regulations – including dealing in stolen goods – the authorities ordered the sale of his house and revoked their protection. He was finally saved from this acute threat by his brother-in-law, who lived in the neighbouring village of Buttenwiesen. The village court protocol records that because his brother-in-law "had spoken for him, he has been allowed into his house again".[53] The brother-in-law, David, ultimately assumed the cost of the court proceedings, as well as Meyer's outstanding payments for protection money and imprisonment costs. From further entries in the village court protocol, we can conclude that in the following years Mayer repeatedly fell into financial difficulties. However, he does not appear to have been threatened with the repeal of his letter of protection again. In October 1680 one of his horses died while grazing. Mayer brought the herdsman before the village court, claiming that the animal "had drowned through his [the herdsman's] inattentiveness". Since the court did not grant his petition for "damages",[54] Meyer received no compensation for the costs arising from the loss of the animal. In view of the order of magnitude of his cattle deals, it is understandable that the loss of one animal must have been a significant setback for him, as was the fact that he was not able to engage in travelling sales for an extended period of time.

The factors which might prevent a family from being able to pay the necessary taxes and cause them to lose their protected status were thus manifold. They included the loss of a trade animal, illness and the death of

51. StaatsAA, Adel, Literalien, von Knöringen Herrschaft Binswangen no. 9, fos 22, 24, entries from 2.1.1681, 18.5.1674, 9.7.1674; no. 8, entries from 4.5.1664, 12.9.1664, 14.6.1678, 5.8.1668, 25.2.1669, 14.10.1670, 22.3.1671, 11.3.1671, 17.7.1671.
52. StaatsAA, Adel, Literalien, von Knöringen Herrschaft Binswangen no. 8, entry from 6.12.1671.
53. *Ibid.*, entry from 21.12.1672.
54. StaatsAA, Adel, Literalien, von Knöringen Herrschaft Binswangen no. 9, entry from 10.10.1680.

a spouse, and familial disputes which hindered the smooth operation of a small business. Since only a small minority of poorer households could make provisions for an emergency, even minor losses could have serious consequences for them.

IV

It thus remains all the more astounding that, despite the dangers described here, poor families were often able to maintain their protected status. Simon and Merle Ulman were veritable "survival artists" in this regard. In the end, however, they could no longer prevent the forced sale of their business as a result of their increasing debt. Yet, in spite of this, they were able to avoid losing their protection document. What patterns of behaviour emerge here? Where did the Ulmans receive support and what did their situation look like in the end?

In the course of the Ulmans' compulsory sale trial in July 1723, a long list of creditors and their demands was drawn up. This list also contains references to the support which the couple had received in the form of different kinds of loans. In spite of the Ulmans' increasing outstanding payments, Christian business partners repeatedly supplied goods for their business. In the end, the Ulmans owed the Augsburg businessmen, Johann Jakob Guttermann and Johann Jakob Kolb, a total of 800 fl. and 37 kr. Considering the order of magnitude of Simon's business deals, these loans must have been granted over a long period of time. Simon was also given numerous loans within the Pfersee Jewish community. He received 50 fl. from the community orphan coffers (Salomon Kitzinger demanded this amount as the "guardian of Samuel Weyl's heirs").[55] David Jakob Ulman testified in the protocol of the trial that "among the loan-givers he must have suffered the greatest losses".[56] Understandably, we are rarely able to identify intra-Jewish clientele relations – it was evidently a matter of such relations in Simon Ulman's case – from sources in the Christian province. In spite of this, such relations may have played an important role, given the significant differences in wealth within rural Jewish communities.

Social hierarchies were particularly pronounced within the Pfersee Jewish community. This community included a number of very wealthy families of "court Jews" – who had acquired their wealth by lending money and supplying goods to the rulers and armies of various royal courts in southern Germany[57] – as well as a whole series of families with no assets other than

55. StaatsAA, Reichsstadt Augsburg, Literalien, St. Jakobs Pfründe no. 207, fo. 108. See also fos 120, 127, 137.
56. *Ibid.*, fo. 131.
57. Mordechai Breuer and Michael Graetz (eds), *Deutsch-Jüdische Geschichte in der Neuzeit 1600–1780*, (Munich, 1996), pp. 106–125; Friedrich Battenberg, *Das europäische Zeitalter der Juden. Zur Entwicklung einer Minderheit in der nichtjüdischen Umwelt Europas*, 2 vols (Darmstadt, 1990), vol.

their houses.[58] The functions of the elite group within the community's social and economic life can be traced through Lazarus Günzburger, Löw Simon Ulman (the Elder), and Salomon Kitzinger. In 1703, Günzburger – who according to tax lists was by far the wealthiest member of the community – loaned Elias Ulma over 1500 fl., for which the latter pawned half of his house as well as his synagogue seats.[59] In addition to this, Günzburger also functioned as business partner for retailers. In 1684, he imported coins valued at 350 fl. and distributed them among the Jewish merchants in the village as an advanced payment. The majority of household heads in Pfersee had borrowed money from him.[60] This economic intertwining within the community would support the assumption that a well-organized network of intermediaries and negotiators, made up of the numerous Jewish cattle and goods merchants – for whom the court Jews functioned as buyers and wholesalers – was necessary in order to supply courts and armies with provisions on the order of magnitude we know to have been the case.[61] To what degree Günzburger also made special contributions to the communal coffers for the poor is unclear. However, records regarding compulsory sales indicate that Salomon Kitzinger, the member of another wealthy family, functioned as the administrator of the guardianship coffers. And in 1755 Löw Simon Ulman (the Elder), one of the most important Pfersee court Jews of the eighteenth century, signed a contract together with Abraham Samson Model concerning the support of the village poorhouse, in which he assumed a large part of the costs involved.[62] Turning to the support of wealthy fellow Jews was thus also possible – be it through the communal coffers for the poor and the orphan coffers, or through a direct loan.

In addition to this, the authorities also extended the term of payment for the Ulmans' protection money in the sum of 25 fl. 40 kr. – which accorded with the amount due for one year. This extension by the authorities fits with the tax policies, described earlier in this article, concerning widow households, and again illustrates that fiscal demands were by no means always immediately and rigorously applied. Simon Ulman was also given another reduction of his protection tax in 1724.[63] Thus, at least for a limited period of time, the family was carried by the network of loans from business partners and from fellow Jews, as well as by the protection authorities who,

2, pp. 245–249; Jonathan I. Israel, *European Jewry in the Age of Mercantilism 1550–1750*, (Oxford, 1985), pp. 123f.; Felix Priebatsch, "Die Judenpolitik des fürstlichen Absolutismus im 17. und 18. Jahrhundert", in *Forschungen und Versuche zur Geschichte des Mittelalters und der Neuzeit. Festschrift für Dietrich Schäfer* (Jena, 1915), pp. 564–651.

58. Ullmann, *Nachbarschaft und Konkurrenz*, pp. 360f.

59. StaatsAA, Adel, Literalien, von Langenmantel no. 34, fo. 13.

60. StaatsAA, Reichsstadt Augsburg, Literalien, St. Jakobs Pfründe no. 202, fos 49, 614v.

61. On comparable clientele and loan relationships in Christian travelling peddlers, see Laurence Fontaine, *History of Pedlars in Europe* (Cambridge, 1996), pp. 121–139.

62. StadtAA, St. Jakobs Pfründe, Fach 123 Fasz. A, fo. 34.

63. StadtAA, St. Jakobs Pfründe, Fach 118, Fasz. A, fo. 140.

through a well-considered tax policy, allowed the family a certain temporal latitude.

When the Ulmans' debts could no longer be brought under control, even through clientele relations, it was ultimately the support of relatives which proved to be decisive – as had also been the case with Mayer from Binswangen cited above. Ulman's son-in-law, Sigmund Bacharach from Steppach, was prepared to buy the Ulman house for 1600 fl., and this intervention prevented the expulsion of the Jewish couple. With this, the Ulmans did lose the property rights to their house, but they were able to continue living in it and thus to retain their protection privileges in Pfersee. However, this support was not offered without services in return, but rather was tied to a series of concrete conditions and demands. The proceedings concerning the purchase of the house and the assumption of the Ulman debts reveal conflicts within the family as well as within the Jewish community.

The disputes here were marked by the fact that the total of the Ulmans' outstanding debts was significantly higher than the price agreed upon for their house (1500 fl.). As a result, protracted negotiations arose between creditors and potential buyers. After the first prospective buyer, Leb Ulman, decided not to purchase the house – evidently because of the magnitude of the debt – the Ulmans' son-in-law was, at least initially, the only potential buyer. The latter had to fend off the demands of creditors, which evidently exceeded his financial capacities as well. Initially, he doubted the legality of several of the debts. In a second step, he attempted to ward off the liability to the community which had arisen through Simon's pawning of the family's synagogue seats. There was a heated conflict on the matter between the son-in-law and Salomon Kitzinger who, as administrator of the community coffers, insisted on the return of the amount during the public auction proceedings. Sigmund Bacharach, on the contrary, claimed that the two seats should be included in the purchase price, as the house itself – according to his argument – was "not worth the purchase price, and no Jewish house had ever been purchased without synagogue seats".[64] The son-in-law was finally able to work out a compromise. He paid only 50 fl. rather than the original demand of 75 fl., and the interest which had accrued on the payment was also waived.[65]

After this point in the conflict had been settled, the dispute between Bacharach and Kitzinger again became extremely heated when, shortly before the purchase contract was to be signed, Kitzinger decided to make an offer on the house himself. Faced with the rigid limitation of protection privileges set by the Pfersee authorities – which since 1713 had consistently kept the number of protected Jewish households to twenty-eight, and had

---

64. StaatsAA, Reichsstadt Augsburg, Literalien, St. Jakobs Pfründe no. 207, fo. 109.
65. *Ibid.*, fo. 108.

refused to grant residency rights for further households[66] – Kitzinger attempted to acquire property along with a protection document for his son by purchasing the Ulman house. In addition to this, he planned to build a new house on the property, thus enabling his son to establish his own household. The Pfersee court prevented this plan by maintaining a prohibition which had been issued in the fall of 1721, according to which the Kitzinger family was forbidden from acquiring protection privileges for "children and grandchildren".[67] The occasion for this decree had been a conflict two years earlier regarding an honorary post within the synagogue, which had escalated to such a degree that it had not been possible to carry out an orderly election of the Jewish community leader. Because the dispute was thought to have called the authorities' power into question, Kitzinger – who was regarded as a "ringleader" – was given this severe sanction.[68] The sanction itself again clearly underlines the fact that Jewish population growth was a volatile issue, given the rigid limitation of the number of protected Jewish households in Pfersee.

This attempt by the wealthy Kitzinger family to expand its privileges at the expense of the Ulmans, by exploiting the latter's acute financial straits, was not successful. However, considering the significant social hierarchies within the Pfersee community, it was probably not an isolated occurrence. In her petition from 18 February 1727, the Pfersee widow Rifga requested reduced protection money from the authorities, complaining that her husband had left her with six small children and that now "several people from the Jewish community intended to acquire the protection rights for themselves, and want to drive out myself with my poor abandoned orphan children".[69] Life in the Jewish community consisted not only in various forms of assistance and economic connections; it also included a significant potential for conflict. In this regard, competition around the limited numbers of protection documents in the village could also become a dangerous risk for poorer members of the community.

The agreements which the son-in-law, Bacharach, finally made with Simon and Merle Ulman indicate further that support from relatives was not the expression of unselfish solidarity, but rather rested upon services in return. Communal relations, as well as relations to relatives, in other words, should not be misunderstood in terms of romantic clichés. Rather, they were characterized by reciprocities which again produced conflicts of their own. What did the contractual conditions for the purchase of the house look like in detail? First, Sigmund Bacharach had to agree to assume the debt contracts of his parents-in-law, and in future to pay the annual protec-

66. Ullmann, *Nachbarschaft und Konkurrenz*, pp. 80f.
67. StaatsAA, Reichsstadt Augsburg, Literalien, St. Jakobs Pfründe no. 207, fo. 130.
68. On this, see Ullmann, *Nachbarschaft und Konkurrenz*, pp. 183f.
69. StadtAA, St. Jakobs Pfründe, Fach 118 Fasz. A, fo. 158.

tion fees of 16 fl. 40 kr. for "as long as they live".[70] In return, he secured free, lifelong living rights for a member of his own family, the sick and elderly husband of his dead sister. Merle Ulman also had to give him half the income from her business for seven years, and following this, one-third of her profits. Simon Ulman's business activities were not mentioned in this context, but rather only those of his wife. Since no more of Simon's trade contracts appear in the officials records after the summer of 1723, but only further waivers of protection money, it is possible that Merle was able to establish his legal incapacity. Or perhaps Simon was no longer able to work due to illness.

By purchasing the house, the son-in-law from Steppach secured residency and business rights in Pfersee for his wife's family. This support, however, was only provided for the appropriate services in return: another needy family member – Bacharach's sick brother-in-law – was to be accommodated there, and Bacharach himself was to have a share in the Ulmans' business in the future. For Simon and Merle Ulman, assistance from relatives meant a lifeline in an extremely precarious situation. The assistance, however, was tied to new obligations and dependencies – this time to their son-in-law from Steppach.

V

What effects did the specific risks to Jewish existence and the strategies adopted by Jewish households to counter those risks have on the structure of rural Jewish families? Is it possible to derive typical characteristics for protected Jewish households from this?

One initial dimension might be the intensity of intrafamilial cooperation through which such families sought to improve their economic possibilities. The Jewish peddling trade could only function through the cooperation of all members of the household capable of working. This led to the great economic independence of Jewish women, an independence which was also evident in Jewish marital law. I recapitulate Merle Ulman's situation. She possessed a dowry of 400 fl. Her husband was able to use this money, but required her approval in order to do so, and had to pay the money back if they were divorced. Consequently, it was Merle who countersigned the debt contract for 50 fl. with Andreas Wagner from Kaufbeuren, as she was the one who assumed liability for this sum with her own capital. In the course of their increasing debt, the couple not only lost their house, but Merle's dowry as well – both of these sums are recorded in the proceedings of public auction trial.[71] The loss of Merle's "female privilege" – which evidently occurred in steps through several debt contracts – was thus a result of the

---

70. StaatsAA, Reichsstadt Augsburg, Literalien, St. Jakobs Pfründe no. 207, fos 69–71.
71. *Ibid.*, fo. 141.

couple's financial plight. The use of her dowry, however, was not possible
without her express consent, and in the contracts with her son-in-law, Merle
continued to be treated as an independently acting business woman. Among
rural Jews, the optimal use of all potential labour resources led to the largely
autonomous economic position of wives, even if, in Merle's case, this economic autonomy was ultimately sacrificed to the necessities of the couple's
economic plight. The conflicts in the Ulmans' marriage – which are documented in a number of places in the surviving records – might have had
their origins here.

Jewish women found themselves in a particularly precarious situation
following the death of their husbands. They were not always able to maintain their protected status and had to fight resistance from within their own
community as well, i.e., it was often only possible for widows to lead an
independent household for a limited period of time. This is perhaps the
reason why widow households in rural Jewish society were something of an
exception.[72] The compulsion to remarry or to transfer protection rights may
have also been affected in the long run by the disparity between the very
limited number of protected households permitted and the increase in
population within the Jewish community.

In addition to the small number of widow households, there is a further
peculiarity in the structure of Jewish families, one which was also the
immediate consequence of protection practices and the result of specific
counterstrategies developed by Jewish society: the comparatively large
number of servants within Jewish households, even among poorer families.
I offer a few numbers to illustrate this. According to the 1730 census, there
were a total of thirty-five servants and maids living with sixty-three families
in Kriegshaber, a Jewish settlement near Pfersee. Individual wealthy families,
such as those of Moises and Lazarus Neuburger, had up to ten domestic
servants. The families of Joseph Mändle and Abraham Mändle each had
five servants within their households. Yet, in addition to these families of
court Jews, the cantor Seeligmann, Alt Hitzig and Hitzig Levi, as well as
the households in "altes Bäschenhaus" – which were among the poorest in
the village – also employed maids and servants. Only thirteen families had
no servants listed as members of their household.[73] A census of the Jewish
population in 1722 reveals a similar situation in Pfersee. In the thirty-one
protected households, there were twenty-six servants. As one might expect,
the court Jews had the greatest number of employees, but some of the less
wealthy families also had a maid or a servant. Only the poorest families –
such as Simon and Merle Ulman (the Small), the three widow households,

---

72. Ullmann, *Nachbarschaft und Konkurrenz*, pp. 527–536. With four widow households in 1722,
the Pfersee community was an exception. Judging from my current knowledge of the sources, this
was probably connected to the community's engagement in the pawn business, a typical enterprise
for women and one which created a particularly favourable situation for them.

73. *Ibid.*, p. 527.

the old butcher Leb, and Joseph Behr, as well as the cantor and the current butcher – were not in a position to have additional people live with them.[74] In the case of Simon and Merle Ulman, however, this situation changed in 1723 after the conclusion of the public auction trial, when they had to take in their son-in-law's relative (who, however, was not yet listed in the census from 1722).

The large number of servants in Jewish families becomes understandable when we consider the origin of the people involved.[75] The restrictive policies in issuing protection documents meant that many families could not accommodate their children or related widows and widowers in their own village, and were thus compelled to find places for them in other communities. When a family could afford it, these people were often allowed to participate in the residency rights of relatives who took them in as "servants". The case of Lev Ulman's widow illustrates that people designated as "maids" or "servants" in the Christian tax lists were often not household employees in the actual sense of the term, but rather relatives. When Ulman's widow transferred her right of protection to her son, the administrator of the judicial authorities allowed this transfer – already mentioned earlier in the article – under the condition that "the mother gives up her protection and remains as a maid".[76] Thus the language of the authorities found a category for this specific Jewish phenomenon, which was then adapted to Christian linguistic traditions. At the same time, the example of Simon and Merle Ulman shows that solidarity among relatives did not always occur voluntarily, but could also be the expression of financial difficulties within that household. If this taking-in of relatives was voluntary, then each household had to weigh how much a particular "servant" would require in additional food, or how much that servant could contribute to the household as a whole. On the basis of existing sources, we are not able to determine whether this contribution consisted in work, money or a portion of business profits earned.

The small number of widow households and the large number of servants are indications of the same phenomenon, i.e., the attempt to accommodate as many people as possible within a single household. This increased size of protected households accords with a strategy worked out within Jewish society, a strategy which sought to expand the letter of protection issued to the head of a household so as to include a broad circle of people and thus to evade restrictive Jewish policies. The case of Simon and Merle Ulman

74. *Ibid.*, pp. 535–539.

75. On the composition of protected Jewish households and the "hidden" population in the late Middle Ages, see Michael Toch, "Die soziale und demographische Struktur der jüdischen Gemeinde Nürnbergs im Jahre 1489", in Jürgen Schneider (ed.), *Wirtschaftskräfte und Wirtschaftswege. Festschrift für Hermann Kellenbenz* (Stuttgart, 1981) pp. 79–91, 82f. For the early modern period, see Sabelleck, *Jüdisches Leben*, pp. 82–88.

76. StadtAA, St. Jakobs Pfründe, Fach 118 Fasz. A, fo. 161.

indicates that the concrete manifestations of this basic structural tendency produced a variety of conflicts on a communal as well as a familial level.

An increase in the members of a household, however, did not necessarily mean that these members also made up a single economic unit or that they were all integrated within the family business run by the head of the household. Rather, Jewish servants also operated independent businesses – a practice which was forbidden by the authorities. The fact that Jewish servants made independent contributions to households is indicated by the decrees issued regarding such activities. In January 1699 the authorities in Pfersee felt it necessary to enact a mandate concerning "the Jewry's servants", which ordered that "servants should refrain from all private trading",[77] since the privilege of operating an independent business was tied to the possession of a separate document of protection. The activities of Jewish servants and maids are actually documented numerous times in the official protocols. When, in April 1738, the maidservant Vögele moved to Oettingen from Pfersee, where she had lived in the household of Elias Heium, she attempted to settle the unpaid debts from her pawn business. She was able to pass on a portion of the deposits to a Jewish man named Joseph, who was employed by David Ulman as the schoolteacher – for example, the $16^1/_2$ ells of black cloth which a woman from Augsburg had left with her for 10 fl.[78] Similarly, the independent pawn deals of a servant named Isaak Meyer are also documented in the records: in 1726, a shopkeeper's daughter from Augsburg pawned her inferior jewellery with him for 5 fl.[79] And in Binswangen, Rubin Gerstle, who was employed in Leb Jonas's household, bought seeds from a peasant in Bonstetten for 9 fl. in May 1740.[80] In the autumn of that same year, he reported to officials the peasant owed him 20 fl. 15 kr. from a deal in leather goods.[81]

The relatively independent economic status of servants within protected Jewish households in the countryside again accords with the particular conditions of Jewish existence there, and the external pressures exerted upon that society. On the one hand, as many people as possible attempted to participate in the protected status of a household; on the other hand, the small trade businesses could hardly provide everyone in the household with a livelihood, so that independent economic opportunities had to be exploited as well – by wives as well as by "servants" and "maids". In all probability, however, there was a qualitative difference between the cooperative work organization between husbands and wives within the peddling business and the activities of servants, which were probably significantly more independent. Yet both forms arose from the same strategy, a strategy

77. *Ibid.*, fo. 24.
78. StaatsAA, Reichsstadt Augsburg, Literalien, St. Jakobs Pfründe no. 210, fo. 495.
79. StaatsAA, Reichsstadt Augsburg, Literalien, St. Jakobs Pfründe no. 207, fo. 505.
80. StaatsAA, Adel, Literalien, von Knöringen Herrschaft Binswangen no. 26, fo. 120.
81. *Ibid.*, fo. 151.

which can be expressed as follows: as much residential unity as possible so as to enable the optimal exploitation of a protection document, combined with great economic independence for the individual members of the household. As a result, Jewish households were not set economic and social units, but rather were characterized by a certain independence for individual members. In the battle for survival, the composition of the households could be altered. However, we must also bear in mind that our reflections on the size of Jewish families as well as on the inner structure of the "household economy" always moves in a grey zone, due to the peculiarity of existing sources. In this sense, I understand my interpretation as an initial approach to a complex reality, a reality which can only be grasped with difficulty. Finally, differences between Jewish and Christian worlds should not be over-emphasized, as networks of relatives, the necessity of replacing role functions in widows' households and the vocational activity of women as conditioning factors of early modern familial forms were also components of Christian agrarian societies.[82]

Translated by Thomas Lampert

---

82. Michael Mitterauer, *Historisch-anthropologische Familienforschung. Fragestellungen und Zugangsweisen*, Kulturstudien 15 (Vienna [etc.], 1990), pp. 131–141.

International Review of Social History 45 (2000), pp. 115–135
© 2000 Internationaal Instituut voor Sociale Geschiedenis

Industrious Households: Survival Strategies of Artisans in a Southwest German Town during the Eighteenth and Early Nineteenth Centuries*

DENNIS A. FREY, JR

In the last two decades, scholars have significantly expanded, through the use of probate inventories, our purview of early-modern European households. Their work has tended to focus on the social and cultural implications of the material culture found in these inventories.[1] Seldom, however, have they used these sources to study the family economy found in many early-modern European households, and since artisanal small-scale production remained the predominant mode of urban economic activity, this has produced a conspicuous gap in our knowledge.[2] This essay, which contains a comprehensive investigation of probate inventories from artisanal households during the eighteenth and early nineteenth centuries, is a modest attempt to fill some of that gap by providing a more nuanced understanding of the social, cultural, and economic survival strategies employed by the

* The Fulbright Commission and the Daimler-Benz-Stiftung provided generous assistance that facilitated the research for this paper, and the insightful and thought-provoking criticisms of Frederick Marquardt served this essay well. I extend my heartfelt gratitude to them. Any faults herein are my own.
1. Among many diverse studies, see the following: Anja R. Benscheidt, *Kleinbürgerlicher Besitz: Nürtinger Handwerker-inventare von 1660 bis 1840* (Münster, 1985); Cissie Fairchilds, "The Production and Marketing of Populuxe Goods in Eighteenth-Century Paris", in John Brewer and Roy Porter (eds), *Consumption and the World of Goods* (London, 1993), pp. 228–248; Andrea Hauser, *Dinge des Alltags: Studien zur historischen Sachkultur eines schwäbischen Dorfes* (Tübingen, 1994); Peter Höher, "Konstanz und Wandel in Wohnausstattung und Hauswirt-schaft (1630–1899): Das Beispiel Nürtingen am Neckar", in Günter Wiegelmann (ed.), *Beiträge zur Volkskultur in Nordwestdeutschland 55* (Münster, 1987), pp. 309–331; Barbara Knüttel, *Manns- und Weibskleider in Unterfranken* (Würzburg, 1983); Uwe Meiners, "Zur Wohnkultur der münsterschen Bevölkerung in der zweiten Hälfte des 18. Jahrhunderts: Eine Fallstudie anhand von Nachlaßverzeichnissen", in *Rheinisch-westfälische Zeitschrift für Volkskunde*, 25 (1979/80), pp. 80–103; Ruth-E. Mohrmann, *Alltagswelt im Land Braunschweig: Städtische und ländliche Wohnkultur vom 16. bis zum frühen 20. Jahrhundert* (Münster, 1990); Daniel Roche, *The People of Paris: An Essay in Popular Culture in the 18th Century* trans. by Marie Evans (Berkeley, CA, 1987); Roman Sandgruber, *Die Anfänge der Konsumgesellschaft: Konsumverbrauch, Lebensstandard und Alltagskultur in Österreich im 18. und 19. Jahrhundert* (Vienna, 1982); Sylvia Schraut, *Sozialer Wandel im Industrialisierungsprozess: Esslingen 1800–1870* (Esslingen, 1989); Carole Shammas, *The Pre-industrial Consumer in England and America* (Oxford, 1990); and Lorna Weatherill, *Consumer Behaviour and Material Culture in Britain, 1660–1760* (New York, 1988).
2. Hans Medick's work, i.e. *Weben und Überleben in Laichingen 1650–1900: Lokalgeschichte als Allgemeine Geschichte* (Göttingen, 1997), is a clear exception, and serves, in fact, as one of the models for my own work.

poorer households as they struggled to avoid the abject indigence of the truly destitute.

Among scholars who study inventories, the work of Pierre Bourdieu has provided not only the inspiration but also a conceptual framework for using these sources. In *Distinction*, Bourdieu revealed all of the available strategies that individuals and social groups rely on as they move through their social space. According to Bourdieu, movement through this social space has never been – and never will be – random; numerous forces act on individuals, pushing and pulling them through society, as they consciously or unconsciously accept some of those forces while consciously or unconsciously resisting others.[3] Since an intrinsic and reciprocal relationship exists between individuals and the social space that surrounds them, all components of that space whether material (i.e. material culture) or immaterial (i.e. practices) simultaneously reflect and shape the "*habitus*", or behaviors and strategies, on which individuals depend. Therefore, argues Bourdieu, all elements of material culture should be considered as forms of economic, social, and cultural capital. These persuasive conclusions further buttress the need for a more nuanced study of early-modern probate inventories that adequately reflects the social, cultural, and economic aspects of material culture.

These relatively new source materials can, however, be problematic.[4] While the inventories from Württemberg were supposed to list the entirety of a family's property, including any outstanding loans or debts, items could have been hidden or liquidated before the notary visited. Worse yet, the death inventories oftentimes captured household economies at strikingly different stages, depending on the circumstances of the deceased. If death came too early for the husband or wife, then the probate inventory came from a household economy that probably had not yet reached its full potential. Inventories from particularly old individuals could reflect household economies that had clearly passed their prime. Lastly, the inventories from Swabia rarely listed the rooms, or location, in which the items were found. Still, these documents offer an unparalleled glimpse into the material culture of ordinary families and households. This has provided scholars with the incomparable opportunity to study the material culture of many households

---

3. Pierre Bourdieu, *Distinction*, transl. by Richard Nice (Cambridge, MA, 1984), p. 110.

4. For further details on the problems inherent to studying inventories, see, among others: Peter King, "Pauper Inventories and the Material Lives of the Poor in the Eighteenth and Early Nineteenth Centuries", in T. Hitchcock, P. King, and P. Sharpe (eds), *Chronicling Poverty: The Voices and Strategies of the English Poor, 1640–1840* (New York, 1997), pp. 161–166; Hildegard Mannheims, *Wie wird ein Inventar erstellt? Rechtskommentare als Quelle der volkskundlichen Forschung* (Münster, 1991), pp. 121–134; Medick, *Weben und Überleben*, pp. 398ff.; Ruth-E. Mohrmann, "Archivalische Quellen zur Sachkultur", in Günter Wiegelmann (ed.), *Geschichte der Alltagskultur, Heft 21* (Münster, 1980), pp. 69–86; and Bernard Vogler (ed.), *Les actes notariés: Source de l'histoire sociale XVIe–XIXe siècles* (Strasbourg, 1979).

from a variety of social groups in this region.[5] The inventories from the "orderly-built, friendly city" of Göppingen, which date back to 1738, have yet to be examined.[6]

Göppingen, which still lies on the major thoroughfare between the large, regional centers of Stuttgart and Ulm, was well situated in the "urban network" of southwest Germany.[7] As a consequence of this ideal setting, handicrafts, but especially those involved in the manufacture of woolen worsteds (*Zeuge*), and in the production of foodstuffs, dominated this economy. These trades, and others, experienced the vicissitudes common to the proto-industrial economies of the eighteenth and early nineteenth centuries. The annual commercial registers, which listed the yearly, variable tax paid by all artisans according to their profitability, recorded these ups and downs in Göppingen's economy (see Figure 1 below). Numerous events, both from within and without, affected the economic activity of the small-scale producers in this town. A cataclysmic fire, for example, burnt nearly the entire city to the ground in 1782. There was also a burgeoning population in the late eighteenth and early nineteenth centuries that expanded from 2,912 inhabitants in 1760 to 5,490 in 1837.[8] This undoubtedly put yet further strain on an economy that, for the most part, remained in the doldrums. However, beginning with the 1820s, two quiet decades brought not only new opportunities for economic growth but also new pressures before economic and political tumult once again hit in the 1840s.[9] Thus, Göppingen is an excellent case study for investigating the strategies used by poor households as they wrestled with these economic tribulations.

A sample set of 348 probate inventories was studied for the years from 1738 to 1827. In order to provide a frame of reference, the total wealth, or net worth, of each single inventory was calculated through the following formula:

5. Among many studies, see Benscheidt, *Kleinbürgerlicher Besitz*; Peter Borscheid, *Textilarbeiterschaft in der Industrialisierung* (Stuttgart, 1978); Hauser, *Dinge des Alltags*; Heilwig Schomerus, *Die Arbeiter der Maschinenfabrik Esslingen* (Stuttgart, 1977); and Schraut, *Sozialer Wandel im Industrialisierungsprozeß*.

6. Karl Chr. Fr. Pistorius, *Taschenbuch auf Reisen durch Würtemberg; mit einem Anhang über die besuchteren Bäder Würtembergs, einem Ortsregister und zwei lithographirten Abbildungen, auch auf Verlangen mit einer Charte* (Stuttgart [etc.], 1827), p. 111. Unless otherwise noted, all translations are mine.

7. For more details, see Karl Kirschmer, *Die Geschichte der Stadt Göppingen*, 2 vols (Göppingen, 1953); Emil Hofmann, *Die Industrialisierung des Oberamtsbezirkes Göppingens* (Göppingen, 1910); Walter Troeltsch, "Die Göppinger Zeugmacherei im 18. Jahrhundert und das sog. Vayhinger-buch", in G. Schmoller (ed.), *Jahrbuch für Gesetzgebung, Verwaltung und Volkswirtschaft im Deutschen Reich* (Leipzig, 1896), pp. 165–187; and Alexander Dreher, *Göppingens Gewerbe im 19. Jahrhundert* (Göppingen, 1971).

8. Cf. Stadtarchiv Göppingen (hereafter StAG), B.II.6.a, Seelentabellen und Bürgerlisten, 1760; and Hofmann, *Die Industrialisierung*, p. 168.

9. See Dreher, *Göppingens Gewerbe*, pp. 9–18; and Hofmann, *Die Industrialisierung*, pp. 3–10.

Dennis A. Frey, Jr

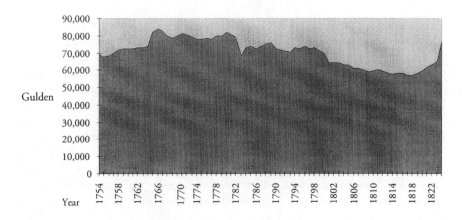

Figure 1. Total annual commercial tax of all trades in Göppingen (1754–1824)
Sources: StAG, Commerzienregister

Net worth or total wealth =
aggregate property[10] + loans outstanding (*Activa*) – debts owed (*Passiva*).

With net worth calculated, the households were then sorted into three thirty-year intervals (i.e. 1738–1767, 1768–1797, and 1798–1827). And, finally, using a normal distribution, the households were partitioned into the following three wealth strata:

Table 1. *Social stratification of cases by net worth in Gulden (1738–1827)*

Decade	Lower stratum (25%)	Middle stratum (50%)	Upper stratum (25%)
1738–1767	21.35 ≤ 360.83	361.04 ≤ 1,385.88	1,392.48 ≤ 12,205.63
Average	229.18	675.14	3,073.69
Number	29	58	30
1768–1797	21.77 ≤ 483.70	486.14 ≤ 2,330.87	2,332.37 ≤ 8,996.10
Average	257.82	1,155.14	4,291.60
Number	31	61	31
1798–1827	–54.03 ≤ 571.65	572.70 ≤ 3,253.18	3,588.18 ≤ 18,482.75
Average	264.55	1,603.08	6,027.95
Number	27	54	27

Sources: StAG, Inventuren und Teilungen

10. The corresponding categories from the probate inventories were as follows: Aggregate property = real estate + cash + precious items + books + male clothing + female clothing + bedding + linens + brass utensils + tin utensils + copper utensils + iron utensils + tinplate utensils + wooden utensils + furniture + barrel and binding materials + common household goods and tools + harness, tack, and building materials + craftsman tools, supplies, and wares + livestock + produce + foodstores + supplies + wine and other drinks.

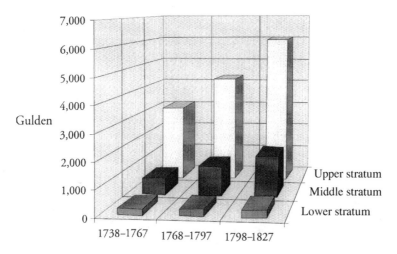

Figure 2. Average net worth in Gulden by wealth stratum (1738–1827)
Sources: StAG, Commerzienregister

With the 348 cases separated into their respective social strata, it was simple to chart the average net worth for each social stratum, and the results were startling (see Figure 2). The net worth of the families in the lower stratum clearly stagnated throughout the period, holding steady somewhere between 200 and 300 Gulden.[11] While they were not the poorest of the poor in their town, the lower-stratum families were clearly struggling to make ends meet. The average total wealth of the other two strata showed, on the other hand, steady growth over the ninety years studied, with the upper stratum clearly outpacing the middle stratum. Therefore, the basic trend in wealth was one of growing disparity among the strata, which had, as will be shown below, serious consequences for the poorer artisanal households in Göppingen.

Evidence from the inventories suggests that even as these disparities grew, households in all three strata employed a striking resourcefulness as they tried to piece together a variety of sources of income. Ernst Jacob Vayhinger, a *Zeugmacher* (woolen worsted weaver), who lived from 1729 to 1791 and kept a chronicle during the years from 1756 to 1784, epitomized this. This eighteenth-century weaver, who would become part of the upper stratum, started off his adult life in an inauspicious manner when at the age of twenty-five or twenty-six he married his spouse, Anna Barbara, née Schaupp, in 1755. According to their wedding inventory, the parents of the newlyweds showered them with generous gifts worth 289fl. 13x., which gave them when combined with their own property (i.e. 174fl. 59x.) a net worth

---

11. During this entire period, the currency in Württemberg was: 1 *Gulden* (fl.) = 60 *Kreuzer* (x.).

of 464fl. 12x.[12] During the "golden years of the eighteenth century" inherited wealth (*Startkapital*) could, as argued by Hans Medick, play a decisive role in how a family fared later in life, because it often saved young families from serious capital outlays.[13] Indeed, their parents' gifts certainly helped the Vayhingers get off to a good start in their wool-weaving business, for Ernst Jacob recorded annual profits for the first ten years of his own business.[14] Those times were not easy ones; the Seven Years' War (1756–1763) disrupted trade so much, that "no one had any worsted wool" and the craft went into dire straits.[15] From this solid start, the Vayhingers methodically increased their net worth to 2,950fl. 32x. in 1792 when Ernst Jacob died.

The generosity of Vayhinger's parents did not stop with the aforementioned gifts, for they agreed in 1758 to sell the "upper part" of their house to Ernst Jacob and Anna Barbara for 215fl. Even though Ernst Jacob and Anna Barbara came up with "no more than 75 Gulden" of the 100fl. down payment, the elder Vayhingers apparently did not mind, for the transaction was completed without further mention.[16] And, following the death of his mother in 1773 – his father had died in 1763 – Ernst Jacob acquired his mother's portion of the building, which meant that he now owned "three-fourths" of it.[17] He would eventually acquire the entire building when, in 1775, he purchased the "bottom part" of it for 200fl. from one of the town's curates, named Stimmel.[18] This "three-story building" with a garden "behind the house [...] and [stretching to] the city wall", was worth 2,000fl. in 1789.[19] It housed three of the Vayhingers' four economic activities: weaving woolen worsteds, raising pigeons and canaries, and renting out space in their home. The fourth economic activity (i.e. farming) took place primarily on the community plots that the family apparently leased from the town.[20] However, they may have also used "the half of [a] ¹/₂Vrtl. [i.e. a *Viertel* of cultivable land] under the paper mill", which was worth 34fl., or perhaps the garden behind the house, for small horticulture.[21] All told, then, the

---

12. See Kirchenregisteramt Göppingen (hereafter KrtG), Familienregister, 1558–1800, Sch–Z, 608–636, p. 432; and StAG, B.II.2g, Zubringens Inventuren vom 23. Jan. 1750 biß 20. Febr. 1756, p. 561b.

13. Medick, *Weben und Überleben*, pp. 212–228.

14. StAG, B.I.1.a, Hauschronik des Zeugmachers Ernst Jakob Vayhinger, pp. 8–19.

15. *Ibid.*, p. 9. See also Troeltsch, "Die Göppinger Zeugmacherei", p. 185.

16. StAG, B.I.1.a, Hauschronik des Zeugmachers Ernst Jakob Vayhinger, p. 10.

17. StAG, Wirtschaftliche Lage in Stadt u. Amt 1622–1819; Schulden 1824/25, "1774 Tabellen wirtsch. Art".

18. StAG, B.I.1.a, Hauschronik des Zeugmachers Ernst Jakob Vayhinger, pp. 35 and 50.

19. StAG, B.II.2.g, Inventuren und Teilungen, 23.2–209.5 (1789).

20. Unfortunately, the Vayhingers' inventories do not make clear how households gained access to these community plots. This was not unusual, for the probate inventories rarely listed the terms of use. Occasionally, the inventories did list the value of such community plots under the household's immovable property. This was, however, not the case with the Vayhingers.

21. StAG, B.II.2.g, Inventuren und Teilungen, 23.2–209.5 (1789). The land measurements during this period were as follow: 1 Viertel = 0.25 Morgen; and 1 Morgen = 0.78 acre = 0.32 hectare.

Vayhingers owned real estate that totaled 2,034fl. in 1789. At the same time, the net worth of the Vayhingers' estate (including the additional value of loans extended but not collected, and subtracting the value of debts still owed) was 2,727fl. 37x. Therefore, as a percentage of net worth, real estate equaled 74.57 per cent. Between the time of Anna Barbara's death (1789) and Ernst Jacob's in 1792, the value of the Vayhinger real estate did not change, but their total wealth did, increasing to 2,950fl. 31.5x.[22] Thus, in 1792, the house on Pfarrstraße and the plot of land under the paper mill constituted 68.94 per cent of the Vayhingers' total wealth. In general, then, real estate consistently made up about 70 per cent of their total wealth; in effect, immovable property was the cornerstone of the Vayhingers' wealth. This behavior resembled that of their fellow middling-to-wealthy artisans in Göppingen and other artisans elsewhere in Swabia.[23]

The significance of real estate, including both buildings and arable lands, for the *Handwerker* in general and for the Vayhingers in particular, cannot be understated. After all, the land and the building(s) which usually stood on it housed not only the *Handwerker* family, but also the very workshop which kept them solvent. In fact, the two spaces were firmly intertwined. In the case of the Vayhingers, they may have devoted three rooms in their house to *Zeugmacherei*. They had had, according to Ernst Jacob's chronicle, "three ovens" in their home prior to the city-wide fire on 26 August 1782; hence he could have easily heated three different rooms for weaving.[24] He and his family certainly had more than one loom operating at a time. Their first loom came as a wedding gift from Ernst Jacob's parents. In mid-to-late 1763, Ernst Jacob used the profits of the preceding year to improve this loom and to have a yarn mill built. Then, in his chronicle entry from 1767, Ernst Jacob mentioned that "on Martini [11 November]" he gave his "*Gesellen Feier-Abend*", which clearly indicates that he worked with journeymen. And, since both of Vayhinger's sons eventually became *Zeugmacher*, they probably assisted him in weaving, too. Moreover, the Vayhinger household also engaged in putting out, for after the city-wide fire of 1782 consumed their home, the wife of one of "his [out-]workers" in Lorch, a town 16 km to the north, offered Vayhinger "their entire house" as temporary housing.[25]

Thus, the Vayhingers owned only 0.04875 acres or 0.02 hectares. David Sabean, in *Property, Production, and Family in Neckarhausen* (Cambridge, 1990), argues that anything less than 1.5 hectares was "clearly less than adequate land to live from agriculture alone" (p. 39). Obviously then, this tiny plot of land did not mean annual self-subsistence for the Vayhingers.

22. Cf. StAG, B.II.2.g, Inventuren und Teilungen, 23.2–209.5 (1789), and 24.2–405.5 (1792).

23. See Medick, *Weben und Überleben*, pp. 183–228, where he argues that real estate often made up the largest chunk of wealth among his linen weavers. When, for instance, the linen weaver Michael Schwenk died in 1748, landed properties, according to Medick's calculations, constituted seventy per cent of his estate's total worth (p. 198).

24. StAG, B.I.1.a, Hauschronik des Zeugmachers Ernst Jakob Vayhinger, p. 53.

25. *Ibid.*, pp. 16–23.

The probate inventories from Anna Barbara and Ernst Jacob shed even more light on the way in which the Vayhingers conducted their household economy. In 1789, when Anna Barbara died, the notary wrote that the craft tools in the household "were estimated in general, together with all items, at 50fl".[26] Although the notary failed to take an item-by-item list of those tools, he was more precise with his list of the *"Handthierungs-Waaren"* (i.e. supplies and wares) found in the Vayhinger household, describing twelve items that were worth a sum total of 632fl. 30x. With a good number of supplies and wares, the Vayhingers plied their trade vigorously. In fact, craft tools, wares, and supplies constituted in 1789 just over 25 per cent of the Vayhingers' net worth. Because none of those wares and supplies were found three years later in Ernst Jacob's death inventory, this statistic dropped dramatically to 0.44 per cent in 1792; according to his probate inventory, Ernst Jacob had liquidated most of his *Handthierungs-Waaren* in August 1791 by selling them, on credit, to his sons. [27] Like his father before him, Ernst Jacob provided his sons with some *Startkapital*.

Aside from the large number of supplies and wares, Anna Barbara's inventory of 1789 also listed numerous and expensive loans worth 1,464fl. 57x. that the Vayhingers had extended. In terms of total wealth, this category of loans extended, or *Activa*, comprised over fifty per cent of the Vayhingers' net worth. In real terms, all of these loans came from merchandise that the Vayhingers gave on credit to "various friends" and "merchants" located well outside the walls of Göppingen.[28] These far-reaching credit lines for finished woolen worsteds suggest that Vayhinger followed the common behavior of cutting out the middleman by participating in the trade and marketing of his merchandise. The extension of generous credit lines was not only an innovative behavior, but it was also, according to Medick, essential to "the maintenance and expansion of [...] a *Weber-Marchand's* (weaver-merchant's) activities" in a constrictive economy.[29] With multiple looms, outworkers, stockpiled goods, and their own merchandizing, the Vayhingers therefore practiced their trade in not only an assiduous, but also a venturesome manner.

The Vayhingers were, as the chronicle constantly implies, active gardeners. Ernst Jacob noted in one of his entries from 1771 that, after gathering produce "from [his] community plots", he "immediately sold" it for 27 Gulden.[30] Two years later (1773), Vayhinger wrote that "[t]his year I had, thank goodness, a robust year". He then proceeded to list the sources of his revenue:

26. StAG, B.II.2.g, Inventuren und Teilungen, 23.2–209.5 (1789).
27. StAG, B.II.2.g, Inventuren und Teilungen, 24.2–405.5 (1792).
28. StAG, B.II.2.g, Inventuren und Teilungen, 23.2–209.5 (1789).
29. Medick, *Weben und Überleben*, p. 239.
30. StAG, B.I.1.a, Hauschronik des Zeugmachers Ernst Jakob Vayhinger, p. 31.

From 3 [of his] community plots [he] cut 40 bushels barley, from the fourth plot 30 bushels potatoes [and] 2$^1/_2$ bushels beans. From [the sale of] four of my male canary birds came 48 fl [*Gulden*]. Because this year, they were quite rare. [And] because everything came off [well] due to the rise in prices; [he] won with the help of God 210 fl [...].

Only after explaining that some of this profit was consumed by an outstanding debt owed for taking over the entire house from his recently deceased mother, did Vayhinger turn to the primary trade of his household: weaving woolen worsted. Here, he briefly mentioned that seventeen *Centner* of wool "from the town shepherds" of three surrounding towns had been worked.[31] Apparently then, throughout their adult, married lives, the Vayhingers made good use of their share of the common lands, even hiring farmhands to assist in their endeavors.[32]

The Vayhingers also engaged in a third economic pursuit: animal husbandry. In 1755, as the notary took down the marriage inventory of Ernst Jacob and Anna Barbara, he recorded "two bird cages" and "twelve pairs of pigeons" worth a total of 2fl. 15x. Carefully cultivating these original twenty-four pigeons, Ernst Jacob more than doubled their number by 1782, for that was when "not more than five of [his] fifty pigeons escaped [the city fire] with their lives".[33] Expanding his efforts at animal husbandry, Ernst Jacob even began to raise canaries during the difficult years between 1764 and 1766. These birds were a significant source of the household's annual income in late 1772, when they comprised nearly one-quarter (i.e. 22.9 per cent) of the annual profit for that year (i.e. 210fl.). Perhaps more significantly, the solid income came at a particularly good time for the Vayhingers. During the years from 1770 to 1772, they, along with the rest of Göppingen, lived through famine and its concomitant, a severe rise in prices. Sometime during this famine, their canaries led Ernst Jacob and one of his sons on a journey to Schwäbisch Gmünd, "because the bird merchants were there".[34] Since the Vayhingers could not control the outside forces that led to the downturn in weaving, they aggressively tried to compensate for that lost, or slackened, enterprise by increasing their other undertakings.

Besides animal husbandry, Ernst Jacob and Anna Barbara profited from a fourth economic activity: renting out the bottom floor of their three-story house. They became landlords as soon as they took over the lower part of the house in 1775. Although leasing space in one's house was quite common among artisans and others in many large and medium cities throughout

31. *Ibid.*, p. 33.
32. *Ibid.*, p. 14.
33. Cf. StAG, B.II.2.g, Zubringens Inventuren vom 23 Jan. 1750 biß 20 Febr. 1756, p. 561b; and StAG, B.I.1.a, Hauschronik des Zeugmachers Ernst Jakob Vayhinger, p. 54.
34. StAG, B.I.1.a, Hauschronik des Zeugmachers Ernst Jakob Vayhinger, p. 47.

early modern Europe,³⁵ Vayhinger's chronicle implies that this type of
activity was relatively new to Göppingen. The Vayhingers had a succession
of three different tenants between 1775 and 1782, but when the city-wide
fire consumed the house in the latter year, the Vayhingers' tenants also lost
their quarters. Although Ernst Jacob discussed how difficult it was to rebuild
the "lower floor", he made no further mention of any other tenants in the
last two years of his chronicle.³⁶ Nor could a statement of how much money
he made from this rental property be found. While it would be useful to
know what percentage of the Vayhingers' income derived from their tenants, in this case it does not really matter. What matters is that they demonstrated their flexibility and an entrepreneurial attitude by employing yet
another strategy available for their use.

Here was a family that expanded and diversified its household economy
in a number of ways, evidently in an attempt, not only to remain competitive in trying economic times, but also to aggrandize its wealth. And the
Vayhingers' efforts yielded high dividends. Between 1755 and 1789, their
total wealth increased sixfold, moving from about 464fl. in 1755 to just over
2,720fl. in 1789. This household net worth placed the Vayhingers, according
to the wealth stratification for the period from 1768 to 1797, firmly in the
upper stratum in Göppingen. In the three years between Anna Barbara's
death (1789) and Ernst Jacob's death (1792), the total wealth of the Vayhinger household increased by just over 200 Gulden from about 2,720fl. to
2,950fl. This increase apparently came from two significant moves by Ernst
Jacob. First, he liquidated most of the wares and supplies in his workshop
just before his death, and second, he drastically reduced the loans outstanding and debts owed. With decreases in both loans and debts, it appears that
Vayhinger tried to clear his books so that the slate would be clean for his
sons after his death. He had, in fact, paid down all of the outstanding debts
for cash that had appeared on his wife's probate inventory in 1789. Only
one of the three *Passiva* in 1792 stemmed from cash (78fl. 45x.) that was
owed. The other two came from services rendered by the "barber Laiching-
er" (3fl. 10x.) and from back taxes in the amount of 10fl. 5x.³⁷ By reducing
the debt burdens that would be passed on to his successors, he provided his
sons with a rather large patrimony (*Startkapital*) that furnished them with
a solid foundation for their own industrious households.

The Vayhingers' high yields attest to the successful combination of a
number of economic strategies for dealing with an unpredictable world.
However, not all *Handwerker* households had the same resources. Three
case studies from the lower stratum make this crystal clear. The Greiners,

35. See Wolfgang von Hippel, Ute Mocker, and Sylvia Schraut, "Wohnen im Zeitalter der Industrialisierung. Esslingen am Neckar 1800–1914", *Esslinger Studien*, 26 (1987), pp. 137f.; Roche, *The
People of Paris*, pp. 103–110; and Schraut, *Sozialer Wandel*, pp. 252–258.
36. StAG, B.I.1.a, Hauschronik des Zeugmachers Ernst Jakob Vayhinger, pp. 42–63.
37. Cf. StAG, B.II.2.g, Inventuren und Teilungen, 23.2–209.5 (1789), and 24.2–405.5 (1792).

for instance, were shoemakers that lived and worked in "half of a two-story house" valued at 350fl. in 1779. They owned no other real estate. This portion of a building was a mere fragment of the Vayhingers' immovable property, worth 2,034fl. in 1789.[38] The Greiners – Georg Adam Greiner and Maria Barbara, the widow of Andreas Schieck, a stone-cutter in the neighboring town of Winterbach – had married in 1768; unfortunately, their marriage inventory could not be located, so it is impossible to determine their *Startkapital*. However, since Maria Barbara came into the marriage from outside Göppingen and from a different trade, it would seem likely that Georg Adam did not inherit an already established household economy, as was frequently the case when one married the widow of an artisan.[39] Apparently, the newlyweds lived in a residence owned by others until 1772, when, according to the annual tax register, they first began to pay property taxes of their own.[40]

The tax rolls also indicate that the Greiners' shoemaking business was not nearly as dynamic as the Vayhingers' weaving business. Whereas the Greiners paid 75fl. for commercial taxes in 1779, the Vayhingers paid 300fl. in the same year. In fact, throughout the 1780s, the taxes assessed on the Vayhingers were no less than 250fl., while those assessed on the Greiners were no more than 150fl.[41] To be sure, though, Maria Barbara's probate inventory, which lists a "four-poster bedframe [and an] old trunk in the journeyman's room", implies that the Greiners may have had someone outside the immediate family circle working with them.[42] The possible existence of a journeyman or an apprentice would have been offset by the rather heavy debt burden that they carried in 1779. As listed in the inventory, the Greiners had extended loans worth 45fl., but had incurred outstanding debts totaling 303fl. 35x.; while about one-quarter of that debt came from back taxes (i.e. 14fl. 40x., or 4.83 per cent) and from back rent (60fl., or 19.76 per cent), the remainder of the debt came from the two noteworthy categories of borrowed cash and supplies taken on credit.[43] The Greiners had borrowed 121fl. 66.5x. in cash from various wealthy creditors, like the *Gerichtsverwandt* (justice of the court) Erhardt, and institutions, like the *Armenkastenpfleg* (the poor relief fund). In addition, they had taken on credit leather valued at 40fl. from the wealthy tanner Widmann and another 60fl.-worth of

38. StAG, B.II.2.g, Inventuren und Teilungen, 19.2–49.5 (1779).
39. KrtG, Familienregister, 1558–1800, A–G, 608–634, p. 861, and Göppingen Familien-Register, Bd. 2, 608–2, p. 429. Winterbach is located about 25 km northwest of Göppingen.
40. Cf. StAG, B.II.5.d, Steuervermögensregister, 1764–1773 Haußgenoßen, Strb. [blank]; and Steuervermögensregister, 1764–1774 Drittes Viertel. Löw, Strb. 129.
41. See StAG, B.II.5.d, Steuervermögensregister, 1779–1782 Löw No. 78; Steuervermögensregister, 1783–1787 Haußgenoßen; Steuervermögensregister, 1783–1791 Ochs No. 89 1/8; Steuervermögensregister, 1779–1782 Löw No. 96; and Steuervermögensregister, 1783–1991 Löw No. 12.
42. StAG, B.II.2.g, Inventuren und Teilungen, 19.2–49.5 (1779).
43. *Ibid.*

leather from the tanner Schaufler.[44] This household of impecunious cobblers thus lived close to the edge, perhaps even *von der Hand in den Mund*, for if the Greiners defaulted on their numerous debts, then their real estate, the only significant asset of their net worth, would have been jeopardized. What happened to the Greiner household following the death of Maria Barbara is not entirely clear, for Georg Adam's probate inventory could not be located. Surrounding sources, however, suggest that Georg Adam remarried less than six months after Maria Barbara's death. He and his new wife, Anna Maria, née Beisser, had six children, four of whom apparently survived to adulthood, and their household economy continued to plod along, paying a steady 25fl. in commercial taxes throughout the 1790s, until Georg Adam died in 1806.[45]

Although the Endriß household engaged in a different trade, their situation did not differ much from that of the Greiners. In 1798, Johann Georg Endriß, a twenty-three-year-old butcher, married Margretha Schrag, the twenty-six-year-old widow of Johann Georg Bacher, also a butcher.[46] Since their marriage inventory was not found, their early material culture and *Startkapital* remain unknown. According to the annual tax rolls from 1801 to 1811, though, the Endrißs paid substantial property taxes of 462fl. in 1801, 391fl. in 1802, and 453fl. in 1806; their commercial taxes during the same period paled in comparison (i.e. 25fl. for 1801, 1802, and 1806).[47] While they owned considerable and wide-ranging farmland, which they evidently turned to agriculture and pasturage, Johann Georg and Margretha had a dismal trade in butchering. In fact, the Endrißs would request and receive a grant of 500fl. from the *Armenkastenpfleg* in 1803, using their extensive real estate as collateral.[48] As far as can be gathered, the Endrißs acquired this loan in order to purchase more land. Perhaps they had hoped to expand their farming endeavors. If so, they were unsuccessful, for when Johann Georg's death inventory appeared twenty-four years later in 1827, this debt was still pending, along with nineteen other outstanding debts for a total of 1,546fl. 23x. The largest portion of this debt came from borrowed cash, which totaled 1,373fl. 39x.; the second largest portion was for services rendered on credit, tallying 70fl. 40x.; another 62fl., the third largest, stemmed from administrative costs; the fourth chunk came from raw materials and goods in the amount of 20fl. 8x. that had been purchased on credit; and lastly, the household owed 19fl. 39x. in back taxes.[49] Like the Greiners, the Endrißs had turned to the town's poor relief institution for an injection

44. *Ibid.*
45. KrtG, Göppingen Familien-Register, Bd. 2, 608–2, p. 429.
46. *Ibid.*, p. 140.
47. StAG, B.II.5.d., Steuervermögensregister, 1801–1811 Ochs, fo. 395.
48. Cf. StAG, B.II.2.b, Gerichts Protocolle, p. 207 (5 Sept. 1803); and StAG, B.II.2.g, Inventuren und Teilungen, 239–12a (1827).
49. StAG, B.II.2.g., Inventuren und Teilungen, 239–12a (1827).

of hard capital, but unlike the Greiners, the Endrißs did not turn to the wealthy for additional loans. Instead, these poor butchers had turned to their apparently wealthy brother-in-law, Christoph Endriß, a tanner who loaned them 423fl. between 1813 and 1826.[50] Ultimately, the Endrißs' total debt owed was greater than their aggregate property (i.e. 1,522fl. 35x.), which meant that, like the Greiners, they had a precarious existence, always on the brink of disaster. In 1823, four years before Johann Georg's death, the tax roll listed the household industry as without journeymen or apprentices and as procuring only "humble earnings".[51] Evidently, the heavy debt load, which the Endrißs created by borrowing significant amounts of cash since at least 1803, sapped the vitality of their household economy, and the only way to survive was to borrow heavily from their generous brother-in-law.

The third case study, the Maiers, established their household economy in 1783 when Johann David Maier wedded Sibilla Magdalena, née Vöster. According to their marriage inventory, they began with 460fl. 10x. in *Startkapital*. About two-thirds of it came from their parents, who presented them with cash wedding gifts: Johann David's father gave them 200fl., while Sibilla Magdalena's mother gave 100fl.[52] At their nuptials, Johann David, a turner originally from the town of Adelmannsfelden, was four days short of his twenty-fourth birthday, while Sibilla Magdalena, the daughter of a cowherd in Göppingen, had just turned twenty-five.[53] Whether they lived at first with Sibilla Magdalena's parents or elsewhere in Göppingen is unclear, but the tax rolls do clearly indicate that they did not pay any property taxes until 1791, when they began to pay 35fl. in taxes on their "half of a two-story *Häuslen* [i.e. a small house]".[54] The value of this building could not be established, because neither the tax documents nor the probate inventory for Johann David listed its value. In fact, according to Johann David's probate inventory, the Maiers had at some time before 1827 lost all proprietary rights to this small house.[55] The tax registers also suggest that the Maiers had little success at their lathe-operating business. They were never assessed for more than 25fl. in commercial taxes during the period from 1783 to 1801; they paid no commercial taxes whatsoever in 1787, 1791, and 1792; and in 1823, their household economy was listed as "very poor [because father and son] pursued the trade quite feebly", with the son, Johann Georg,

---

50. *Ibid.*
51. StAG, B.II.7.c, Gewerbe Steuer 1823, p. 4b.
52. StAG, B.II.2.g, Zubringens Inventuren vom 13. Jun. 1779. bis 31. Merz. 1784., p. 427.
53. KrtG, Göppingen Familien-Register, Bd. 4, 608–4, p. 147. Adelmannsfelden is located about sixty km northeast of Göppingen.
54. See StAG, B.II.5.d, Steuervermögensregister, 1783–1787 Haußgenoßen; Steuervermögensregister, 1787–1790 Haußgenoßen; Steuervermögensregister, 1791–1801 Wolf No. 288; Steuer und Guther Buch. Renoviert 1790. IV. Viertel Wolf, p. 288; and Gewerbe Steuer 1823, p. 43b.
55. StAG, B.II.2.g, Inventuren und Teilungen, 239–11a (1827).

apparently serving as the single journeyman employed by the household business.[56] To be sure, at sixty-four years old, Johann David's household industry had most likely passed its prime, but still the household industry had not come even close to the solid rewards that were reaped by the Vayhingers' business. Indeed, the net worth of the Maier household in 1827, when Johann David died at the age of sixty-eight, was the paltry sum of 8fl. 9x. His *Schulden* (debts) played a significant role in reducing the estate to such a negligible level, for they totaled 149fl. 56x. Maier owed "71fl. [in] outstanding *HausZins* (rent)" to Michael Endriß (a tanner in Göppingen), "70fl. 56x." in borrowed cash, and "8fl." from wares that he had purchased on credit.[57] No evidence could be found of Maier making provision for providing his son with a solid patrimony as Vayhinger had done with his two sons.

With fewer resources, the lower-stratum artisans had fewer economic strategies available to them. Households, such as the Greiners, Endrißs, and Maiers, did not have the wherewithal to diversify their economic pursuits, and as we have seen, this flexibility was crucial for the survival and success of the Vayhinger household. This also seems to have been the case in nearby Laichingen, where Medick's linen-weavers weathered the economic fluctuations of the eighteenth and nineteenth centuries by changing their economic behaviors accordingly. When new opportunities in the linen industry presented themselves during the golden years of the second half of the eighteenth century, many linen-weavers expanded their small-scale production by investing more heavily in that sector than in land, even though "landed resources remained important". But when stagnation hit at the end of the eighteenth century, the linen-weavers who survived best were the ones, like Peter Näher, who turned their resources to the older economic ventures, like working the land, or to newer ones, like extending large "credit lines".[58] Flexibility and pragmatism were, therefore, typical hallmarks of the *Handwerker* household. In fact, as argued by Richard Wall, the basic economic unit during the early modern era might best be described as the "adaptive family economy," where the "key characteristic [was] flexibility".[59]

In Göppingen, arable lands were a crucial component of that flexibility for wealthier households. For instance, when Anna Maria Widmann died in 1770, the notary recorded that her and her husband's household consisted of not only "a three-story house, with a barn entrance [...]" worth 1,600fl., but also a collection of "fields, gardens, and community plots", which was

56. StAG, B.II.7c, Gewerbe Steuer 1823, p. 43b.
57. StAG, B.II.2.g, Inventuren und Teilungen, 239–11a (1827).
58. Medick, *Weben und Überleben*, pp. 212–228, and 229–243.
59. Richard Wall, "Work, Welfare and the Family: An Illustration of the Adaptive Family Economy", in L. Bonfield, R. Smith, and K. Wrightson (eds), *The World We Have Gained: Histories of Population and Social Structure* (Oxford, 1986), p. 265.

worth 1,430fl.[60] In fact, farmland was apparently a resource that significantly set the middling and wealthy *Handwerker* apart from the poor ones (see Table 2). Few, if any, of the poorer households owned enough landed property to pursue agriculture; the *Handwerker* of the lower stratum were lucky if they owned more than a section of a building. Thus, it is not surprising that ownership of other categories related to agricultural production – i.e. produce and livestock – also distinguished the households of the poorer families from those of the other strata in Göppingen (see Table 2).

Renting out space within one's household as an economic strategy would have also remained limited to better-off households. Again, the poorer households simply did not have enough property for empty space. Indeed, the average value of the lower stratum's real estate always paled in comparison to that of the wealthier households in Göppingen (see Table 2). Moreover, as shown in Table 3, the lower stratum always had a higher percentage of house- and landless members as compared to the other two strata. Therefore, the typical household among the poorer artisans lived in cramped quarters, and in some cases those quarters were not owned by the family which inhabited them. This, in turn, meant that the lower-stratum artisans must have crowded their workshop into their living space, which would have left little room for tenants or subtenants and for journeymen or apprentices, too. For those poor artisans who did own their homes and perhaps some arable land, their real estate was much more than just the cornerstone of their wealth. Oftentimes, it was the whole sum of the lower-stratum family's wealth, constituting close to, if not over, 100 per cent of its net worth (see Table 2). Of course, owning real estate could in itself be an important strategy for lower-stratum households; they could use it as collateral in acquiring loans, as the Endrißs did, or they might use it as a form of insurance against times of severe crisis. However, beyond the residences that housed their businesses, the poorer households possessed few liquid assets. So, if anything went wrong, then the whole kit-and-caboodle could easily be lost. Fettered by this, the industrious households of the lower stratum lacked the versatility that characterized the middling-to-wealthier households in Göppingen.

The poorer artisans did, nonetheless, explore other strategies in an effort to adapt to the changing world around them. The households in the lower stratum tried, like most small-scale producers, to rely on the strategy of reallocating more of their total wealth to their craft tools, supplies, and wares to take advantage of good economic times. But, when it came to the average amount of Gulden allocated to this category (Table 2), the poorer

---

60. StAG, B.II.2.g, Inventuren und Teilungen, 16.2–250 (1770). The Widmanns were wealthy tanners, and incidentally this probate inventory, unlike the Vayhingers', categorized the their "community plots" as part of their permanent real estate. The Widmanns presumably had a long-term lease on those plots.

Categories of possessions by stratum (1738–1827)

Category	Lower Stratum Average value in fl.	As % of net worth	Middle Stratum Average value in fl.	As % of net worth	Upper Stratum Average value in fl.	As % of net worth
Real estate:						
Buildings						
1738–1767	184.97	80.69	377.66	55.93	724.62	23.57
1768–1797	237.70	92.27	676.96	58.39	1,470.48	34.26
1798–1827	298.70	112.91	1,024.63	63.92	1,943.22	32.37
Arable lands						
1738–1767	12.93	5.64	99.17	14.69	543.47	17.68
1768–1797	13.55	5.25	259.18	22.73	964.71	22.48
1798–1827	69.02	26.09	256.60	16.01	741.81	12.36
Craft tools, wares, etc.						
1738–1767	10.69	4.66	19.41	2.88	174.64	5.75
1768–1797	57.94	22.47	146.26	12.61	293.96	6.85
1798–1827	21.28	8.04	288.68	18.01	514.00	8.56
Loans extended						
1738–1767	35.39	15.44	124.38	18.42	827.24	26.91
1768–1797	17.85	6.92	158.61	13.68	1,148.71	26.77
1798–1827	11.64	4.40	240.69	15.01	2,036.13	33.92
Debts owed						
1738–1767	−112.56	−49.11	−159.93	−23.69	−198.06	−6.44
1768–1797	−201.95	−78.32	−421.28	−36.33	−553.26	−12.89
1798–1827	−238.40	-90.11	−637.52	−39.77	−789.38	−13.15
Cash						
1738–1767	10.47	4.57	38.26	5.67	452.73	14.73
1768–1797	13.88	5.38	47.39	4.09	273.57	6.37
1798–1827	6.89	2.61	64.07	4.00	470.46	7.84
Clothing and jewelry						
1738–1767	25.18	10.99	40.70	6.03	82.29	2.68
1768–1797	36.02	13.97	81.34	7.02	124.74	2.91
1798–1827	23.36	8.83	85.72	5.35	131.98	2.20
Furniture, bedding, linens						
1738–1767	48.54	21.18	76.16	11.28	189.92	6.18
1768–1797	58.30	22.61	113.69	9.81	212.33	4.95
1798–1827	52.73	19.93	152.27	9.50	279.76	4.66
Produce and livestock						
1738–1767	0.42	0.18	7.79	1.15	63.15	2.05
1768–1797	0.33	0.13	22.83	1.97	96.17	2.24
1798–1827	4.52	1.71	29.60	1.85	114.74	1.91
Household items[61]						
1738–1767	10.16	4.43	46.64	6.91	202.70	6.59
1768–1797	20.14	7.81	62.69	5.41	252.10	5.87
1798–1827	13.05	4.93	93.54	5.83	554.94	9.24

Table 2. *continued*

Category	Lower Stratum Average value in fl.	As % of net worth	Middle Stratum Average value in fl.	As % of net worth	Upper Stratum Average value in fl.	As % of net worth
Books						
1738–1767	3.04	1.33	4.94	0.73	9.00	0.29
1768–1797	3.88	1.50	7.47	0.64	8.09	0.19
1798–1827	1.75	0.66	4.80	0.30	5.93	0.10
Net worth (sum of categories)						
1738–1767	229.22		675.18		3,073.69	
1768–1797	257.84		1,159.46		4,291.62	
1798–1827	264.55		1,603.08		6,003.59	

Sources: StAG, Inventuren und Teilungen

Table 3. *Percentage of each stratum without real estate (1738–1827)*

Period	Lower stratum	Middle stratum	Upper stratum
1738–1767	17.24	8.62	3.33
1768–1797	32.26	4.92	0.00
1798–1827	14.81	7.41	0.00

Sources: StAG, Inventuren and Teilungen

households simply could not keep up with their socioeconomic superiors. While the wealthiest and middling families made steady increases over the course of the ninety years studied, the poorest families increased only between the first and second interval. Simply stated, the rich and middling could afford the costs involved in expanding their small-scale production, whereas the poorer could not. Their poverty, in effect, negated this economic strategy for survival. This forced most of them into an untenable position, where all focus was on a household industry that could not be made competitive when new economic opportunities and pressures arose in the late eighteenth and early nineteenth centuries.

The indefatigable artisans of the lower stratum did, however, seek a way out of this dilemma. One possible course of action was to increase the economic capital available to their industrious households by borrowing more and paying back less. This was most likely the motive behind the 500fl. grant that the Endriß applied for in 1803, and it was clearly the motive behind the Greiners, the shoemakers, who took 100fl. in leather

61. This category includes the following items from the probate inventories: brass utensils + tin utensils + copper utensils + iron utensils + tinplate utensils + wooden utensils + barrel and binding materials + common household goods and tools + harness, tack, and building materials + foodstores + supplies + wine and other drinks.

supplies on credit from two tanners. According to Table 2, a good number
of other households hit upon this strategy as the average amount that the
lower stratum borrowed continued to outpace the loans that they extended.
On the other hand, the families of the upper stratum evidently became the
creditors as they continued to loan out more than they borrowed. For many
of the poorer households, these increased debt burdens were a logical way
to increase their resources, but the overwhelming nature of these debts could
also spell doom, as shown above by the cases of the Endriß and Maier
households. Ultimately then, the strategy of increasing stagnant resources
through enlarged debt burdens was a double-edged sword: one edge may
have increased economic viability, but the other introduced even more risk
of disaster. Whether conscious or unconscious, this behavior was both cause
and effect of the limited flexibility and adaptability found among the poorer
households.

The least wealthy families had yet another strategy designed to deal with
the changing world around them. Even before they tried to rouse their
small-scale production with more fluid capital, the poorer artisans concentrated more of their net worth on items that carried social and cultural
capital, rather than just economic capital. Indeed, when it came to noneco-
omic goods, like clothing, jewelry, furniture, and bedding, the lower-
stratum households always devoted to them proportions of their net worth
that clearly exceeded the rates of their socioeconomic superiors (see Table
2). To be sure, in absolute values the poorer families did not own as much
of these items as the middling and wealthy, but they did keep pace with
the new fashions and styles that came with the sartorial revolution of the
late eighteenth and early nineteenth centuries. In 1738, for example, the
lower-stratum Weiß, who worked as tailors, owned a number of novel
items in their rather abundant wardrobes. Justina Weiß had a necklace and
a number of colorful skirts and bonnets, and Johannes had a pair of woolen
cloth trousers.[62] The trousers were particularly unusual, for during much of
the eighteenth century, leather was the material of choice for trousers among
artisan-craftsmen.[63] Given their trade, though, it would have made good
business sense for the Weiß to advertise their wares and craftsmanship in
tailoring through their own wardrobes. Justina and Johannes would have
been likely "trend-setters", because new trends and fashions create great
potential for business among tailors.[64]

All three of the poorer households mentioned above had trendy items
among their possessions. The Greiners, who struggled as cobblers during
the 1770s, owned clothes and jewelry, such as a blue waistcoat, numerous

62. StAG, B.II.2.g, Inventuren und Teilungen, 1.38–109.5 (1738).
63. See Benscheidt, *Kleinbürgerlicher Besitz*, p. 116; and Ernst Schubert, "Daily Life, Consumption,
and Material Culture", in Sheilagh Ogilvie (ed.), *Germany: A New Social and Economic History*,
vol. 2: *1630–1800* (London, 1996), p. 362.
64. See Medick, *Weben und Überleben*, p. 419.

colorful skirts, and a necklace, that did not differ much at all in style and fashion to those of their socioeconomic superiors. Maria Barbara and Georg Adam also owned a *"Trisure"* [i.e. sideboard], which was considered a luxury item in the 1770s.[65] Similarly, the Endrißs had among their possessions a *"Seßel"* [i.e. easychair], which was still a novelty in 1827. In their wardrobes could be found the following up-to-date and fashionable items: *"a zizene* [i.e. colorful lightweight cotton] skirt, a *zizene* apron, [and] a taffeta apron" for Margaretha; and "silver shoe buckles, silver suspender buckles, woolen worsted trousers [and] a dark blue overcoat" for Johann Georg.[66] And, lastly, even the elderly turner, Johann David Maier, had among his household possessions in 1827 certain novel furnishings, such as "two nonupholstered *Canapee* [i.e. sofa/daybed], a *Seßel*, two portraits, and a birdcage".[67] By acquiring a relatively wide array of the latest styles, these households, like many other members of the lower stratum, engaged in the new behavior of keeping in fashion. However, while the middling and wealthy families comfortably acquired the new fashions with little trouble, the least wealthy artisans diverted larger portions of their net worth away from revenue-generating, economic goods to noneconomic, consumer goods. The poorest households, therefore, paid the highest price as the lure of new fashions snared most families in Göppingen, and in general, contemporaneous auth-orities and social commentators quickly focused on such negative ramifi-cations. Complaints about the *"Kleiderluxus* (clothing luxury)" of the petty bourgeois "run through the entire [eighteenth century]".[68] These writers, according to Helmut Müller, realized that "[w]ith the scanty economic leeway of the *Kleinbürgertum*, clothing luxury [could have] ruinous conse-quences".[69]

The lower-stratum artisans in Göppingen, however, may have had good motives for devoting larger portions of their wealth to these goods. They had, as demonstrated by their stagnant wealth, little success in taking advan-tage of good economic opportunities, whereas their wealthier contemporar-ies not only grew more wealthy but also acquired the trappings – both in clothing and jewelry and in household furnishings – that signified such wealth. In a situation where they had little flexibility and, hence, could not truly compete economically with their richer and middling colleagues, the lower-stratum households could, at least, acquire the new styles and fashions as soon as, if not sooner than, their colleagues in the upper and middle strata. By adopting the new trends in clothing, jewelry, and furnishings, they made what Bourdieu might consider "an excellent investment in social

65. StAG, B.II.2.g, Inventuren und Teilungen, 19.2–49.5 (1779).
66. StAG, B.II.2.g, Inventuren und Teilungen, 239–12a (1827).
67. StAG, B.II.2.g, Inventuren und Teilungen, 239–11a (1827).
68. Helmut Möller, *Die Kleinbürgerliche Familie im 18. Jahrhundert: Verhalten und Gruppenkultur* (Berlin, 1969), p. 143.
69. *Ibid.*, p. 146.

capital".[70] Clothing, after all, served – and continues to serve – as outward expression of one's position in society, and hence, such items carried social utility. Indeed, as argued by Möller, when it came to proclaiming one's identity, "magnificence in clothing was not only the most effective – because it fell on the most eyes and at the same time distinguished one from others – but it was also the cheapest compared with other forms of representation".[71]

Unfortunately for the poorer artisans, though, this strategy could only benefit them and their households superficially. On the surface, their outward appearance would have kept them "competitive" with the more profitable craftspeople, but by consciously or unconsciously utilizing this strategy, these lower-stratum families most likely accelerated the depletion of their already meager resources. When thrust into dire straits, where even finding one's daily bread became a frantic and grave struggle, the only economic benefit that diverse wardrobes and stylish furnishings had was the quick cash that might be generated by liquidating them. But owning relatively large and diverse wardrobes and novel furnishings did not, of course, single-handedly cause the immense difficulties that the lower-stratum artisans experienced during the late eighteenth and early nineteenth centuries. There were other, more momentous events, such as the city-wide fire of 1782, and thereafter the crisis years of the Napoleonic period, that were certainly nearer the root cause of their difficulties.

Still, the poorer households continued to persevere. In fact, even though the families of the lower stratum in Göppingen had always lacked the means for establishing a truly flexible, patchwork household economy like the Vayhingers, they nevertheless attempted to carve out more room for maneuver. They aggressively expanded their debt burdens as they continued to allocate significant portions of their wealth to material commodities that carried both social and cultural capital. To be sure, they may not have had much choice in the matter, for if they wished to hold on to their status and their position in society as their economic capital declined, then they had to turn to these means. Even with more loans, though, the investments in economic capital (i.e. equipment, stores, real estate, etc.) could oftentimes be too expensive for the poorer households. Hence, the predetermined choice would have been to continue their concentration on social and cultural capital. There was always the possibility that they may have disdained the novel cultural goods of the late eighteenth and nineteenth centuries, but with the strong communal pressures for and societal expectations of conformity in the German hometowns, charting such a course would have been extraordinarily difficult and potentially disastrous.[72] Instead, out of a desperate resourcefulness, the poorer craftspeople in Göppingen used the

70. Bourdieu, *Distinction*, p. 375.
71. Möller, *Die Kleinbürgerliche Familie*, p. 146.
72. See Mack Walker, *German Home Towns* (Ithaca, NY, 1971).

novel cultural goods and growing debt burdens as a kind of last ditch effort to salvage their precarious livelihoods. And, although their precise motivations and reasoning are not self-evident in the inventories, it is nonetheless striking that the least wealthy artisans tried to compensate for their lack of access to economic capital by increasing their fluid capital and by investing in social and cultural capital. Within an economy of scarcity, the poorer households tried to stretch what little flexibility and adaptability that they had by employing not only economic but also social and cultural strategies for survival.

International Review of Social History 45 (2000), pp. 137–157

Individualization Strategies Among City Dwellers in Contemporary Africa: Balancing the Shortcomings of Community Solidarity and the Individualism of the Struggle for Survival

ALAIN MARIE

In urban Africa today, like elsewhere, the purported survival strategies of individuals are determined constantly by severe material constraints. The poor and the new poor are overwhelmingly new city dwellers dependent on precarious, intermittent odd jobs (*petits boulots*);[1] single women with small children; young school dropouts (*déscolarisés*), condemned to the expediencies of the streets, illicit actions and, in many cases, delinquency; unemployed graduates (*diplomés-chômeurs*), without opportunities for paid employment; as well as those designated successively in the vernacular as *conjoncturés, déflatés* and *compressés* (i.e. workers affected by wage reductions, permanent employees downgraded to temporary contracts or casual labour, and workers who have lost their jobs through massive redundancies). These individuals can meet only the most basic needs (eating, feeding their children, paying the rent). When survival becomes an issue, long-term strategies tend to be constrained by the need to fulfil the most basic needs and daily necessities. At any rate, pursuit of this objective does not involve selective mobilization of optimized means, when those who admittedly are looking out for themselves (*se cherchent*), rummage about (*grouillent à droite [et] à gauche*), pursue small jobs in unskilled manual labour or portering, or as night watchmen (*racolage pour trouver des petits contrats de manoeuvrage, de manutention ou de veilleur de nuit*),[2] search constantly for opportunities to sell items that they bought for a little bit less, inland or across the border. They may also try to establish a business or small craft shop and, during the interim, get by with difficulty thanks to sporadic aid from relatives who are also unemployed. All rely on circumstances, encounters, the economic situation, luck and what they call fortune (*la chance*). Except for some graduates and former wage employees (some of whom have cultural and social capital), they very rarely have the relative latitude of a choice of means and ends justifying what we might call strategies, which are often

1. The expressions in italics are from the French African vernacular in the major cities of West Africa.
2. These activities are occasional, irregular, temporary, isolated and very poorly paid jobs. The trick is to discover them by expanding one's network and increasing the interactions, offers and applications.

merely grass-roots activism and efforts to reach out in all directions.
While they certainly seem very busy, their activities do not offer genuine
prospects or opportunities to pursue coherent ambition.

These survival strategies are indeed rigidly defined by poverty (the
common feature of want – *manque de moyens* – in conjunction with the
obsessive "there is no money" – *y a pas l'argent*) and consequently by
the informal economy and illicit activities, amid scarcity and anomic
laissez-faire that both imposes and promotes individualism as imperative
in the struggle for survival. Nevertheless, all these means of survival are
embedded in a social and cultural setting marked by anti-individualist
community traditions that clearly attribute a specific style and significance. In this respect, they always seem associated with a strategy. On
the one hand, individualism is prescribed by economic need and is based
on the universal inclination to impose one's own interests (of which
Africans have as many as anybody else). On the other hand, the solidarity
ethic derives from longstanding cultural traditions that are deeply
internalized, but are also sustained by requests for help that are more
urgent than ever in this crisis. Between these two contradictory forms
of logic, individuals therefore need to practise well-informed strategies of
compromise. Noting the shortcomings of community solidarity and the
worsening threats of witchcraft sanctioning these shortcomings, they
resort to avoidance, protection and greater individual autonomy involving
extracommunity religious and political involvement.

Though their economic survival methods are often far from strategic or
original, they resort to existential and social survival strategies. Their conduct comes to reflect a specific world state, implicitly and often explicitly
involving transformation of both the person and of the ways that the overall
being and they themselves pursue this objective, from reinterpreted traditions and reclaimed modernity, a specific combination of means.

Analysis of this complex and often ambivalent process will benefit
from relating the social and cultural logic to the basis of community
solidarity. After this anthropological digression, the microsociology of
concrete situations and the meanings attributed by the city dwellers
facilitate highlighting this explicit and reasoned strategic dimension of
their social conduct.

I ANTHROPOLOGICAL FOUNDATIONS OF COMMUNITY SOLIDARITY

First of all, a classical empirical observation comes to mind. In traditional
African societies, most of the different forms of social milieux (consisting
of family relationships, or links among neighbours based upon production,
reciprocal consumption, or political-territorial records) are interwoven so
well that all social relationships are constantly imbued with affects, that the

distinction between the public and the private spheres is hardly relevant, and that solidarity appears as an *a priori*, ontological and axiological principle, largely out of range of analytical and critical considerations.[3]

Anthropological tradition has long settled for a cultural-functionalist perspective focusing on the virtuous specificity of community solidarity – as opposed to the individualism of Western modernity – that directly integrates individuals in groups and turns people into their own recourse (*Ouolof adage*).[4] The group's primacy with respect to the individual is thus manifested by the absence of the household concept (of a conjugal family) which is not recognized as a specific category in the language. Nor is it acknowledged as an independent entity in practice: the individual is relevant only in collectives of inclusive parentage (the extended family, the lineage, the clan).

Solidarity as the embodiment of the realism of mutual assurance

Nonetheless, a less culturalist perspective, based on the simple idea that societies sanctified the basis of their operations and reproduction, reveals that solidarity's importance derives primarily from the objective need for reciprocity over the short and long term.

Simultaneously, there is a daily need for ordinary cooperation to cover risks and provide protection from life's dangers.[5] Diachronously (over the course of seasons, years and generations), the reciprocity principle underlies loan and restitution cycles.[6] While awaiting the upcoming production, the collectivity consumes the preceding production under the supervision of the eldest, who run the annual system of services and redistributions. Over time, the ascendant generations sustain the descendant ones, which, after receiving these advances, provide compensation in the form of aid and services when they in turn enter the production cycle and later become responsible for supporting the generation of grandparents, when the birth of grandchildren starts a new cycle.

From this materialist perspective, the community henceforth appears as

3. A detailed description of the implicit and explicit socialization procedures that give rise to individual habits driven by a natural inclination toward solidarity appears in the study by Jacqueline Rabain, *L'enfant du lignage. Du sevrage à la classe d'âge* (Paris, 1979), on informal education among the Ouolof in Dakar.

4. This tradition remains significant in Louis Dumont, *Essais sur l'individualisme. Une perspective anthropologique sur l'idéologie moderne* (Paris, 1983).

5. Greater mobilization of the workforce for tasks exceeding the capacities of domestic units; gifts of food, various services and prized commodities that sustain support networks and offer entitlement to various gifts in return to cope with daily needs, such as social obligations or production hazards; recurring gestures of hospitality and commensality; reciprocal participation in wedding or funeral expenses; sets of services to the eldest and the chiefs in return for guaranteed return disbursements on their part, etc.

6. Cf. Claude Meillassoux, *Femmes, greniers et capitaux* (Paris, 1975).

a mutual organization based on the reciprocity principle. Far from being considered original, this principle is to be interpreted as the modality of an objective need for protection from the insecurity of the present and insurance covering future uncertainties and economic and human resources wherever the material circumstances compel an immediate mutual management of resources.

The question nevertheless arises as to how this reciprocity is actually protected from any shortcoming by three forms of social logic operating in a context of necessary circular involvement: the debt logic, the hierarchical logic and the anti-individualist logic.

The realistic gift: the debt logic

The debt logic underlies the relationship between a donor (who takes charge as the creditor) and a donee (who is subordinate as the debtor and is obliged to repay the debt incurred sooner or later). This practice legitimizes his permanent right to receive mutual aid and cooperation and, more generally, to support (or accumulate) social capital: such relations are so much more useful that they are vital.

This perspective places the act of giving in a more realistic light. According to Mauss's formula *do ut des* (I give so that you will give):[7] if an initial gift inspires a return gift, it is basically an investment to be recovered in the long run. Giving means taking out insurance on the near or distant future. Such insurance is secured by the law of reciprocity (i.e. personal interest in honouring one's debt to safeguard one's place in the cycle of reciprocal exchanges), and everything passes before the tribunal of public opinion (which is quick to impose sanctions on unscrupulous or insolvent debtors).[8] This debt logic, however, exists continuously in African societies.

The debt logic is first of all the ontological and metaphysical debt of mortals with respect to Gods, civilizing heroes, ancestors, preceding generations, and those who died recently. It underlies everything (customs, know-how, territorial prerogatives) and is a condition for everything (health, fecundity, fertility). Individuals also have an existential debt toward their social surroundings: a person's ontosociological debt (always/already in debt) toward the parents who transmit life, enter within a lineage, attribute status and identity, raise, educate, organize the rites of magic protection and initiation and later arrange a marriage marking the transition to adulthood; a husband's debt toward his in-laws who have given the wife ensuring his offspring, who are the ultimate insurance for old age and survival (this

7. Marcel Mauss, "Essai sur le don", in Marcel Mauss (ed.), *Sociologie et anthropologie* (Paris, 1960).
8. For a critique of the culturalist orientation of Maussian theory, from a materialistic point of view, cf. Alain Marie, "L'échange: sous le don, la dette", *Sciences humaines*, 23 (1998), pp. 28–31.

progeny is responsible for caring for elderly parents before giving them honourable funerals that are the key to a peaceful life after death);[9] the debt of ordinary people to their chief and the eldest in the lineage, who, because they are at the heart of a system of tributary or ritual services, accumulate wealth for redistribution as aid in case of need and as ceremonial spending (intended to honour the ancestors and divinities, on whom the living depend for their wellbeing).

The debt logic thus perpetuates such a close network between creditors and debtors that a debtor's balance with one individual may be offset by a creditor's balance with a third party. Any debtor, upon becoming economically independent, is in turn responsible for helping others incur debts, both because of his social obligations and his world view and because of his personal interest (upward social mobility, insurance for the future).

The hierarchical principle

In return, this socially pre-established harmony between the debt's social logic, individual rationality of running into debt, and personal desire for acknowledgement presumes and implies intrinsically hierarchical relationships between the members of the community. Disregarding exchanges of equivalent services[10] – which impose no obligation other than that of the giver, giving for rather short terms – debt relations, however, are unequal. Whether as accompanying[11] or constituent factors,[12] they always affirm a relationship between the dominant and the dominated party.

Anti-individualism: witchcraft and its effectiveness

The beliefs concerning witchcraft that prevail among different African societies somehow complete this consubstantial liaison between debt logic and hierarchical logic. Understanding their deep-seated rationality will elucidate their hidden functionality.

If these beliefs make sense to the social agents invoking them to explain the various misfortunes attributed to the evil and occult actions of witches around them, they are not as senseless as they might appear. Regarding

9. This is why among the Dan from Ivory Coast, for example, regardless of the amount of matrimonial compensation initially paid for the wife, the husband's debt toward his in-laws is infinite: it is said that "the dowry never ends", in that the husband has a never ending obligation to give gifts, to accommodate, and to help his in-laws (personal observation).

10. E.g. land clearing and work in the fields of others, joining collective hunts, mutual aid in house building, reciprocal guarding of part of the herds.

11. The relation between parents and children, between older and younger generations, between chiefs and subjects.

12. The relation between givers of a wife and recipients, between patron and client, between protector and protégé, between benefactor and beneficiary.

Durkheim's formula about the religious sphere,[13] if they seem like a delirium, as soon as this delirium becomes collective, it must be based on solid foundations. It should relate (symbolically and therefore indirectly) to reality (objective) and should have a realistic significance (expression or revelation of some of its properties). Without going into detail, we will recall the main assertions.[14]

(1) Mankind's unhappiness is caused largely by other people, who, endowed with magic occult and evil powers, are responsible for most misfortunes, of which the accumulation or repetition reveals that they arise from malicious intentions. According to the theory of witchcraft, certain individuals are responsible for, and are therefore guilty of, misfortunes that afflict those around them.[15] This position relieves society of all blame.[16]

(2) Witchcraft is all the more effective and malicious, because it pitches people against those around them, parents, husbands and wives, spouses in polygamous unions and their respective children, matrimonial alliances, neighbours (nowadays schoolfellows, colleagues or competitors). Within their social circle, all people therefore find both those who are inclined to help them and others who turn out to be their worst enemies. Thus, like any rather cohesive environment, but with a more intense role as the site of daily life and a "unit of survival",[17] communities are presented as essentially ambivalent, very remote from all Western fantasies of being harmonious and equipped to weather any serious internal conflict.

(3) This community ambivalence arises from ambivalence among people. Witchcraft is not the attribute of certain predesignated categories of individuals. Anybody can become a witch or sorcerer: by heredity, by particular circumstances of conception or birth; by accidental contamination; by a magic spell; by deliberately joining a secret fraternity of sorcerers; or quite simply because the distinction between common empirical reality and the surreality of the ruling occult powers is fluid. A vast clandestine and mysteri-

13. Emile Durkheim, *Les formes élémentaires de la vie religieuse* (Paris, 1912).
14. A more detailed analysis appears in Alain Marie, "Du sujet communautaire au sujet individuel. ne lecture anthropologique de la réalité africaine contemporaine", in Alain Marie (ed.) *L'Afrique des individus. Itinéraires citadins dans la société contemporaine (Abidjan, Bamako, Dakar, Nyamey)* (Paris, 1997), pp. 53–110.
15. Business failures, poor harvests, accidents, deaths of young children, infertility, impotence, stillborn babies, successive illnesses, decline, madness, epidemics, death in the family, death of the victim etc.; in today's world, also traffic accidents, losing one's job, dropping out of school, bankruptcy, etc.
16. Ideas about witchcraft help exonerate society from any semblance of a cause for criticism or subversion (in addition to sanctifying the social order in the stories of the world's creation by the gods and the divine heroes and society's establishment by our forebears). The community order is thus sanctified according to Durkheim's definition of the term: the profane shall not affect it; individuals have no alternative but to submit. For an analysis related to this perspective, cf. Max Gluckman, "Crises morales et solutions magiques", *Economies et sociétés*, Cahiers de l'I.S.E.A., 2 February 1967, pp. 5–48.
17. Norbert Elias, *La société des individus* (Paris, 1991, fourth French edition).

ous underworld of antisocial sentiments and aggressive impulses can submerge anybody at any time, and unknowingly even force them to the other side of the spectrum of community sociability, into the invisible and formidable mirror world, where sorcerers interact, take up with each other, sometimes get into confrontations and always feed on each other's misfortunes. Every human being has the potential to become a sorcerer.

(4) Surely, this means that the sorcerer is the individual himself as envisaged in his most intimate dimension, the most individualized, least socialized and even most resistant to all socialization undertaken: hidden, often subconscious, affects and secret, often unknowing, impulses. The different dispositions attributed to the sorcerers depending on the cases correspond with an all-encompassing characterology. It provides a framework for identifying abuses of power or successes of eminent individuals,[18] that are sometimes too overwhelming or too quick for comfort, and for stigmatizing ordinary people who may be suspected of using sorcery to indulge in vengeance, jealousy, envy or unbridled ambition, or refusing to remain in their social station.

Through these representations, community societies thus stigmatize individualism as a threat, while acknowledging implicitly that it is a universal potentiality and temptation. In this respect, these societies are quite anti-individualist.

(5) From this perspective, sorcerers are optimally suited by virtue of their individualism to challenge the debt logic and the hierarchical principle. Magically controlling those around them,[19] feeding on their vital strength to reinforce their own, offering some of those close to them as sacrificial meat at cannibalistic feasts of their brotherhood, sorcerers are just the people to violate the debt law. As creditors fearing neither God nor man, they take without giving, accumulate without returning, exploit, steal, pillage, and kill, assume no obligation but take everything. Simultaneously, they subvert the hierarchical principle: as men of power, they use it arbitrarily (they always want more and use it for their own benefit without redistributing); as common people, they rebel against their situation, are devoured by jealousy or by ambition, attack things and people and sometimes even become serial killers.[20]

18. Chiefs, distinguished individuals, exorcists, religious officials, great warriors, political entrepreneurs, rich merchants; in today's world, political officials, successful businessmen, outstanding pupils or students etc.
19. For example by making their "invisible" doubles work as slaves on their "invisible" plantations.
20. This account presumes a view of the social world as a "closed society" devoted to simple reproduction, excluding expanded reproduction that indefinitely increases the resources and diversifies the positions to be conquered. In a closed society, individualism therefore automatically has a detrimental effect on others. Generally, a "materialist" explanation prevails for this symbolic representation. Following a case study on witchcraft in France today, Jeanne Favret-Saada noted that faith presumed a closed conception of the social universe and its economic resources: each individual is in charge of a domain; once all domains have been appropriated, sorcerers need to

(6) Beliefs in witchcraft thus concern power as well,[21] in that all temporal power and all extraordinary abilities are considered based on the surreal – local divinities, genies, ancestors – as well as on the magic gatherings. Chiefs (the political leaders in modern contexts), exorcists with supernatural powers, dignitaries, clan elders, and the elderly in general, are believed to wield magic powers of defence and aggression, enabling them to protect themselves and their dependants from attacks by jealous sorcerers, and to inflict punishment as defenders of the established order, on those guilty of individualism that threatens the community law. They are the ones most likely to organize or control the rituals for detecting and neutralizing sorcerers.[22] Moreover, by implementing the universal scapegoat mechanism, the beliefs concerning witchcraft are intrinsically conducive to maintaining the community order. People understand that they can always resort to witchcraft (even unknowingly) and are aware of what happens to those labelled as sorcerers after a trial or simply by rumour.[23] Especially among the common people known as "simple" (as the people without magic powers are known in Ivory Coast), everybody, therefore, tries to suppress all evil (i.e. individualist) ideas, and ostensibly to manifest conviviality and benevolence (i.e. altruism) toward others.

(7) The individualist temptation, however, remains omnipresent (nobody escapes), as the witchcraft theory implicitly acknowledges, and as several ethnographic observations noting the frequent recurrence in community society of suspicions of witchcraft and, sometimes, legal-therapeutic rituals following an accumulation of misfortunes. Overall, indigenous socioanthropology supports, metaphorically, the powerful belief in the indomitable duality of society and the individual: society and mankind are equally ambivalent in that both harbour disturbing and threatening twilight zones beneath their ordinary, reassuring and convivial surfaces.[24]

Far from weakening individualist tendencies, however, the postcolonial

remove resources magically from other domains to expand their own. See Jeanne Favret-Saada, *Les mots, la mort, les sorts. La sorcellerie dans le Bocage* (Paris, 1979).

21. On political aspects of witchcraft in societies based on lineage, see Marc Augé, *Théorie des pouvoirs et idéologie* (Paris, 1975), and *idem, Pouvoirs de vie, pouvoirs de mort* (Paris, 1977). Regarding the phenomenon's context with respect to "modern" political stakes in contemporary Africa, see Peter Geschiere, *Sorcellerie et politique en Afrique. La viande des autres* (Paris, 1995).

22. For an especially demonstrative case study, see Pierre Bonnafé, *Nzo Lipfu, le lignage de la mort. La sorcellerie, idéologie de la lutte sociale sur le plateau Kukuya* (Nanterre, 1979).

23. Rumour itself is fraught with danger: it activates the magic forces of powerful men and exorcists.

24. Representations depict persons as consisting of several psychological components: a vital force, defensive and aggressive powers, shadow, mirror images. Thus, the idea of the individual's essential duplicity appears rational ("I am another" and even several others). We understand why an individual accused of witchcraft accepts this accusation: he knows that his double may have acted maliciously and beyond any conscious control of his, and that it is very believable if his double has been captured or manipulated without his knowledge by a sorcerer's double. See *La notion de personne en Afrique noire*, Colloques du CNRS (Paris, 1973).

regimes have assumed responsibility for this community regime – based on plans for debts, hierarchy and anti-individualism – by operating a type of conservative modernization entailing supercommunitarization of global society through political domination based essentially on clientelism (i.e. the extension of the debt to the macrosociological scale).

II MODERNITY: SUPERCOMMUNITARIZATION AND SOCIOPOLITICAL DEBT

Establishing itself as the exclusive agent in building the nation, as the eminent owner of the collective wealth, and as the principal actor for development, the postcolonial state inevitably became the privileged instrument and main site of the accumulation of wealth and extortion implemented with impunity by a kleptocratic oligarchy, obtained primarily through tributary withholdings on the export revenues, customs receipts, and foreign aid.

This *politique du ventre* (gut politics)[25] also works according to the debt logic: acceding to the prebend positions requires an invitation either from the prince or his entourage, support from a political sponsor, a network of friends in high places, or appointment as a leader by a sufficient number of people willing to stake their careers on somebody they expect to become their protector. The oligarchy also comprises several clientelist networks with which the members are associated, as well as the relations of creditors to debtors and mutual complicity, while remaining linked to those who enabled their rise from below and expect support, aid, intervention, and financial generosity from them.

In fact, these acts of redistribution provide protection from jealousy and possible vengeance by the surrounding community, who are inclined to perform the most scrutinizing evaluation of the services rendered by the one who has succeeded, finding him ungrateful if he seems to forget everything that his relatives (of the clan, the lineage, the village) have done for him, and mobilizing the power weapons of aggression (maledictions, misfortunes, attacks through witchcraft) to remind him that individualists risk all kinds of sanctions (bad luck, disaffection by a superior, accident, family misfortunes, loss of employment, illnesses, death), intended to reimpose the community value system on those inclined to abandon it or to punish them if they continue along this course.

Nonetheless, an urban middle class (professionals, teachers, university and secondary school students, subalterns, junior managers, permanent employees and workers, businessmen and small entrepreneurs) wield considerable force with respect to politicians. In economic crises accompanied by austerity measures, they form social movements that are a much greater threat to politicians because they are joined by the lower classes from the

25. Jean-François Bayart, *L'Etat en Afrique. La politique du ventre* (Paris, 1989).

cities (especially by the young people without jobs and those existing on the margins of society).

The postcolonial state has long averted this threat through a clientelist redistribution to the different components of this middle class. This has also given rise to a very pivotal role between state and society: therefore, directly or indirectly, part of the state manna is redistributed among the working classes. All modern city dwellers have an obligation to share their advantages with their less fortunate relatives in the towns and the villages. They must be hospitable toward visitors, provide lodgings to newcomers in search of jobs in the city, take responsibility for a schoolchild of relatives, contribute toward health expenses, build homes for older generations remaining behind in the village, contribute toward ceremonial expenses (funerals, weddings, baptisms), pay dues to associations modernizing the village, donate money at the request of a member of the community or to support a relative in need, speak to a relation with connections regarding a request for employment or an administrative procedure etc.

The redistribution of solidarity, however, derives from this debt logic that underlies community sociality. Everybody knows all that they owe from birth to their creditors, and depend on them. Likewise, everybody knows when lack of respect (shortcomings toward the different guarantors of the community hierarchy), and lack of acknowledgement (literally the individualist attitude of whoever fails to "acknowledge" his debts) will incur heavy penalties. On the one hand, in case of adversity, a person would no longer be able to count on others, and would forfeit the right to collect from his own debtors.[26] On the other hand, he would immediately risk punishment by malediction, misfortune or attacks by witchcraft.[27]

Upon taking stock of this group of causalities, both objective and subjective, real and imaginary, sociocultural and sociopsychological, cognitive and affective, sociological and religious,[28] the hold on citizens of community structures (i.e. extended families, lineage networks, gatherings of people from the same village or region, ethnic associations) may be interpreted as if they pertain simultaneously to specifically associative and urban-style

26. Reciprocity is intrinsically an extremely rigorous and effective constraint: if an individual abstains from attending large funeral gatherings, he risks being left alone to bury his loved ones in shame and, worse still, being buried all alone himself "like a dog". He will be doomed to wander eternally and to oblivion, which is tantamount to hell.
27. This explains the sudden changes of fortune, the accidents, the diseases, death of a loved one, loss of a job, disaffection of one's patronage, professional failure, and persistent failures on examinations or recruitment tests. The suddenness, accumulation, or repetition of all such events reveals that they are far from fortuitous.
28. Though analytically distinct, they are in reality united in "a wealth of imaginary social meanings" that stick together and form a bond between the social actors, who think in their world and act strategically within it without needing to disassociate the one from the other. See Cornelius Castoriadis, *L'institution imaginaire de la société* (Paris, 1975).

structures, even if they increase in number, moreover, as they become more integrated in urban society.[29]

III INDIVIDUALIZATION STRATEGIES AS A MEANS OF ADJUSTING AND RECONSIDERING SOLIDARITY

Benefiting from the services of this mutuality, based on the community of origin, clearly requires ongoing participation in the underlying reciprocities and honouring one's debts, while in turn placing others in one's debt. Amid this endemic economic crisis exacerbated through neoliberal structural adjustment plans, the stories of African city dwellers today reveal that the renowned community solidarity is needed more than ever but is also increasingly a source of dissatisfaction.[30] This contradiction conveys all previously concealed ambivalence: the benefits of mutual aid and gifts without apparent interest harbour a utilitarian logic of social standing; the apparently spontaneous inclination to sacrifice for the sake of solidarity embodies constraints of debt and the terrorist arsenal of anti-individualist repression guaranteed by witchcraft.

Dysfunctional aspects of solidarity: individualization among city dwellers

"You Europeans are different from us Africans: you feel solidarity!" The preceding analyses obviously substantiate this paradoxical statement by a young unemployed citizen of Abidjan. This assertion appears to reverse the generally recognized stereotypes. Understanding that the man was not referring to the same type of solidarity resolves the paradox.

On the one hand, he was emphasizing to what extent, given their absence in his society, our minimum wage and our different types of insurance (unemployment, sickness, old age etc.) express genuine macrosocial solidarity in European society (which implicitly raises questions as to whether our private individualism is the counterpoint to general conditions providing anonymous guarantees against risks, thereby rendering solidarity with the surrounding community unnecessary).

On the other hand, like many other speakers,[31] the young man also notes

29. These are ad hoc gatherings based on free individual accessions and released from the community framework: mutual aid and mutual savings groups – *tontines* – between neighbours and colleagues; sports associations, recreational groups, committees of parents of schoolchildren, neighbourhood associations, self-defence groups against crime, syndicates, political parties, churches, prayer groups, fundamentalist Islamic communities etc.

30. See Alain Marie, "'Y a pas l'argent': l'endetté insolvable et le créancier floué, deux figures complémentaires de la pauvreté abidjanaise", *Revue Tiers-Monde*, 36 (1995), no. 142, pp. 303–324.

31. Statements recorded in Abidjan between 1992 and 1997 in several working-class neighbourhoods. See François Leimdorfer and Alain Marie (eds), *Individualisations citadines et développement d'une société civile: Abidjan et Dakar*, Research report commissioned by the ministry's representative for cooperation and French language, I.E.D.E.S. (Université de Paris I), June 1998; Alain Marie (ed.), *Paradoxes de l'individualisation dans la société abidjaaise. Etudes de cas en milieu social*

that amid the hardships of the economic crisis (which has been largely endemic since the late 1970s) and structural adjustment plans, community solidarity has been found wanting. From becoming *conjoncturés* and subsequently *déflatés* and *compressés*, the middle classes of Abidjan are no longer able to serve as much and as consistently as before as liaisons between the state's clientelism and the working-class circles, or to redistribute to the surrounding community. Wage freezes followed by pay cuts, diminishing revenues from independent activities,[32] insecure company jobs,[33] early retirement, abrupt redundancies without compensation, unemployment of several graduates condemned to the expediencies of the informal economy, unpaid traineeships, and reliance on relatives, the dissemination of survival activities among young people forced to leave school because their parents could not afford the tuition, are all factors of relative and absolute impoverishment that drastically reduce the resources for achieving community redistribution. As victims of plummeting prices all over the world, the farmers (coffee and cacao planters, cotton growers and peanut farmers), far from being able to help their relatives in the cities, are also becoming ever poorer and appeal to them for help in increasing measure. When all is said and done, however, these city dwellers have either maintained their position or in a minority of cases managed to succeed in the system.

Basically, a serious question arises, amid this correlative blockage of the clientelist and community redistribution, regarding this underlying debt logic. Little wonder in these circumstances that African societies are permeated by a drive toward individualization (existential itineraries and subjectivities) that suggests rising individualism.[34]

This progressive individualization (privatization of practices, strategies and aspirations, growing independence, a devil-may-care view of community establishments, a major struggle to survive and to protect or promote personal interests to the detriment of solidarity) marks the four main fields of everyday life.

Against impoverishment: the every-man-for-himself strategies

This individualization appears first of all in the economy. As they say in Ivory Coast, "these days everybody is out for himself", and "everybody has

---

précarisé; final report, GIDIS-CI, ORSTOM, Centre ORSTOM de Petit Bassam, Abidjan, December 1994; Marie, "'Y a pas l'argent'", *idem*, *L'Afrique des individus; idem*, "La ruse de l'histoire. Comment, au nom du libéralisme, l'ajustement structurel accouche l'Afrique de ses classes sociales", in M. Haubert *et al.* (eds), *Les sociétés civiles face au marché. Le chargement social dans le monde post-colonial* (Paris, 2000, forthcoming).

32. The clientele becomes poorer, the deadbeats increase, as competition rises as laid-off workers and jobless graduates join the ranks of the self-employed.

33. Dismissals after rehiring workers formerly paid monthly with part-time contracts or as day labourers, thus alternating periods of uncertain and poorly paid employment with periods of forced inactivity.

34. See Marie, *L'Afrique des individus*.

his own thing" (*aujourd'hui chacun se cherche* and *chacun est dans son chacun*). These adages reveal a prevailing quest for remunerative activity that makes the most of all opportunities, with virtually no regard for community support or corresponding obligations.

In Bamako, the modernist neo-entrepreneurs (unemployed graduates or skilled workers who have lost their jobs) thus affirm their will as self-made men by refusing to take out family loans which they would have to repay.[35] As owners of popular restaurants in Abidjan, they try to disassociate their business from their family environment.[36] Some avoid hiring relatives (they are difficult to dismiss, refuse wage advances to or absences for family events; demanding that they show up for work on time and are productive is another problem). Even if they dodge their financial obligations entirely, they do as little as possible (Bamako entrepreneurs indulge in salaries that secure the company's income and their personal income; they allocate a share for inevitable social spending from their personal income only).

In Mali young unemployed graduates understand that they are responsible for their fates.[37] Aware of the limits of family solidarity (the system barely guarantees basic food and housing needs and is not equipped to resolve employment problems) in addition to the constraints it entails, they prefer to solve their problems themselves (*s'en sortir*) or enlist aid anonymously from institutions or even lobby through corporate organizations to impose their claims on the state (adjustment of hiring quotas for public offices, unemployment benefits, free transport and healthcare etc.).

More generally, many others get by with individual income improvised through haphazard opportunities, encounters and the ability to take advantage of anything that comes their way. In Abidjan, former employees brave the shame of loss of professional and social status associated with informal activities previously left to immigrants:[38] a former accountant starts a small residential cleaning business; a former driver for a transport firm becomes a *diallo* (as the Nigerian owners of coffee houses are known); a former bank employee travels inland to buy up local products and resell them back home in the hope of opening a small shop one day; a worker laid off from an industrial company uses his compensation benefits to buy a used car and becomes the driver of a *woro-woro* (a small, cheap city taxi). Young adults without credentials form associations to collect household rubbish from neighbourhood enclaves, while others who have diplomas but lack job

35. R. Vuarin, "Les entreprises de l'individu au Mali. Des chefs d'entreprise innovateurs dans le procès d'individualisation", in Marie, *L'Afrique des individus*, pp. 171–200.
36. F. Leimdorfer, "Individus entre familles et entreprises : patrons et patronnes de restaurants populaires à Abidjan", in Marie, *L'Afrique des individus*, pp. 113–169.
37. E. Gérard, "La lettre et l'individu : marginalisation et recherche d'intégration des 'jeunes Diplômés' bamakois au chômage", in Marie, *L'Afrique des individus*, pp. 203–248.
38. G. Kponhassia, "Reconversions professionelles, reconversions mentales. L'irruption des salariés ivoiriens au chômage dans le secteur des activités informelles autrefois abandonnées aux étrangers", in Leimdorfer and Marie, *Individualisations citadines*, pp. 149–158.

opportunities set up small companies offering computer services, for example.[39]

The precarious existence of these companies (which face intense competition, low profitability and thousands of annoyances arising from the predatory actions of a corrupt government), the fact that they were established through encounters between classmates or people sharing the same problems rather than family proximity, as well as their obligation to meet standards of economic profitability and to comply with legal regulations, all give rise to a certain distance from community solidarity obligations. Unable to afford the ostentatious ceremonial expenses or the demands for gifts associated with family visits, they return to their villages less frequently, concentrate their ability to help on their close relatives and, even if they do not abandon the solidarity ethic entirely, they postpone any such practices ("solidarity obligations are for the rich"). More generally, the lack of confidence in modalities of social integration, whether traditional (community solidarity) or modern (sociopolitical clientelism), paves the way toward personal efforts and an individualism with little concern for means ("nobody cares how you made your money: what matters is that you have enough to eat") in an unbridled quest for money, as an omnipresent divinity amid scarcity, inequality, competition and heightened materialism ("in Ivory Coast, if you have no money you are nobody in your own eyes and in the eyes of the members of your family you are nothing").

Against the debt logic: strategies of selective solidarity

This individualization coincides with subjective questioning of the debt logic that is objectively compromised by impoverishment. Debtors are therefore hardly able to repay their debts or do so very scantily and selectively; no longer can they initiate a new cycle by doing others favours to benefit from their ulterior solidarity. Creditors note bitterly that those whom they had helped in the past still lack the means to honour their debts.[40] This knowledge is all the more painful when creditors, who are themselves *déflatés or compressés* or suffer the more general effects of poverty, are in great need.

Thus, following the complaints by young people (they vary in age from fifteen or younger to twenty-five or older) who left school early because their fathers lacked money, but were nevertheless accused of not doing all the necessary favours for their children ("my father did not help me continue my studies"), the parents respond with recriminations against the

39. B. Ori, "Initiatives d'insertion socio-économique et démarches d'individualisation chez les jeunes citains d'Abidjan", in Leimdorfer and Marie, *Individualisations citadines*, pp. 159–178.
40. Such help may have included support during their studies, help with finding a job, funds to get them started, gifts of money, accommodation etc.

laziness of these good-for-nothings. Many young city dwellers, tired of being insulted for their ongoing dependence, throw themselves into street life: they work as shoeshine boys, scarf or newspaper salesmen, car valets, windscreen washers, vendors of assorted trinkets for a larger merchant, guards for political parties, bodyguards or petty thieves, and sometimes dabble in drugs or organized crime.[41] Young girls often join the ranks of the *freshnies* and the *quinzanies*,[42] cashing in on their freshness and their fifteen years for a few dozen francs quickly spent.

In turn, those who formerly held permanent jobs regret the social investments to which they devoted much of their resources when they were relatively prosperous. They find, at their own expense, that this money was wasted. The former company mechanic, after being laid off following a cutback in staff, lives frugally from occasional car repairs and has had to move into very small accommodation he shares with a girlfriend who has suffered similar misfortune and is unable to contribute anything to support the four children he had with former girlfriends during better times. He broods over having given far too much to others, especially to relatives who, compounding their ingratitude and deepening the shame he feels, now even ignore his existence: "They do not even know where I live. They never come see me!"

A former stockboy, a father of three forced to entrust his children to relatives who owed him favours from the past (a younger brother and a cousin), also notes the failure of the community solidarity network and the reciprocity principle according to which "a good deed is never in vain": not only do his former social investments bring him nothing today (except for caring for his children, albeit with many strings attached), but they have also prevented him from making other economic investments that would enable him to have his own small business ("I had fifteen people asking me for favours when I was working: solidarity prevents investments!").

A former technician at a refinery has difficulty coping with the transition from a privileged situation (a good salary and benefits derived through all kinds of fraud in the company's upper echelons) to being unemployed and in need. His predicament is all the more humiliating, because he is staying with an older brother who does not want him and refuses to help him start a small business. The technician emphasizes the ingratitude of those he helped in the past, especially his relatives with connections who, now that he needs them, disappear from him so that he is ashamed of contacting them and prefers to avoid them.

All these individuals question the debt logic. More specifically, without

41. Alain Marie, "L'insécurité urbaine: l'engrenage des violences", in G. Hérault (ed.), *Jeunes, culture de la rue et violence urbaine en Afrique*, Proceedings from the international symposium in Abidjan, 5–7 May 1997 (Ibadan, 1997).
42. Ouattara, S., "Freshnies et quinzanies: la prostitution juvénile au secours des familles", in Marie, *Paradoxes de l'individualisation*, pp. 269–309.

disputing the solidarity ethic that is the rose-coloured version, explicitly valorized and, as such, internally established, they learn with disappointment about its instrumental, utilitarian version. This is the one that now emerges as the naked truth.

The former mechanic, dreaming of opening "a modern garage of his own", but "currently unable to for lack of money", and the impossibility of enlisting any aid from this family to which he had "given far too much", learned that this community solidarity had failed, and that he had been swindled. He and his wife started to economize and began to live frugally, eating only one meal a day so that they would some day open the garage of his dreams. To this end, as the couple had to join forces to take distance from both his own parents and his in-laws, he formed a close partnership with his wife, who thus became an equal partner in the undertaking ("my wife has joined my project"). He said that he no longer let relatives live with him ("I will not let anybody stay with me anymore"). Without denouncing the solidarity ethic, if he succeeded, he would prefer to help individuals who were trustworthy rather than anybody taking advantage of being a relative. He now asserts that "it is better to help one's friends than one's family", thus expressing his preference for a limited, contractual solidarity, governed by an explicit rational principle of conditionality (based on deferred generosity), to the traditional, unconditional, imperative and massive solidarity (any individual from the same community is fully entitled to this solidarity, regardless of his relationship to the person from whom he is requesting aid).

Likewise, the former stockboy emphasized that he would dedicate his energies exclusively to his immediate family[43] (his procreative family), and would no longer practise solidarity with the extended family of his origins, except as a strategic measure: selective, rational and conditional help, especially to assist those who had provided him with significant and tangible aid (in practice, close relatives or people who had acted as such), as well as those considered "likely to succeed" and thus able to repay their debt some day. Mainly, however, he devotes all his efforts to his conjugal family, and with the support and approval of his wife, who had become a full partner here as well, (his business was decisive for the household's survival): "Now I want to fight for my children and my own family. My wife helps me in my struggle."

The former technician has adopted the same view. He notes with pride that in his new solitude only his "little woman" with whom he cohabits "helps him with his small business". He therefore "listens to her advice", as, ultimately, "she is the only one on whom he can rely". He, too, has learned an important lesson from his own disappointment with community solidarity: the time of the "policy" of generosity (investing in favours to others)

43. They have no word for the conjugal family.

is over. All he thinks about now is to "establish himself for his children". If one day he realizes his ambition of becoming a transporter, "he will no longer help others". Now, he "votes for himself". "Everything is for the wife and children, for the [conjugal] family". He will continue to see his true friends but will no longer give anything whatsoever to his original family.[44] In the meantime, he will ask only his true friends – former colleagues who still hold their jobs – for small amounts of money and perhaps for leads that might help him find a job again.

Thus, against the logic of the community debt, the infinite debt (it is interminable, as it is never repaid in full), the indefinite debt (neither its amount nor its terms nor the recipients are predefined), and finally the unconditional debt (based on a true culture of altruism and constituting a categorical imperative for need imposed by the terrorist arsenal of witchcraft), and the dysfunctional aspects of the community solidarity network in a context of impoverishment and scarcity imposing an individualism of need required by the struggle for survival, African city dwellers aim to promote a radical revision of the actual principle without a dramatic break with the system. Without questioning solidarity as a value, they affirm their individuality in this respect and use their abilities to analyse and criticize, to redefine, each in his own way and according to his means, its conception and style of implementation. Henceforth, they all perceive the debt as somewhat relative and conditional (based on a rationale of generosity in that those who have given help will receive it), a limited and selective debt (they criticize ostentatious spending at large ceremonial gatherings; they distinguish between true creditors and others; they value supporting close relatives – father and mother, brothers and sisters "of the same father and the same mother"; they reject the idea of a debt toward more distant categories of relatives and especially toward the community in general; they affirm that they will indeed continue, if possible, to help a given individual but on the condition that his personal right to aid is recognized), and finally a strategic debt (the recipient of the aid is judged according to his specific aptitude to provide tangible and effective help in the long run).

The categorical imperative that is embedded intrinsically in hierarchical holism is replaced by the rational strategy principle and contractual negotiation between individuals able to impose their personal interests.

Against witchcraft: strategies of religious protection

Nevertheless, this community weapon, so perfect for calling to order individualists violating the debt law, is useful for accomplishing this

---

44. On the evolution of views regarding conjugality and the procreative family, see Alain Marie, "Les structures familiales à l'épreuve de l'individualisation citadine", in M. Pilon *et al.* (eds), *Ménages et familles en Afrique. Approches des dynamiques contemporaines*, Les études du Ceped, 15 (Paris, 1997), pp. 279–299.

renegotiation and for seeking protection from the dangers of witchcraft. Rather than fading, witchcraft is more pronounced than ever in urban environments: countless educational or professional failures, individual redundancies, and sudden illnesses are blamed on witchcraft.[45]

The former stockboy who henceforth expects to "wage a personal struggle for his children and for his family" has become a zealous member of an evangelical church: "In Christ's hands, I do not fear witchcraft". And he has a compelling formula: "Now, I am no longer guided by the dead, as I belong to Jesus". Does this statement not reflect, in fact, this subjective reservation, this disengagement of a subject (in philosophical respects) thanks to mediation by an extracommunity and universalist religion, to the heteronomy of community roots and the retrospective temporality (that aptly captures the legal adage according to which "the dead seize the living") of the principle of linear solidarity, which, on the contrary, still subordinates the period of personal and individual projects to the cyclical and retrospective period of the debt toward one's elders and community of origin?

Increasingly, city dwellers are joining extracommunity religions (prophetic therapeutic and anti-witchcraft movements,[46] Islamic associations, prayer groups, sects inspired by Oriental values, freemasons, Evangelical and Pentecostal churches), where they learn to disassociate from certain traditions:[47] while we find a microsocial refuge and forms of mutual aid in hard times, we also observe a more personal approach in the search for meaning and new models of sociality that come between community solidarity (which is all the more threatening when defective) and the indifference of global society. These new communities are based on individual membership, where people experience new, more egalitarian fraternities (they are "brothers and sisters through Christ"), purged of the tensions inherent in family and village life, where an ethic of asceticism prevails, adapted to the existing personal hardship. They are also places where people seek effective protection from the witchcraft that is so threatening, in these times of individualization and questioning of the established order, that feelings of guilt arise, despite the assorted compromises reached with the debt regime.

One of the main reasons for joining these extracommunity religious movements is the desire to escape the contradictions of community solidarity, and to satisfy aspirations for individual autonomy, which are even greater than the dysfunctioning of the debt system would suggest. The

45. See Alain Marie, "Avatars de la dette communautaires. Crise des solidarités, sorcellerie et procès d'individualisation (itinéraires abidjanais)", in Marie, *L'Afrique des individus*, pp. 249–328.
46. On this subject, see Colette Piault (ed.), *Prophétisme et thérapeutique* (Paris, 1975); Jean-Pierre Dozon, *La cause des prophètes. Politique et religion en Afrique contemporaine* (Paris, 1995), for case studies of Ivory Coast.
47. For a case study of the role of these Pentecostal religions in Ghana, see Birgit Meyer, "Les églises pentecôtistes africaines, Satan et la dissociation de la 'tradition'", *Anthropologie et sociétés*, 22 (1998), pp. 63–84.

extra-community religious circle (more generally, the spiritual renewal movements), by promoting new types of social links based on a fraternity mediated by a central institution prohibiting ambivalence toward others, form a social sphere from which individuals, still imbued with a religious perception of the world that excludes agnosticism, derive support.

Against the hierarchical principle: the strategy of political commitment

There is still another sphere, however, where the same individuals question their submission to their community that they previously took for granted and come up with opposing ideas. In politics, through recognizing the arguments of their own revolts and their previously rather diffuse aspirations in the analyses drafted by the opposition parties, as well as on international radio stations, they learn new words to identify their existential problems, thereby giving them a different, objective and secularized meaning.[48] Along with their attribution of individual misfortune to witchcraft, they appropriate other general explanatory principles: the predatory state, the oligarchy's exclusive concern with individual enrichment and power retention, the failure of authoritarian development modes, the corruption of politico-administrative elites, embezzlement, nepotism, clan favouritism. With the impact of globalization and the anticorruption conditions imposed these days by international moneylenders, modern society becomes a generator of exclusion. In this society, clientelism, as an instrument of the state's legitimation and reproduction of the consent by those dominated to their domination without appeal, no longer serves in this capacity as it did in the past.[49] This trend signifies a new, political conception of solidarity now being adopted by city dwellers: as fully individualized political subjects, citizens can impose the macrosocial solidarity that the conjunction of social justice and political liberty provides in a democracy, once democratic settlement of political conflicts and sanctioning of those with political power through free and transparent elections become possible.

Thus, referring sometimes to their recent militant involvement (since 1990, upon the rise of the multiparty system) in new opposition parties or autonomous syndicates (i.e. independent of the Union Générale des Travailleurs de Côte d'Ivoire, enfiefed in the former single party in power), the citizens of Abidjan are now very able to invoke all aspects of this universal

---

48. See Alain Marie, "Pas de société civile sans démocratie. Contre l'État et sa société, l'exigence démocratique des jeunes chômeurs abidjanais engagés dans l'opposition", in Leimdorfer and Marie, *Individualisations citadines*, pp. 63–111, "La ruse de l'histoire".

49. This crisis of the sociopolitical debt is highlighted, for example, in the following statement: "Among our ministers, there are many to whom we have given money [often the entire extended family, including all the heads of a village family, contributed toward their study costs]. And they do not help. There has been a break in contact."

causality that attributes meaning to their misfortunes, their revolts, and their aspirations. For example:

> Ivory Coast is wealthy [...]. Unemployment among young adults is wrong [...]. Too many injustices exist in this country [...]. In France, they have a minimum wage. Here, they have nothing.

> They have taken all the money. They are the ones who eat. Not the rest of us.

> Unemployment, hooligans, bandits are all the outcome of the course of events, failure in school, lack of skills [...]. All this mismanagement has arisen from lack of criticism or opposing debate.

Establishing a link between political authoritarianism and community authoritarianism and denouncing the culture of submission long maintained by these two accessory orders is becoming a widespread preoccupation among young city dwellers. On this topic, the following statements are significant:

> We, the children of this country, lacked the right to express ourselves [...]. We paid for our PDCI [the former single party] membership cards, which we called "taxes" [...]. The village chief ordered us to purchase the cards.

> Our elders are exhausting us and exploiting us.

> Our leaders are responsible. But, according to an African adage "when you are an earthworm, do not complain if they step on you" [...]. We Africans bear primary responsibility. We need to change our attitude.

> A democracy offers freedom of association, religion, and opinion.

IV CONCLUSION

Individualization of itineraries and awareness of oneself and others does not culminate in postmodern individualism (the self-inverting kind), which entails valorization of individual independence and dissolution of assigned sociality bonds. Individualism remains impossible amid a crisis in which an organized and accessible system of social protection is lacking. Resorting to community solidarity continues to be a form of security and insertion in contemporary society (access to school, employment, and the city). Nevertheless, individualization is apparent in the analyses and criticism of the community solidarity logic (that of an individual's debt to the community), called into question by the emergence of a major contradiction. On the one hand, the economic crisis, by rendering solidarity increasingly necessary, makes the system more akin to an anti-individualist categorical imperative (eroding solidarity's traditional self-evidence, the crisis turns it into an explicit, urgent necessity and places it in a context of suspicion and resentment expressed in the witchcraft idiom). On the other hand, as the available resources dwindle while costs rise, the economic crisis leads to severe dysfunctions in the system's reproduction and legitimation: the process of individuals incurring debts – especially while they are in school and are embarking on their professional careers – is often unfinished, unsatisfying, and riddled with failures and disappointments. The debtors, who remain or become insolvent, are bitter toward parents that they consider inadequate or malicious, while fearing their rancour for having made unproductive investments. On the other hand, the creditors feel they have been cheated and dwell on their disappointment at not being repaid by their "children", or that these "children" have "succeeded" but are "ungrateful".

In this context of constraints, as well as the feasible and conceivable opportunities arising from this contradiction, critical (reformatory) awarenesses emerge that herald the individual's rise as a subject inclined toward autonomous ideas and actions. This process becomes apparent along the social and cognitive trajectories that are determined both by objective conditions of existence and by strategic intent: recourse to achieved forms of sociality with the valorization of elective social investments and the selective and contractual recomposition of relations with the community social surroundings; questioning the unconditional and massive debt for the benefit of a social, conditional, negotiated, and reasonable debt; the quest for personal new identities and new forms of sociality (reconstruction of collective identities), through diversified religious itineraries and syndicated and political commitments as well. All these processes coincide with the advent of a civil society, a "society of individuals" (Elias), henceforth individualized as subjects increasingly affirm their own needs and demands as much against community despotism as against postcolonial state despotism.

Translated by Lee Mitzman

International Review of Social History 45 (2000), pp. 159–177
© 2000 Internationaal Instituut voor Sociale Geschiedenis

Finding the Right Balance: Financial Self-Help Organizations as Sources of Security and Insecurity in Urban Indonesia*

HOTZE LONT

Financial self-help organizations can be found in many parts of the world, and the cities of Java are among the areas where they are particularly widespread. Since about the 1950s, interest in these institutions among anthropologists and development sociologists has increased considerably.[1] Analyses of financial self-help organizations have most often focused on their economic or their social function; few scholars have pointed to their function as providers of security and identified self-help organizations as typical forms of local social security institutions.[2] The main shortcoming of most of these studies is that they base their conclusions solely on an analysis of the financial arrangements provided by these self-help organizations, neglecting the accommodating practices that people undertake in order to fit the provisions of self-help organizations to their own household needs. This essay explores the observation that financial self-help organizations do not simply provide

---

* I am grateful to Peer Smets for the helpful comments I received from him while writing this article. The article is based on quantitative and qualitative data gathered during fieldwork that took place between August 1997 and August 1999. This research is sponsored by the Royal Netherlands Academy of Arts and Sciences (KNAW).

1. For a good overview of the literature on financial self-help organizations, see J.N. Kerri, "Studying Voluntary Associations as Adaptive Mechanisms: A Review of Anthropological Perspectives", *Current Anthropology*, 17 (1976), pp. 23–47; F.J.A. Bouman, "ROSCA: On the Origin of the Species", *Savings and Development*, 19 (1995), pp. 117–148; and Hari Srinivas, "The Virtual Library on Microcredit [Online]", available at: http://www.soc.titech.ac.jp/icm/icm.html (accessed 17 February 2000).

2. See for example F. von Benda-Beckmann *et al.*, "Introduction: Between Kinship and the State", in F. von Benda-Beckmann *et al.* (eds), *Between Kinship and the State: Social Security and Law in Developing Countries* (Dordrecht, 1988), pp. 7–20, 16; F.J.A. Bouman, "ROSCA and ASCRA: Beyond the Financial Landscape", in F.J.A. Bouman and O. Hospes (eds), *Financial Landscapes Reconstructed: The Fine Art of Mapping Development* (Boulder, CO, 1994), pp. 375–394, 375, 381; J. Midgley, "Social Security Policy in Developing Countries: Integrating State and Traditional Systems", *Focaal*, 22/23 (1994), pp. 219–229, 223; G.R. Woodman, "The Decline of Folk-Law Social Security in Common-Law Africa", in von Benda-Beckmann *et al.*, *Between Kinship and the State*, pp. 69–88, 81; W. van Ginneken, "Overcoming Social Exclusion", in W. van Ginneken (ed.), *Social Security for the Excluded Majority: Case Studies of Developing Countries* (Geneva, 1999), pp. 1–36, 20–26; V. Gerdes, "Precursors of Modern Social Security in Indigenous African Institutions", *The Journal of Modern African Studies*, 13 (1975), pp. 209–228. J.-P. Platteau, "Mutual Insurance as an Elusive Concept in Traditional Rural Communities", *The Journal of Development Studies*, 33 (1997), pp. 764–796, has very justifiable reservations as to whether these institutions, and other "traditional" collective arrangements, really embody the concept of mutual insurance as we understand it in developed market economies.

security through the different kinds of insurance mechanisms they might contain, but that, particularly through the way in which people use them and participate in them, these institutions become meaningful for coping with insecurity. It examines the question of whether participation in financial self-help organizations contributes to the ability of households to cope with adversities and deficiencies in a concrete social context. Research aiming to answer this question was conducted in Bujung, an urban ward on the outskirts of Yogyakarta, on the island of Java.[3]

The argument of this essay requires concise introductions to the characteristics of financial self-help organizations in Bujung, and of households and their financial insecurities. It then goes on to explain the different ways in which people try to cope with the financial insecurities they face and how financial self-help organizations play a role in this.

FINANCIAL SELF-HELP ORGANIZATIONS

A financial self-help organization is an association of a number of people who decide to pool money in a collective fund. There are three basic types of arrangement found in the Bujung area. The first is the *arisan*, an arrangement whereby the participants regularly contribute money to form a kitty. The kitties that are built up in this way are distributed to each participant in rotation; the sequence being usually determined by lot, and sometimes by bidding.[4] The second type is the *simpan pinjam*, whereby participants do not contribute to a kitty but to a loan fund. Members of the organization can borrow money from the fund and repay these loans at a modest rate of interest. This way the total capital of the self-help organization can accumulate over time.[5] The third arrangement, which in practice is found only in addition to the *simpan pinjam*, is the "special fund". In this system money is contributed to a collective fund used to make disbursements to its members in the event of adversity (such as death, illness or accidents). The sums provided through these arrangements are relatively small and the support they provide is more symbolic than substantial.[6] One single financial self-

---

3. Bujung itself has around 6,000 inhabitants, whereas the city of Yogyakarta as a whole contains around 500,000 people. The inhabitants of Bujung range from civil servants to scavengers, from pedicab drivers to traders, from poor to lower middle class basically. The poorer inhabitants of Bujung tend to live together along the rivers, more or less separated from their wealthier neighbours.
4. In the literature on financial self-help organizations these arrangements are usually termed ROSCAs (Rotating Savings and Credit Associations). A formal definition can be found in S. Ardener, "Women Making Money Go Round: ROSCAs Revisited", in S. Ardener and S. Burman (eds), *Money-Go-Rounds: The Importance of Rotating Savings and Credit Associations for Women* (Oxford, 1995), pp. 1–19, 1.
5. This arrangement is usually termed ASCRA (Accumulating Savings and Credit Associations). A formal definition can be found in Bouman, "ROSCA and ASCRA", p. 376.
6. This type of arrangement has been termed SAVA (Savings Association). See P. Smets, *Informal Housing Finance in Hyderabad, India*, Urban Research Working Papers No. 40 (Amsterdam, 1996), p. 55.

help organization can host several of these arrangements. Such organizations are often termed *arisan*, even if they have a *simpan pinjam* and special funds as well. In Bujung these *arisan* and *simpan pinjam* have become prominent institutions in daily life, with several meetings being held in different places every day.[7]

A rich variety of financial self-help organizations can be found in Bujung. There are, for example, organizations managed by individuals and by committees, organizations with membership based on gender, occupation, or neighbourhood, organizations with meetings and without meetings, officially-registered cooperatives and "informal" organizations, organizations with one single financial arrangement and organizations with a myriad of activities, obligatory and voluntary organizations, large organizations and small organizations, organizations initiated by the government, and independent organizations. The most numerous category are the self-help organizations linked to the Rukun Tetangga, or neighbourhood section. In urban Indonesia, each Rukun Tetangga (RT) has obligatory associations for the men, the women, and the youngsters, usually one per approximately forty households. These organizations form the basis for coordinating all kinds of neighbourhood activities, and lotteries are held to attract people to the meetings and to generate funds for various social projects and local initiatives.

Altogether, the inhabitants of Bujung participate in hundreds of different financial self-help organizations,[8] and each of them is unique. Even so, apart

7. There are many references that mention or discuss the existence of ROSCAs in Java, referred to locally as *arisan*. The most important are C. Geertz, "The Rotating Credit Association: A 'Middle Rung' in Development", *Economic Development and Cultural Change*, 10 (1962), pp. 241–263; and H. Papanek and L. Schwede, "Women are Good with Money: Earning and Managing in an Indonesian City", in J. Bruce and D. Dwyer (eds), *A Home Divided: Women and Income in the Third World* (Stanford, CA, 1988), pp. 71–98. ASCRAs, referred to locally as *simpan pinjam*, have been discussed by *inter alia*: (in west Java) T.J. Scheepens, "Socio-economic Research about Traditional Savings and Credit Associations in Comparison with Modern Organizations in Desa Bojong, Jawa Barat, Indonesia" (M.A., Wageningen Agricultural University, 1974); (in central Java) G. Williams and M. Johnston, "The Arisan: A Tool for Economic Development?", *Prisma – The Indonesian Indicator*, 29 (1983), pp. 66–73; and (in east Java) S. Cederroth, *Survival and Profit in Rural Java: The Case of an East Javanese Village* (Richmond, VA, 1995), pp. 181–187. Selosoemardjan, *Social Changes in Jogjakarta* (Ithaca, NY, 1962), pp. 314–323, mentions a number of ASCRAs started as a private initiative by people in and around Yogyakarta as early as the 1940s.
8. The average number of financial self-help organizations per household in Bujung is 4.81 (total 156). There was not a single household in our sample in which none of the members participated in financial self-help organizations. Compare this with two surveys – one in Bolivia: D.W. Adams and M.L. Canavesi de Sahonero, "Rotating Savings and Credit Associations in Bolivia", *Savings and Development*, 13 (1989), pp. 219–236, 224, and one in India: P. Smets, *My Stomach Is My Bishi: Savings and Credit Associations in Sangli, India*, Urban Research Working Papers No. 30 (Amsterdam, 1992), pp. 11–12. The participation rate in financial self-help organizations was found to be between 30 per cent and 40 per cent (total 450) in the case of Bolivia and 58 per cent (total 326) in the case of India. The data were gathered in a different manner, but it is clear that the participation rate in Bujung is very high; to a large extent this can be explained by the obligatory character of the *arisan* RT.

from money being pooled, there are a few other commonalities. First, the participants have some role in the decisions made about the activities of the organization; thus the organizations are self-administering and free to determine, for instance, selection criteria and the size of loans and interest rates. Secondly, the participants can acquire lump sums from financial self-help organizations, ranging from Rp. 10,000 to Rp. 10,000,000.[9] This way, what financial self-help organizations basically do is to transform small sums of money (contributions, instalments) into larger amounts (loans, kitties).

HOUSEHOLDS AND MONEY

In practice, it is very difficult to discern the boundaries of Javanese households because there may be relatives or friends who regularly join in at meals or spend the night, and children and parents may work somewhere else and spend considerable time outside the house. Conceiving households loosely as home-based budget-pooling units, one can say that most households in Bujung comprise two parents with one or more children.[10] Occupational multiplicity is the standard for households in Bujung. Not only does the household income come from various household members, each person generally derives an income from various sources. In most households the income of both partners is substantial, but that of the husband is usually higher than his wife's.[11] In cases where unmarried youngsters earn an income of their own, they are generally free to spend it for themselves. With a few exceptions, they are asked to contribute only in the event of deficiencies.

The generally accepted view among anthropologists of Indonesian households as budget-pooling units is that women, much more than in other societies, have decision-making power over the household budget.[12] In my

9. During my fieldwork the rate of the Indonesian rupiah fluctuated between Rp. 2,400 and Rp. 15,000 to the US dollar. For comparison, over this period the daily wage of an unskilled construction worker rose from Rp. 5,000 to Rp. 10,000.

10. In the two neighbourhood sections where I concentrated my fieldwork, there were fifty households consisting of two parents and one or more children (55.6 per cent), twelve households consisted of two parents, one or more children, and one or more grandparents (13.3 per cent), and nine households with a single mother and one or more children (10 per cent). The remaining nineteen households fell into other smaller categories.

11. It proved to be very hard to quantify the size of the contributions of women in these households because there is a strong tendency among both women and men to dismiss the income earning activities of the wife as "just helping the husband" (*bantu-bantu suami*).

12. Examples of authors observing a strong position for women in the household are R.R. Jay, *Javanese Villagers: Social Relations in Rural Modjokuto* (Cambridge, MA, 1969), pp. 92–93; L. Manderson, "Introduction", in L. Manderson (ed.), *Women's Work and Roles: Economics and Everyday Life in Indonesia, Malaysia and Singapore*, ANU, Development Studies Center, Monograph No. 32, (Canberra, C.T., 1983), pp. 1–14, 6; and Papanek and Schwede, "Women are Good with Money", pp. 89–91. Others observed some involvement by men in decisions, especially those on major expenditure: H. Geertz, *The Javanese Family: A Study of Kinship and Socialization* (New

view this is an oversimplification. The degree to which women control household money is severely limited in many cases. This becomes clearest by looking at the different components of the household budget. Zelizer[13] has shown, in a quite different context, that not all money is the same, and that people might distinguish between different kinds of money based on its origin, destination, amount, etc. It is possible to make a somewhat artificial, but realistic, distinction between three different kinds of money within the household budgets in Bujung. This distinction is based on who is entitled to decide about the money. Shopping money (*uang belanja*), which is used to cover daily household expenses, is controlled by the wife, and only a few husbands keep a close eye on how she spends this. Apart from that, individual members of the household can use pocket money (*uang jajan*) for private purposes. Husbands, children and elderly all have pocket money, while wives have to manage with their shopping money. The third kind of money is stocked savings. This is money locked for future expenditures. This money might be kept in a special jar in the house, at the bank, with a financial self-help organization, or in the form of durable goods. Whether and when this money will be used is usually the joint responsibility of the husband and wife. Which of them has the biggest say in this is partly determined by the origin of the money, but there is ample scope for negotiation.

Even though the wife has sole responsibility for the way shopping money is spent, the husband has the final say on the actual quantity earmarked as shopping money, since that money consists of the earnings of the wife *plus* whatever additional contribution is made by the husband. A few "good" husbands simply contribute all their income and ask for money every time they want to buy cigarettes, for example. Their wives are often able to save relatively large amounts of shopping money, sometimes in secret jars, so expanding their own financial room for manoeuvre by creating stocked savings under their own authority. Other husbands take a small amount from their own income before they give it to their wives, and use this for buying cigarettes, an occasional snack, and for gambling. Finally, there are

York, 1961), p. 125; and W. Keeler, "Speaking of Gender in Java", in J.M. Atkinson and S. Errington (eds), *Power and Difference: Gender in Island Southeast Asia* (Stanford, CA, 1990), pp. 127–152, 129. D.L. Wolf, *Factory Daughters: Gender, Household Dynamics, and Rural Industrialization in Java* (Berkeley, CA, 1992), p. 65, argues that proper observation shows that men make the decisions in the household. Keeler, "Speaking of Gender in Java", p. 128; Wolf, *Factory Daughters*, p. 66; and A. Stoler, "Class Structure and Female Autonomy in Rural Java", *Signs*, 3 (1977), pp. 74–89, emphasize that any economic role that women may have in the Javanese household does not lead to their having a similar position in other social spheres.
13. V. Zelizer, "The Special Meaning of Money: 'Special Monies'", *American Journal of Sociology*, 95 (1989), pp. 342–377. Zelizer describes the special status of household money for housewives in the United States. She argues that "culture and social structure mark the quality of money by institutionalizing controls, restrictions, and distinctions in the source, uses, modes of allocation, and even the quantity of money", p. 342.

also the "tough"[14] husbands, who make a conservative calculation of the shopping money their wives will need, and keep the rest as pocket money. In these households there are frequent quarrels about money, and wives have to negotiate and cheat in order to obtain a more realistic budget. In the households where the shopping budget is tight, stocked savings or pocket money regularly have to be mobilized for shopping. Where shopping money is generally more than enough, the wife is able to save part of it for future needs.

Obviously, within the limitations caused by these cultural perceptions of money, both husbands and wives have an interest in maximizing their control over household money. Their financial negotiations can go along different lines. Two reasons why it would be fair for a woman to receive more shopping money are that the costs of shopping are higher than estimated, or that her own income is lower than expected. Most men find it very difficult to check whether the financial picture presented by their wives is true or not, and that provides wives with an opportunity to juggle with the truth. Numerous women who have a hard time negotiating over shopping money consistently lie about the size of their own income, conceal their personal savings, and exaggerate household expenses. Many men naturally have a gut feeling that they cannot rely on their wives' version of the story, and therefore they try to restrict their contribution to the shopping budget to some conservatively estimated minimum, and in some cases they even lie about their own income as well. Wives may also try to play on their husbands' sentiments. They can either claim to be pitiful, by begging and whining, or claim he is pathetic by publicly denouncing him as a loser, who is unable to support his family in a decent way. Other women do not opt for confrontation, and choose to look for work if there is not enough money coming from their husbands. Many of them engage in home production or start working as maids, mainly because they want to have more shopping money. However, this may have the adverse effect of encouraging husbands to believe that they can keep more money for themselves and contribute less to the household.

In general, one can say that in Bujung the wife manages the household budget, but it is more precise to say that she is in charge of one of the household budgets. Shopping money is the responsibility of the wife, while stocked savings are managed by husband and wife. The relative sizes of both budgets and thus the financial autonomy of the wife are determined by how much the husband is willing to contribute to the household budget. If the husband is willing to contribute a lot, then the wife will have sufficient financial scope to determine how much money she wants to have for shopping and how much she wants to save. If the husband is not willing, or

14. The qualifications "good" and "tough" (*baik* and *keras* in Indonesian) were used by female informants.

simply unable, to contribute enough, then the wife faces financial problems. Households can be understood as budget-pooling units, but the individual members of the household never pool all their financial resources, and not all members of the household have the same entitlements to the different monies in the household budget. Households cannot and should not be understood as acting as a unit, but rather as an arena for negotiation between interdependent individuals.

EMERGING FINANCIAL INSECURITIES

Because of their occupational multiplicity, most households in Bujung experience a complex mix of income cycles, where part of the money may arrive on a daily basis, another part on a monthly basis, and the rest every once in a while. There is limited access to stable income in Yogyakarta because the competition for regular jobs and good sites for street trading is stiff. Even if one does have access to a stable income, the total amount is rarely enough for a household to survive. Even the civil servants in Bujung depend heavily on irregular bonuses and have to invest in private enterprise in order to make ends meet.

A monthly income is normally associated with civil servants and with employees of private companies (20.1 per cent of workers),[15] but the many housekeepers and laundry ladies in the ward (8.1 per cent) also get their wages once per month. Such a monthly income is conveniently reliable and forms a good basis for taking care of fixed monthly expenditures, like school fees. The disadvantage of a monthly income is that one has to be very careful with spending, otherwise there will be nothing left at the end of the month.[16] Households that rely largely on a weekly income share the same problems of financial planning, but they may find it more difficult to deal with larger expenditures. The weekly income is typical for labourers in small enterprises, such as workshops and retail shops (9.2 per cent). However, most people earn a daily income, which is more or less uncertain for almost all of them. There are daily incomes for small food traders, home producers, pedicab drivers, construction workers, parking guards, taxi drivers, coolies, scavengers, shopowners, etc. These people have to find ways to deal with days on which there is no income, or only very little, and for them especially it is difficult to deal with larger expenditures.

When discussing fluctuations in income with informants in Bujung, the words *sepi* and *rezeki* were used time and again. *Sepi* means quiet, and is often the primary reason for a slackening in income. When things are *sepi*,

15. The quantitative data on Bujung in this article are based on a questionnaire among 156 households in July 1998.
16. For example, wives of civil servants regularly complained that they worried about making ends meet at the end of the month, and a woman who went around houses selling breakfast snacks each morning told me that her turnover was significantly less at the end of the month.

traders have few customers and irregular workers have very few jobs. The word *rezeki* is, in a way, its counterpart, has connotations of luck, and is used to refer to a windfall, a sudden income, relatively large and more or less unexpected. It is a particular feature in the fluctuation of incomes in Bujung. The regular "special bonuses" of civil servants are considered *rezeki*. Pedicab drivers may have many customers on one day, or just one tourist who pays exceptionally well. Coolies can suddenly have a heavy, but well-paid job. The housewives who travel each year to the northern Javanese city of Pekalongan before the Idul Fitri holiday to pack parcels for a few weeks consider this income *rezeki*. And of course winning the lottery is also *rezeki*. People in Bujung like to use their *rezeki* for something special, like buying new clothes or presents for their grandchildren. However, many people are forced to use part of it to repay their debts, as a way to balance money cycles. A civil servant working at the veterinary lab of Gadjah Mada University said:

> Whenever our wages are not enough and the money has already been spent, we pray for *rezeki* from the Lord. If we believe strongly enough, it will come. What might happen is that a person comes to the lab who needs to have a picture for something. If he is a good person he gives me some extra money for that. That can solve our problems. And otherwise I still have my cocks. I just take one of them to the market and sell it. When another *rezeki* befalls me I buy a new one.

Without *rezeki* many people would have difficulty taking care of large or unexpected expenditures.

Also, expenditures are not evenly divided over time. Four of the most important expenditure items for households in Bujung relate to food, education, financial contributions (*sumbangan*) and hospital treatment. The largest part of the household budget is spent daily on shopping at local shops and at the market, and the average amount spent each day is quite stable. Education for children at primary school also requires daily payment, but for children at secondary school fees have to be paid per month, with additional annual fees. Small financial contributions have to be made for ill or deceased neighbours, and considerably higher contributions in the event of a marriage, events that tend to be concentrated in the four popular wedding months. Furthermore, there are regular contributions to the RT for administration and building costs. Finally, the costs of hospital treatment are clearly not regular expenditure, but if people in Bujung are seriously ill it is quite common to opt for hospital treatment, the costs of which are nearly always quite a burden.[17] These, more or less irregular, costs make for a complex mix of cycles of expenditure as well.

Together, the insecure composite incomes and irregular costs make for unbalanced financial cycles within the household economy. For most people in Bujung, these cycles create insecurities in the form of emerging financial

17. For the 39.1 per cent of households that do not own the house in which they live, the annual rent is a problematic expenditure as well.

disparities. A clear example is an independent coolie, who ma
40,000 one day and almost nothing for the next few days. He
difficult to make ends meet on a day-to-day basis. However, in different
ways nearly everybody in Bujung, whether they are "poor" or "lower middle-
class", unskilled labourers, successful traders or civil servants, is to a larger
or lesser degree confronted with unpredictable financial problems. Hardly
anybody can rely on a safe financial buffer, and too large a financial disparity
can have disastrous consequences for a household's living standard. In the
light of this, one could define responsible household management as spending as one earns, not more. However, it has also become clear that in
Bujung, probably like anywhere else in the world, this is an unrealistic
expectation. Costs and loss of income can be uncertain, and some expenditure, like the payment of school fees, cannot easily be postponed. Or income
is received in small daily amounts, while expenditures might be infrequent
and large. In other words, there is often a time lag between expenditure
and earnings, and households have to find ways to balance these unbalanced
financial cycles.

COPING WITH FINANCIAL DISPARITIES

Savings are a useful, and in Bujung generally preferred, resource for dealing
with the financial disparities created by fluctuations in income and expenditure. Obviously, saving money is difficult for those who have small incomes
with few regular extras. In many cases their own desire to consume is the
most dangerous enemy for those who want to save. Many of my informants
felt unhappy about all the money they spent on clothing, gambling, and
the snacks provided by the numerous peddlers frequenting the neighbourhood. Apart from that, people in Bujung are also confronted with frequent
financial claims from others, in and outside their own households. Each
day, women have to confront children and husbands who are looking for
pocket money, and neighbours and relatives regularly visit to ask for gifts
or loans to meet their needs. In view of these problems, people are looking
for some coercive means to save, for a means to hold on to their savings.

Bouman has introduced the notion of illiquidity preference as a logical
response in many social contexts in developing countries.[18] By illiquidity

18. F.J.A. Bouman, "Informal Rural Finance: An Aladdin's Lamp of Information", in Bouman
and Hospes, *Financial Landscapes Reconstructed*, pp. 105–122, 117–118. The same mechanism also
explains why some people prefer to borrow money (from their boss, a moneylender, or *simpan
pinjam*) even when they still have stocked savings somewhere. They will often have acquired their
savings as the result of a windfall or strong self-constraint and therefore consider it a waste to
spend that money too easily. An elderly tailor for instance said: "My gold ring is worth Rp.
250,000. It is a sort of savings, but I never want to sell it. I am too afraid that I will never be able
to buy a new one." A loan is preferred because that way they will be forced to repay it regularly,
whereas savings are not so easily renewed.

preference he means that people are looking for mechanisms through which they find it easier to save and more difficult to spend. This objective can be achieved in many different ways, and several of them can be observed in Bujung as well. For example, many people make use of piggy banks that have to be broken open before the money can be spent. Women often have special purpose tins in their closet, where they save small sums, for example for school fees or sudden costs, not allowing themselves to spend it on anything else. Larger sums are brought to a bank account, invested in building material, or converted into gold. When they want to spend money, people who make use of these techniques are automatically confronted with a mix of physical and moral constraints that they themselves have put in place.

Even though making yourself save is the most preferred and respected way of balancing financial cycles, many people are unable or unwilling to postpone consumption and spending. Instead they buy on credit or borrow money from neighbours, relatives, moneylenders, pawnshops, etc.[19] Various people said that they saw borrowing as a form of saving as well, with the pattern of putting money aside and then spending it reversed. If people use loans as a means to bridge financial disparities, they tend to be in debt continuously. Because most debts require repayment at some stage, the borrowing behaviour of people in Bujung frequently evolves towards a practice that is locally referred to as *gali lobang tutup lobang*,[20] or repaying debts with debts. For instance, a person may urgently have to repay a debt to a pawnshop. Because he has no money, he borrows from a friend, perhaps promising to pay him back when a loan is available from a *simpan pinjam*.

Repaying debts with debts has clear negative connotations in Bujung and is ascribed to irresponsible, lazy and uneducated people. In spite of this generally held perception, held even by those who engage in it themselves, the practice of repaying debts with debts has unmistakably positive aspects, especially for those people with a low level of income stability. It makes it possible to keep debts fresh. This is very important given the pressure that can grow when a debt is not repaid soon enough. Failure to repay debts on time can create tensions, conflicts and loss of reputation, but it can also mean the loss of the goods that served as collateral for the loan, not to mention high interest payments. Repaying debts with debts makes it possible to adjust the repayment time of loans to the income flows of the household; different sources of credit are made complementary. The practice over-

19. For extensive descriptions of the complexities of saving and credit practices, and comparisons between the various sources of finance, see also O. Hospes, *People That Count: Changing Savings and Credit Practices in Ambon, Indonesia* (Amsterdam, 1996), pp. 41–131; and H.B. Lont, "When We are Broke [...]: Managing Unbalanced Cycles of Money in Urban Households, Yogyakarta, Indonesia", in P. Smets (ed.), *Money and Culture*, Urban Research Working Papers No. 44 (Amsterdam, 1999), pp. 7–26, 13–17.
20. Literally the expression means "dig a hole, fill a hole".

comes financial disparities. A preference for *gali lobang tutup lobang* can create insecurities as well. In times of crisis, whether on a personal or a national level, it is difficult to keep the chain of debts under control, and people are aware of this risk. In Bujung, the story of Marzuki, a pedicab driver who liked drinking and gambling, is often recalled. Marzuki was always in debt, but he was always able to repay his debts sooner or later. One day Marzuki, together with his neighbours, was offered the opportunity to buy his house at a relatively cheap price. He took the offer and borrowed money to pay for the house, but the loan turned out to be a little beyond Marzuki's means and he had problems repaying it. Not long afterwards, Marzuki fell ill. According to the stories, it was the stress of having to repay the large loan that made him sick. Marzuki had to stop working and he could no longer repay his debts. When his condition became serious, there was no longer any money to bring him to the hospital, and so he died.

A chain of debts can get out of control if someone fails to estimate his repayment capability correctly. Also, even though that person may well understand that he or she will not be able to repay these debts in the future, the circumstances might be so pressing that they are simply forced to borrow. The practice of repaying debts with debts also creates the problem of a damaged reputation. In Bujung, the creditworthiness of a person is very much determined by his or her reputation in financial affairs. Making regular use of *gali lobang tutup lobang* in order to repay urgent debts can enhance one's reputation, but miscalculations can weaken it.

The way these issues become manifest in practice and the ways in which participation in financial self-help organizations are related to the problems of financial disparities becomes clear from the following case studies of two households in Bujung.

SURONO AND RATMI

Surono and his wife Ratmi work together on Jalan Malioboro, Yogyakarta's main shopping street. Surono is a parking guard for motorcycles and Ratmi sells drinks and cigarettes at the same site. His income as a parking guard is not very much because the revenues have to be shared with the city government and a military officer who owns the site. Surono's daily income may range from Rp. 1,500 to Rp. 5,000. The major attraction of working as a parking guard is that one is entitled to sell drinks and cigarettes. The income from that can easily be Rp. 10,000 a day. On busy days it can be more. "Once, we were very lucky and we made 2 million in a week. That week we had to serve hundreds of cups of coffee to guests at the hotel behind our spot." Occasionally Surono also works as a *makelar* (broker) for people who want to sell motorcycles, land and houses. With their savings they have also built a house further up their alley, which they let for Rp.

500,000 per year. Surono and Ratmi are in their early forties and have three children, who are eight, thirteen, and fifteen years old.

The couple participate in a host of different financial self-help organizations. Like most men in Bujung, Surono participates in the men's *arisan* in his RT. Apart from that, there is also the *simpan pinjam* UKK and the *arisan* Hansip. Ratmi is in the women's *arisan* in the RT and Dasa Wisma. There is also the Absari RT, the Absari RW, the UP2K and the P2WKSS.[21] Together they participate in two privately organized *arisan* in their neighbourhood. In one of them they have one share; in the other they have three. And finally, there is also the *arisan* among the streetside traders of Malioboro, which they participate in as well. Their oldest daughter is a member of the *arisan* for youngsters in their RT. Surono explains that there are various reasons to participate in these self-help organizations:

> The most important reason why we participate in all these organizations is that we like to meet a lot of people. By attending these meetings you can make friends. People will know who you are and where you live. Where else would we meet people? If you and us never went to meetings, we would never have met. Apart from that the financial aspect is also important, especially with organizations such as UKK and the privately organized *arisan*. In Indonesian culture it is important to give gifts when there is a wedding, a child is born, or someone has died. Therefore you regularly have to spend substantial amounts. By joining all these organizations we ensure that there is always some way of meeting these expenditures.

Later, Surono and Ratmi also make clear that participation in financial self-help organizations has a strong direct meaning for their own household. The lump sums that they derive from the various self-help organizations play an important role in expanding and diversifying their enterprise. For example, with money from an *arisan* they bought a second-hand motorcycle in order to make it easier to transport goods to their trading site. With a loan from UKK they paid Rp. 350,000 as security for a vending cart from Sosro, a large soft drinks company. It allowed them to have a much broader assortment of drinks. Later, they used money from financial self-help organizations to purchase two pushcarts in order to sell food and fruit ices as well.

Surono and Ratmi take their participation in *arisan* and *simpan pinjam* very seriously:

21. UKK stands for Usaha Kesejahteraan Keluarga, or Family Welfare Enterprise, a self-help organization set up by local leaders of the ward. Dasa Wisma, or Dawis, is a subgroup for women in each Rukun Tetangga. Absari is an organization for women who follow birth control. RW stands for Rukun Warga and is a coordinated collection of five or six Rukun Tetangga. UP2K stands for Usaha Peningkatan Pendapatan Keluarga (Enterprise for the Enhancement of Household Income). P2WKSS stands for Peningkatan Peranan Wanita menuju Keluarga Sehat Sejahtera (Enhancement of Women's Role in Support of the Health and Welfare of the Family). The last two organizations are voluntary activities of PKK, the national women's organization.

> The advantage with *arisan* is that it becomes a fixed expenditure. You can count on it. Every month there is the electricity bill and the water bill. In the same way, we know that on certain dates we have to spend money on the *arisan*. If we tried to save alone, we would miss all the social contacts and we would also not be able to save as much as we save now. If you join many, this also reduces the risk of not having money to pay an *arisan*. If you see this problem coming, you just borrow from a *simpan pinjam* beforehand. It is a question of financial management. If you have good management, things can be less expensive. You can see the same thing in our enterprise: by buying our own motorcycle we were able to cut back on our transportation costs, and if we have a broader assortment we sell more drinks.

Still, they cannot rely entirely on financial self-help organizations and sometimes they also make use of other sources of finance. When they built their second house there was a mistake in calculating the costs. It became much too expensive and Surono and Ratmi were forced to borrow from a moneylender, whom they had to pay thirty per cent interest per month. Ratmi:

> After we paid back that debt we said to ourselves that we would never borrow from a moneylender again. The loans from the *simpan pinjam* are much nicer because their interest is only two per cent per month. But you never know. Maybe one of us will have to go into hospital; we pray to God that it will not happen, but that could cost us more than we can afford. Normally we can sell our gold, and we have some money in the bank and our *arisan* and *simpan pinjam*, but it might just not be enough. In that case we might go to a moneylender again. The problem with the *arisan* and *simpan pinjam* is that you cannot always get money at exactly the moment you need it. Therefore we have some savings in the bank. A lot of people here in Bujung always go to a moneylender when there is a sudden necessity.

Afterwards they wait for the meeting of the UKK in order to borrow an amount that they can use to repay their expensive debt with the moneylender.

Surono and Ratmi's bank account has an important role in their financial strategies. Ratmi:

> We have a bank account where we bring our extras. When the big sums from the *arisan* come in we usually bring them to the bank first, before we spend them on the expenditure we planned. When there are good days at Malioboro we usually take the money home and save it there. When it has gone up to a few hundred thousand rupiahs we take it to the bank.

IRWANTO AND GUNEM

Irwanto and Gunem are in their early fifties and living along one of the rivers in Bujung. They have four children, two daughters and two sons (aged twenty-three, sixteen, nineteen and ten respectively). During the period of my fieldwork the oldest daughter married and had a daughter. Her husband moved in with her parents until the couple found a place for themselves.

The second daughter went to Jakarta after she had finished junior high school, to receive training as a nurse. The eldest son works in a nearby repair shop and the youngest son is still in primary school. Irwanto himself has a variety of jobs. His main job is digging wells, and he can earn a higher than average income during the dry season. When he is not busy doing this, he tries to look for jobs as a construction worker. The rest of his time is spent digging sand from the river. Irwanto also has a pedicab, but he more often uses it to go to work than as a source of income. Gunem works as a maid for a Chinese family in another part of the city. There she earns a regular monthly income, with additional bonuses for extra jobs such as shopping and massages. At home, she and her daughter occasionally spend time making strings of artificial flowers, which are sold to a trader to be used at weddings.

Like Surono and Ratmi, Irwanto and Gunem participate in a lot of financial self-help organizations, but they are not always happy with this. One day Irwanto complained to me:

> Life is very difficult now. [...] The problem is that I do not have any work in prospect. [...] This month [January] is always very quiet. In the end I used some money left over from shopping by my wife. I need a lot of money to repay debts. In all the *simpan pinjam* that we follow we have debts, in the men's and the women's *arisan* in the RT, Dasa Wisma, Hansip Kecamatan, Hansip Kampung, and the *simpan pinjam* for the leaders of the RT.[22] There is no way in which I can borrow from any of them right now. When I have repaid those debts, I will certainly borrow from all of them again. Then we also have to pay all the *arisan* that we follow, the five I mentioned, the *arisan* for the youngsters, the weekly *arisan* at the mosque, the monthly *arisan* with Bu Wasiran. For these *arisan* and *simpan pinjam* Rp. 100,000 per month is not enough. I really wonder whether I will be able to follow Bu Surat's *arisan* again when it restarts next month. All these things start to play in my head. If you do not keep control of it you are gone. Apart from this I also have various loans with neighbours, but not that much, and I do not borrow large amounts from the moneylenders. But I also have to think of the weekly savings for the youngest child at the *pengajian* [Islamic lessons] in the mosque and at school we also save money for our children. And I've not finished yet. This week two people in this neighbourhood died. I had to pay contributions of 1,000 per person. My wife pays the same amounts through the women's *arisan*. Then we have to pay for the construction programme of our RT, the yearly picnic, etc. Then we also have to pay school fees for two children, Rp. 13,000 per child per month. I have not even mentioned our daily food. [...] Whoa, life is hard these days. I completely depend on people for whom I have worked, who feel sorry for me and give me some extra money. The problem is also that at the moment I cannot take jobs for digging wells because my partner's back hurts and he cannot bear hard work now. Alone I cannot dig any wells.

It is clear that Irwanto is exaggerating at least a little and mentions expenditures twice in order to "sweeten" his story, but the quotation exemplifies how many worries and headaches Irwanto and Gunem have in balancing their income and expenditure. The financial self-help organizations appear only to contribute to the problems. Irwanto and Gunem spend less on self-help organizations than Surono and Ratmi, but they also have a much smaller and more insecure income. One main difference is that Irwanto and Gunem are not engaged in business. Their main priority lies with their house, which they recently purchased. The house is in a bad condition compared to most other houses in the alley. Irwanto continues:

> When I borrow from a *simpan pinjam* I have to use all the money for the expenditures I mentioned. I have already received both kitties from the big *arisan* I'm in. My plans for improving my house will have to wait. I would like to participate in UKK [...], but I just cannot afford it. Even if I were able to pay the initial contribution of Rp. 100,000 the loan repayments would be too heavy for me. *Kalau dapat uang senang-senang, kalau harus membayar nyut-nyut* [When we receive money we are happy, but when we have to pay our hearts are thumping]. The problem is .lso that there are more and more activities that require money. Today we have the *arisan* for the youngsters again. I've never had so many debts as now. I cannot afford to fall ill at the moment. There is no money.

Sometimes Irwanto and Gunem can use lump sums from financial self-help organizations directly to pay school fees, to buy cement or, like when Irwanto received the kitty from the men's *arisan* in the RT, to buy raw materials for his wife to make flowers. Sometimes they are able to save money in the house or buy gold, as savings in kind. However, most of the time they are forced to spend that money on repaying debts with moneylenders, neighbours or other *simpan pinjam*. If a lump sum arrives, Irwanto and Gunem may not always agree on the purpose for which it will be used. After a meeting of Hansip for example, Irwanto told me that he wanted to use the kitty to buy cement for his house. But Gunem overheard us and she immediately claimed the money: "It is for paying school fees, and Rp. 20,000 has to be used to repay the money we borrowed from Sabarno" (their neighbour, from whom they borrowed money to repay a debt to a friend).

DISCUSSION

Mix of motivations

Both the Surono family and the Irwanto family participate in a large number of financial self-help organizations, considerably more than the average household in Bujung. In that sense, these two households should be seen as extreme examples. For Surono and Irwanto, as for most people in Bujung, considerations of social obligation play a role in their motivation to participate in financial self-help organizations. Javanese urban wards are close-knit communities where good contacts between neighbours are highly valued. Participation in financial self-help organizations is one of the ways in which this is expressed, and nonparticipation in neighbourhood organization is perceived as tantamount to saying that one is not interested in one's neighbours. In that sense, participation is in many cases "compulsory". It is also no coincidence that Surono mentions social motivations as the first and foremost reason to participate in self-help organizations. It is the exemplary socially desirable answer. However, we can also see from the case studies that the Surono and Irwanto families, like many other households in Bujung, also make use of the financial resources derived from financial self-help organizations. The main attraction of these institutions is that they appeal to a balanced mix of motivations that can be both financial and social in nature.

Female paradox

We also saw that when Irwanto had received the kitty from the *arisan* Hansip, the money was "confiscated" by his wife Gunem, who eventually decided what the money was going to be used for. In Bujung, financial self-help organizations are a major object of discussion and negotiation within Bujung households. Scholars too often implicitly assume that the person who is a participant of a financial self-help organization and who attends the meetings is also the one who pays the contributions and spends the money. The reality can be different.

With regard to this, there seems to be a paradoxical contradiction when it comes to female participation in self-help organizations. What happens in financial self-help organizations is basically that small sums are converted into lump sums. In the cultural context of Bujung households this means that through *arisan* and *simpan pinjam* shopping money (or pocket money) is turned into stocked savings. Even though women generally have more to say about lump sums derived from self-help organizations in which they themselves participate, in the process of participation women lose considerable decision-making power over their money. Why then are women more actively engaged in financial self-help organizations than men?

One explanation sometimes suggested is that participation in financial self-help organizations is a secret affair and offers a way for wives to conceal money from their husbands.[23] In the context of Bujung this does not seem to make much sense since the meetings are social events, and saving in self-help organizations can never be as secret as a secret jar at the back of a cupboard. It seems more logical to suppose that women participate because they have to cover financial disparities and cope with larger expenditures in the household, and that they take the involvement of their husbands for granted. By participating in smaller self-help organizations, they can build

23. Ardener, "Women Making Money Go Round", p. 15.

up lump sums that are large enough to be useful and small enough not to arouse the suspicions of their husbands. To some degree, women can use their participation in financial self-help organizations in negotiations with their husbands and bargain for more shopping money. Nonetheless, without a doubt, women with more cooperative husbands, who have an eye for the interests of the household, might benefit more from the potential offered by a financial self-help organization.

Right balance

Turning to the techniques used to cope with financial disparities, participation in financial self-help organizations shows the advantage of illiquidity as well. Not only is the money contributed to a financial self-help organization inaccessible most of the time, there is also an obligation to save and contribute on a regular basis. This is an extra advantage, one that piggy banks and savings in kind lack. With regard to this phenomenon, De Swaan speaks of self-constraint through social constraint leading a person to be an exemplary saver.[24] Social pressure, together with potential feelings of embarrassment if one cannot pay, makes participants eager to fulfil their financial obligations. Informants frequently mentioned this mechanism as the primary reason to participate in self-help organizations: "Without *arisan* I cannot save. If I save in the house, I spend my money too easily." Without the self-constraint component of *arisan* and *simpan pinjam*, Surono and Ratmi would have found it much more difficult to save for the investments they made to expand their business. Depending on the income of a parking guard alone would never have allowed them their present standard of living, nor would they have been able to consider higher education for their children, as they do now. But also, it has made their household less vulnerable to financial adversities; they have built up assets and creditworthiness that can be mobilized in times of need.

Obviously, the preference for illiquidity is not absolute because money still has to be accessible for the "right" purposes, such as school fees, hospital costs, etc. If spending constraints are too strong, new insecurities emerge, as we have seen from the example of the Irwanto family, and they can often only be accommodated at high cost. Surono and Ratmi were forced to borrow from an expensive moneylender, even though they had stocked large sums of money in financial self-help organizations. Also, with regard to the future, Ratmi doubts whether funds from *arisan* and *simpan pinjam* would be readily available if she had to be admitted to hospital. Dramatic examples

---

24. A. de Swaan, "Onderlinge Fondsen: Toen en hier nu en daar", in M. van der Linden and J. Sluijs (eds), *Onderlinge Hulpfondsen* (Amsterdam, 1996), pp. 9–22, 12. The argument is further developed in A. Bijnaar, "Wat je zaait zal je oogsten!: Dwang en Zelfdwang in Creools-Surinaamse Onderlinges", *Amsterdams Sociologisch Tijdschrift*, 25 (1998), pp. 329–370.

of this problem are the several people in Bujung who, because of sudden high expenditures, were forced to sell the kitty of their *arisan* before they received it. In that case, they receive an amount equivalent to only around half its value, while they have to keep paying their regular contributions. In spite of their desire to save, people also want to avoid such situations and therefore look for the best balance between liquidity and illiquidity.

Participants can also opt for a different approach, using financial self-help organizations as a means to repay debts with debts. This entails using the lump sums they are about to receive as collateral for other loans.[25] We have seen the example of Gunem, who borrowed from her neighbour, promising that the debt would be repaid as soon money is received from an *arisan* or *simpan pinjam*. *Gali lobang tutup lobang* is the only way Irwanto and Gunem can get through the lean wet season, and they resort to it every year. The more financial self-help organizations they join, the more flexible they are. A very large part of the lump sums derived from financial self-help organizations in Bujung is directly used to repay debts.[26] Such repayments can sometimes be witnessed at the meeting itself or immediately afterwards. Not only do people use lump sums from financial self-help organizations to repay debts, the reverse also occurs. Surono and Ratmi borrow money to pay instalments and contributions to self-help organizations, mostly from the other organizations in which they participate. Other sources of credit are frequently used for this purpose as well. In the hours before the meeting of a financial self-help organization one can often see people roaming the alleys, approaching neighbours, looking for cash to pay their contributions.

People do not always voluntarily engage in *gali lobang tutup lobang*. If they have no ready cash, they can choose only between default and taking a loan to repay the debt. Given that they face huge social pressure to pay their contributions, the choice is easy for most people. But if debts begin to exceed their irregular income peaks (*rezeki*), the debt cycle will get out of hand, with devastating results. The way to avoid this problem is, obviously, to maintain a safe margin between financial obligations and the average income surplus. Many people in Bujung are very careful in trying to do this and mention this as a reason not to participate in too expensive financial self-help organizations. They often point to people like Marzuki who have been less careful and have to juggle with their money in order to make their regular payments. However, this careful calculating attitude is in constant conflict with the illiquidity pref-

25. In discussing this issue, informants did not distinguish particularly between the use of *arisan* and *simpan pinjam*, even though the latter provides loans and the former does not.
26. It is very difficult to establish which part of the lump sums from financial self-help organizations is used for repaying debts. The practice is generally regarded as irresponsible behaviour, which leads to people being very secretive about it. Of the 109 respondents to our questionnaire who said they had ever borrowed money from a *simpan pinjam*, only 2.8 per cent said they had used it last time to repay debts. Based on my daily observations, interviews, and informal conversations I can safely say that this is a considerable underestimate.

erence and the strategy of seeking self-constraint. More money than necessary can leak away, either to relatives and friends or to consumption. Again, it is important to find the right balance.

CONCLUSION

Much of the income of people in Bujung is insecure, and can vary from day to day and from month to month. Similarly, the costs that they have to incur are not evenly spread over the year. Payment of school fees, rent, hospital costs, etc. leads to difficult moments, and people find it problematic making ends meet.

Financial self-help organizations can play a role in cushioning financial adversities and deficiencies in five different ways, two of them direct and three of them indirect. Directly would be through disbursements from funeral funds and sickness funds, or by using a loan or kitty to bridge a financial disparity. The first option provides only limited financial relief, while the second seldom occurs. Participants are generally unable to influence the moment at which they receive the kitty and, mainly because participants of *simpan pinjam* tend to borrow continuously, loans are not readily available. Therefore, *arisan* and *simpan pinjam* are normally more useful for coping with financial disparities in an indirect way. Participants can use them as collateral for other loans, generally to repay debts with debts. Participants can use lump sums to invest in assets or put the money in the bank, thereby creating resources that can be mobilized in times of need. And finally, participation in financial self-help organizations can be useful for strengthening and expanding social networks. These last three practices are particularly relevant in the Bujung context.

In spite of the obvious usefulness of financial self-help organizations for household survival strategies, there is no reason for hallelujahs (or *alhamdulillahs*). In the process, new problems may emerge and payments can be a real burden for participants. The illiquidity of money in financial self-help organizations leads at least some households to enter a potentially expanding debt cycle. Obligations towards those organizations can force participants to accept expensive solutions, for instance in the form of a loan from a moneylender or the sale of a kitty yet to be received. Partly, this is the result of having to walk the line between illiquidity and flexibility. However, it is also important to be aware that participation in financial self-help organizations cannot be purely understood as a goal-oriented and strategic activity. In Bujung, participation is largely a habitual activity, motivated by a desire to be a good member of the "community" and to conform to the expectations of others. The challenge for participants is to use the financial resources offered by financial self-help organizations as effectively as possible. While having to cope with insecurities, they have to cope with *arisan* and *simpan pinjam* as well.

International Review of Social History 45 (2000), pp. 179–196
© 2000 Internationaal Instituut voor Sociale Geschiedenis

Stepping on Two Boats: Urban Strategies of Chinese Peasants and Their Children*

DANYU WANG

INTRODUCTION

During the 1990s, over seventy per cent of the married men and adult children of Stone Mill village in northeastern China have been employed in wage labor each year.[1] Because a vast number of household laborers (i.e. husbands, sons, and daughters) have nonagricultural jobs outside the village, daily agricultural tasks are performed by married women and elderly men, who are fondly described by the villagers of Stone Mill as "Troop Number 3860" (*3860 budui*). The number 38 refers to International Women's Day, March 8, representing the women in the village's agricultural labor force, while the number 60 represents the minimum age of the elderly agricultural workers.

Since the 1980s, Chinese peasants, like those in Stone Mill, have sought to improve their income by working in nonagricultural areas, such as local village-township enterprises and family businesses, or by migrating to cities to seek urban employment. Local nonagricultural employment has been incorporated into rural household economies.[2] With new job opportunities created by the rapid economic development in cities, massive urban migration by the rural population has been taking place. In the 1990s, not including migration within each county, fifteen to twenty-five per cent of

* I would like to thank Joseph Adams and Dona Geyer for their editorial assistance and comments on this paper. I wish to thank the Wenner-Gren Foundation (Grant 6234, 1997), and the Population Studies and Training Center at Brown University for providing funding for my field research.

1. The name of the village and names of the villagers appearing in this paper are all pseudonyms. Unless otherwise noted, the demographic data about Stone Mill is from my 1997 survey of 315 Stone Mill couples, with wives born after 1930.

2. For local or family level studies of peasants' employment in village-township enterprises or private businesses, see Elisabeth Croll, "The New Peasant Economy in China", in A.H. Stephan Feuchtwang and Thierry Pairault (eds), *Transforming China's Economy in the Eighties I: The Rural Sector, Welfare, and Employment* (London, 1988), pp. 77–100; Samuel P.S. Ho, *Rural China in Transition: Non-Agricultural Development in Rural Jiangsu, 1978–1990* (Oxford, 1994); Graham E. Johnson, "Family Strategies and Economic Transformation in Rural China: Some Evidence from the Pearl River Delta", in Deborah Davis and Stevan Harrell (eds), *Chinese Families in the Post-Mao Era* (Berkeley, CA, 1993), pp. 103–138; Victor Nee *et al.*, "Peasant Entrepreneurs in China's 'Second Economy': An Institutional Analysis", *Economic Development and Social Change*, 39 (1991), pp. 293–310; Edward B. Veemer, "Experiment with Rural Industrial Shareholding Cooperatives: The Case of Zhoucun District, Shandong Province", *China Quarterly*, 314 (1995), pp. 75–107.

rural laborers nationwide migrated to cities for six months or longer; notably, fifty per cent of them were people below the age of twenty-three.[3] Nonagricultural employment and nonhousehold-organized economic activities (such as working for local enterprises) have become a substantial component of the peasant household economy. At a national level, the proportion of nonagricultural income in the total income of rural households has increased from ten per cent in 1980 to twenty-five per cent in 1985 and then to thirty-five per cent in 1995.[4]

The extent to which peasant households profit from employment in local village-township enterprises and family businesses or from migration to cities varies in each locality and each household depending on the availability of local employment and on migratory network connections. The case of Stone Mill, examined in this paper, illustrates a community of peasant households in which many work at wage labor jobs. "Stepping on two boats" is a Chinese saying that describes people who commit to two jobs in order to secure their social and economic advancement. Although the expression has a somewhat negative connotation, there is nothing negative implied about the modern Chinese peasant's strategy of combining farming and wage labor. Diversifying household economy by combining farming and wage labor is a vital household strategy that has helped the impoverished Chinese peasants to survive in the rapid economic development of postsocialist China.

Diversifying household economies was a typical survival strategy of traditional Chinese households before the socialist reforms in the 1950s. However, the way peasants diversified their sources of income in the 1980s–1990s changed in response to the new predicaments facing them in the postsocialist state. The goals of each family have remained the same, namely to ensure a subsistence standard of living and to maintain the continuity and prosperity of the family, but the means of achieving these goals are different. As will be shown here, the traditional survival strategy of expanding family farmland has been replaced by that of improving income, since private ownership of farmland is not an option in the postsocialist state and wage labor employment is available. In addition, the socioeconomic disadvantages created by the socialist state since the 1950s have continued to cloud the lives of Chinese peasants in the new era of market development and globalization of the 1980s–1990s. This paper argues that, for the younger generation, acquiring nonagricultural jobs has become crucial to avoiding the fate of peasant life and escaping rural poverty. No doubt, a collective effort by both

3. See Yaer Zhuang (ed.), *Zhongguo Renkou Qianyi Shuju Ji* [*Migration Data of China*] (Beijing, 1995), p. 238.
4. See Huanyan He *et al.* (eds), *Zhongguo Nongcun Zhuhu Diaocha Nianjian* [*Chinese Rural Household Survey Annals*] (Beijing, 1993), p. 9; *idem, Zhongguo Nongcun Tongji Nianjian, 1992* [*Chinese Rural Statistical Annals, 1992*] (Beijing, 1992), p. 216; Xinmin Zhang *et al.* (eds), *Zhongguo Nongcun Tongji Nianjian 1996* [*Chinese Rural Statistical Annals, 1996*] (Beijing, 1996), p. 280.

parents and children to ensure the survival of the family as a whole has compromised the interests of some (i.e. parents) and benefited others (i.e. children). This has thus brought about changes in gender and generational relationships within the household.

In the following sections, this paper first examines the predicament of household agricultural production in the postsocialist state. It will then proceed to investigate the economic strategies used by many peasant households, which can be described, in short, as maintaining agricultural production and prioritizing adult children's urban employment, while maximizing the household's wage labor income. Lastly, this paper will probe the impact of these economic strategies on peasant households with respect to the division of labor, financial management, and generational independence.

THE PREDICAMENT OF AGRICULTURAL PRODUCTION AND RURAL POVERTY

The many facets of socioeconomic change in China have exerted a great deal of pressure on peasant households. Three factors are particularly pertinent to the "two-boats effect" in the peasant population. The first is a surplus of agricultural labor. The national population of half a billion in the 1950s has now more than doubled to 1.3 billion at the start of the twenty-first century. The average amount of farmland per rural inhabitant nationwide is two *mu*, which equals 1,334 square meters,[5] while in the highly populated areas of the east and southeast, this average is much lower.[6] The second factor is the state's socioeconomic policies centering on urban-industrial development, which provided strong state protection and support of industrial production, urban consumption, and urban social welfare. These policies have been the structural basis for urban–rural inequality and rural poverty since the 1950s.[7] A set of dichotomies such as "urban versus rural resident" (*cheng shi ren* vs. *nongcun ren*) and "nonagricultural versus agricultural employment" (*fei nongye*

---

5. One *mu* is equal to 667 square meters or 0.165 acre.
6. See He *et al.*, *Chinese Rural Statistical Annals, 1992*, p. 215; Zhang *et al.*, *Chinese Rural Statistical Annals, 1996*, p. 58.
7. For urban–rural inequality in China's postsocialist economy, see Marc Blecher, "Balance and Cleavage in Urban–Rural Relations", in William L. Parish (ed.), *Chinese Rural Development: The Great Transformation* (Armonk, NJ, 1985), pp. 219–245; Philip C.C. Huang, *The Peasant Family and Rural Development in the Yangzi Delta, 1350–1988* (Stanford, CA, 1990), pp. 288–301; Sulamith Heins Potter *et al.*, *China's Peasants: The Anthropology of a Revolution* (Cambridge, 1990); Jonathon Unger, "The Class System in Rural China: A Case Study", in James. L. Watson (ed.), *Class and Social Stratification in Post Revolutionary China* (New York [etc.], 1984), pp. 121–141; Andrew G. Walder, "Social Change in Post-Revolution China", *Annual Review of Sociology*, 15 (1989), pp. 405–424; Martin K. Whyte, "City Versus Countryside in China's Development", *Problems of Post-Communism*, 43 (1996), pp. 9–22; David Zweig, *Freeing China's Farmers: Rural Restructuring in the Reform Era* (Armonk, NJ, 1997).

gongzuo vs. *wunong*) has separated urban and rural society in the socio-economic hierarchy. The third factor is the development of the market economy on the national level in which peasants have been forced to compete. On the one hand, the rising prices of agricultural production materials have been increasing the cost of agricultural production, while on the other hand, the prices of agricultural products have been dropping throughout the 1990s, because of the limited size of the urban market. High production costs and low sales prices have resulted in little or no profit for many peasant households. These three factors have greatly contributed to rural poverty, as has the substantial economic discrepancies between rural and urban populations in the past five decades. The per capita income gap between urban and rural inhabitants has been as high as 2.5:1.[8]

The villagers of Stone Mill, most of whom earned an annual income equal to the national rural average of 1,600 yuan (i.e. US $200) per person in the mid-1990s, exemplify the average Chinese peasant's struggle to survive agricultural impoverishment in China. The village is located on the Liaodong peninsula in the northeast, one of the most industrialized and urbanized areas in China. It is ten kilometers away from the county seat, which is a twenty-minute trip by bus or an hour by bicycle. A railway and a recently constructed highway also provide villagers easy accesses to Dalian City, the largest urban center of Liaodong peninsula, as well as to other cities in the northeast region. Easy access to cities has allowed Stone Mill villagers to migrate to a city temporarily or commute to the local town on a daily basis. After the implementation of the household farming policy in 1982, the local government allocated to eligible individuals equal shares of grain fields (*kouliang tian*), vegetable gardens (*caiyuanzi*), and apple trees as measured by unit production. Households in Stone Mill received vegetable plots of about 0.1 *mu* per person, farmland ranging from less than 0.1 *mu* to slightly over one *mu* per person, and twenty to forty apple trees per person depending upon the productivity of the trees. Villagers were given the right to farm this land and decide on their own household production, however they were granted neither ownership of the land nor the right to sell or buy land.

The agricultural economy of Stone Mill today combines subsistence and cash economies (i.e. farming and fruit production). The cornfield, vegetable garden, and domestic farm animals supply the household's basic consumption of grain, vegetables, meat, and cooking oil. These subsistence productions of grain and vegetables, which provide a baseline of survival for rural households in China's rapid economic development, are protected by the state through the household farming policy. Fruit production and wage labor, which enable each household to obtain cash income beyond a mere subsistence level, are

8. Charles Goddard, *China Market Atlas, Research Report* (Hong Kong, 1997), p. 193; Whyte, "Cities Versus Countryside".

Table I. *Prices of apples in comparison with prices of rice (yuan/jin 1 jin = 0.5 kg)*

	Before 1975	1975–1983	1988	1996
Apples	0.185	0.23	1.10	0.5
Rice	0.20	0.20	0.25	1.20

permitted by the state, yet the amount of income earned from such activity is dependent solely on the laborers themselves and the market. The agricultural cash economy, such as fruit production, may have helped to generate cash income. However, a competitive fruit market has put peasant fruit producers in a very precarious and disadvantageous position.

The peasants' fortune in agricultural production has changed dramatically several times throughout the history of the People's Republic of China (PRC). In the collective period (1950s–1970s), village households suffered severe poverty, but they were protected from the risks of market production. Under the system of "unified purchase and unified sale" of agricultural products, the scale of apple production and sales was arranged by the state on the basis of a planned economy. Since the 1980s, peasant households have experienced not simply a return to household production, but integration into the national market. Peasants working as independent fruit producers, like those in Stone Mill, have to compete with other fruit producers, namely peasants in other provinces, as well as foreign fruit producers who export fruit to China's markets. In the mid-1990s, China's apple production accounted for one-third of the world total, and ninety-five per cent of this was sold on the domestic market.[9] In the 1990s, the urban markets became saturated as peasant fruit producers began to supply more apples than could be consumed. The price of apples has dropped drastically (see Table 1), while the cost of apple production has increased because of the rising prices of insecticide, fertilizer, and production tools, resulting in high overhead investment and low return from fruit sales.

Except for certain labor-intensive tasks (e.g. planting), one *mu* of corn requires one person to work ten days each year to perform other routine tasks. Thus, for an area of three to four *mu* of corn for a four-person household, one person needs to work less than forty days a year to farm the household's cornfield. In the case of apple production, one person can usually cultivate 100 trees of productive age. If a household of four persons (a couple whose young children are not given an allotment of apple trees) is allocated an orchard of fifty such trees, the household needs only one person to work regularly in the orchard. Therefore, for most of the year, a couple with young children will have one extra agricultural laborer.

9. *The World Apple Report*, January 1998.

P. Huang has pointed out a feature of Chinese agricultural production during the collective period of the 1950s–1970s, namely growth in productivity without growth in agricultural laborers' income (growth without development).[10] In Stone Mill today, households may be able to increase fruit production by an intensive investment of labor; however, the income from fruit sales cannot increase accordingly due to the high cost of overhead investment, the risk of market competition, and a surplus of labor. The household is not organized for the ultimate purpose of agricultural production; instead, agricultural production is but a means for family members to survive and to realize life goals, such as marrying off the children, continuing the family line, and earning the family respect and dignity (i.e. *mianzi* or "face") from kinsmen and neighbors. When income from fruit production became unreliable and when city jobs offered not only a good income but also became socially desirable, Stone Mill villagers began to incorporate wage labor as a vital component of their household economy. This strategy of diversifying the household economy and transferring surplus labor was a characteristic of the traditional Chinese household economy prior to the PRC regime and was simply adapted again by peasants to accomplish both the old and new family goals in the new political-economic regimes of the PRC.

THE ECONOMY AND ORGANIZATION OF PEASANT HOUSEHOLDS

Owning land used to be the means to survive and thrive. In order to own and expand farmland, peasant families adopted a set of survival strategies to draw resources from local economies or to barter with other peasant families. The traditional household economic strategies included constraining consumption, exporting surplus laborers, and diversifying the household economy. An array of other strategies were also used in order to survive severe poverty or famine; these included child control (e.g. giving children out for adoption), migration (e.g *taohuang*, i.e. escaping the famine) and begging (*yaofan*).[11] Which survival strategy was used depended on the level of poverty of the family, the harvest that year, and the availability of economic opportunities in the local area. The organization of the Qian family exemplifies the characteristics of the organization of traditional peasant

10. Huang, *The Peasant Family and Rural Development*, pp. 222–251.
11. For diversifying household economy and wage labor see Philip C.C. Huang, *The Peasant Economy and Social Change in North China* (Stanford, CA, 1985); Huang, *The Peasant Family and Rural Development*; Sidney D. Gamble, *North China Villages: Social, Political, and Economic Activities before 1933* (Berkeley, CA, 1963). For child transfer see G. William Skinner, "Family System and Demographic Processes", in David I. Kertzer and Tom Fricke (eds), *Anthropological Demography: Toward a New Synthesis* (Chicago, IL, 1997), pp. 53–95; Arthur P. Wolf et al., *Marriage and Adoption in China, 1845–1945* (Stanford, CA, 1980).

households and the cultural economy, which relied on land to secure a subsistence existence and continue the ancestral line.[12]

The Qian couple started their family in the 1880s, and they had six sons and three daughters. The family, which eventually reached four generations, had lived in one household for fifty years working together to expand the family farm. The family had lived a very frugal life and rarely spent money on food or housing. As the family grew, nearly thirty people crowded into the house complex of six bedrooms. Like many other families, the Qians preferred to save money so that they could buy more farmland to produce sufficient food and enable sons to marry.

The division of labor was by gender – men worked for the household's agricultural production contributing to the household's common budget; women worked in the kitchen preparing food for the family and wove after finishing their duty in the common kitchen, the income from which belonged to their conjugal units. When the family had a surplus of labor, the father sent family members to take wage labor jobs. Three sons farmed for a rich household in another village, and two younger grandsons went with their fathers to shepherd pigs and cows for the landlord. The two grown-up grandsons worked on the railway owned by the Japanese, earning 50 yuan a month. In the 1930s and 1940s, a monthly income of 40–50 yuan was very high (as compared with the price of corn at 0.38 yuan/kg or 7.5 yuan/*dou*). However, the family didn't consider working at a railway station as a real and respectable job, for land was considered the peasants' root of life and farming was their bound duty (*benfen*). The two grandchildren were later called back to work on the farm when the family bought more land.

The Chinese household has been widely recognized for its elasticity in adjusting itself to meet its economic needs.[13] In the case of the Qian family, male laborers were transferred to other jobs when they had a surplus of farm laborers, and they returned home when the family farm was short of labor. Since the 1980s, some rural households have still been able to maintain a large household and profit from a diversification of the household economy or from the expansion of household production.[14] However, this

12. See James C. Scott, *The Moral Economy of the Peasant: Rebellion and Subsistence in Southeast Asia* (New Haven, CT, 1976), pp. 1–55, for a discussion of the peasant moral economy. Although this paper uses the term "cultural economy", it addresses a similar conception of the traditional peasant economy.

13. See Myron L. Cohen, *House United, House Divided: The Chinese Family in Taiwan* (New York, 1976); Huang, *The Peasant Family and Rural Development*; Martin Yang, *A Chinese Village: Taitou, Shantung Province* (London, 1947).

14. See Barbara Entwistle *et al.*, "Gender and Family Business in Rural China", *American Sociological Review*, 60 (1995), pp. 36–57; Stevan Harrell, "Geography, Demography, and Family Composition in Three Southwestern Villages", in Davis *et al.*, *Chinese Families*, pp. 77–102; Mark Selden, "Family Strategies and Structures in Rural North China", in *ibid.*, pp. 139–164.

has not been the case for many peasant households because the size of households has shrunk since the 1980s. Studies of Chinese peasant families cannot ignore the impact of the intervention by the socialist state. As a result of the implementation of family planning polices, the national average size of rural households had become 4.5 persons with 2.5 adult laborers by the mid-1990s.[15] Couples married after the late 1970s have either one child or two children, if the first born is a daughter. State intervention and socialist reforms have seriously weakened the elasticity of rural households as a labor regime.[16]

Since the socialist collectivization of the 1950s and with the reduced number of children, peasants no long have the legal option to expand the family farm or the labor elasticity to expand household production. Households have to rely on other strategies to improve their income, which in the case of Stone Mill is urban wage labor. The jobs found in the cities are often temporary or limited to short-term contracts, therefore it has become a common economic strategy to combine agricultural production and wage labor in order to secure the household's survival and to maximize its economic opportunities.

NEW DIVERSIFICATION: URBAN WAGE LABOR AND AGRICULTURAL PRODUCTION

The traditional cultural economy of self-sufficiency and thrift continues in the village today. Except for holidays or other special occasions, villagers prefer to save money by not buying groceries (e.g. meat, out-of-season vegetables) for daily meals. Subsistence farming secures a baseline supply of food for the family, which is especially indispensable when income from wage labor or fruit cultivation is unstable. Since apple production has become less profitable and more risky, some households have cut down the trees to plant corn; some households continue fruit cultivation, trying their luck in new varieties or other kinds of fruits (e.g. peaches); while other households invest a moderate amount of labor to maintain an orchard, so

15. For China's family planning policies and their implementations see Xizhe Peng, *Demographic Transition in China: Fertility Trends since the 1950s* (Oxford, 1991). For data on average household size and agricultural laborers see Zhang, *Chinese Rural Statistical Annals, 1996*, p. 45. For the new custom of early household division, see Myron L. Cohen, "Family Management and Family Division in Contemporary Rural China", *China Quarterly*, 130 (1992), pp. 357–377; Danyu Wang, "Flying From the Nest: The Household Formation in a Village in Northeastern China" (Ph.D., Brown University, Providence, RI, 1999); Danyu Wang, "Complex Households, a Fading Glory: Household Formation During the Collective Period in the PRC", *Journal of Family History*, (forthcoming, 2000); Yunxiang Yan, "The Triumph of Conjugality: Structural Transformation of Family Relations in a Chinese Village", *Ethnology*, 36 (1997), pp. 191–212.
16. Susan Greenhalgh, "The Peasant Household in the Transition from Socialism: State Intervention and Its Consequences in China", in E. Brumfiel (ed.), *The Economic Anthropology of the State* (Lanham, MD, 1994), pp. 43–94.

that they can rely on the orchard when apple production becomes profitable again or when urban wage labor jobs are not available.

Regardless of their differences in fruit production strategies, Stone Mill households are commonly involved in wage labor employment. In the past fifteen years, as rapid regional development and foreign investment in Dalian City has created many job opportunities for people in its rural areas, many Stone Mill households have transferred their laborers to nonagricultural sectors. In 1997, about seventy-three per cent of married men, less than five per cent of married women, and eighty-seven per cent of their unmarried adult children took nonagricultural jobs. Typical jobs taken by Stone Mill villagers include that of carpenter or mason on a construction site or with apartment renovation businesses in the city, contract worker in a factory or service industry, or other temporary physical labor jobs (*mao gong*).

The arrangement of household economic activities in Stone Mill can be divided into three types depending on where the household places its priority: on fruit production, on wage labor, or on a combination of both. The households of Xiang, Lian, and Neng, demonstrate the three strategies of economy diversification.

In the Xiang family, the parents are in their early thirties, and their two daughters are aged eight and three. In order to take care of their children, the couple has been working primarily in the family orchard since their marriage. While their major source of income is fruit, they also manage to make extra money by taking temporary jobs in the local area, such as spraying insecticide for other households who have primarily engaged in wage labor. The husband also works as a mason on construction sites when the orchard work is light. The couple relies on the orchard for living, while earnings from temporary wage labor supplement the household's income.

In the Lian family, the parents are in their thirties, and the two daughters are seven and twelve years old. The wife, who is considered one of the hardest working and thriftiest women in the village, does most of the housework, farm work, and orchard work. The husband spends most of his time working and living at construction sites as a mason. The couple has done their best to make money from both wage labor and fruit sales.

In the Neng family, the parents are in their late fifties, and there are two unmarried sons and one unmarried daughter. In addition to daily housework, the wife is responsible for major regular tasks in their cornfield of five *mu*, and in their orchard, the size of a five-person allocation, which is over one hundred trees. She works extremely hard to take over the agricultural work so that her husband and the three children can work in factories. Since the market for apples has been worsening, the family decided to maintain only the basic growth of apple trees. The household's income is from the earnings of the husband and of the children at the factory jobs.

In 1997, thirty per cent of the households in the village were involved primarily in fruit production while expanding their incomes by taking temporary wage labor jobs in their spare time; twenty-five per cent of the households relied primarily on wage labor, while supplementing their income with moderate or below-maintenance-level fruit cultivation; forty-five per cent of the households were involved in both fruit production and wage labor with the husband working mainly at a wage labor job and the wife performing the agricultural tasks in the orchard, with help from the husband in his spare time. All households basically maintained the subsistence production of corn and vegetables, which became the work of the household members who worked at home (usually in agriculture) or other members in their spare time.

THE WITHDRAWAL OF ADULT CHILDREN FROM HOUSEHOLD PRODUCTION

Households generally try to make the best use of their labor resources (i.e. the couple and their adult children) in either fruit production or wage labor, although not all households can do so successfully. Unmarried adult children enlarge a household's potential labor force; however, the principle of maximizing household labor and income is often compromised by or combined with the strategy of finding city jobs for adult children. Obtaining a city job for children, which is an effective means to survive rural poverty, has been the primary goal of both young people and their parents. In the PRC, rural poverty is not only a problem pertaining to survival, but also one of economic inequality and social hierarchy. The economic inequality between urban and rural societies in the PRC has had a far-reaching impact on the lives of rural people. Compared with urbanites, the peasants of Stone Mill lived in poverty during the collective period (1950s–1970s), as did those in many other rural communities.[17] Poverty and the frequent scarcity of food in rural areas were much more severe than in urban areas because the state guaranteed the city dwellers employment and a stable food supply, which was called "iron bowls" (*tie fanwan*) versus the peasant's mud bowls (*ni fanwan*). In light of the very low intake of protein products (e.g. eggs, meat) in the collective period, a daily ration of 250–500g corn per person was hardly enough to cover a household's grain consumption. There is no doubt that the return to household farming in the early 1980s has greatly improved agricultural productivity, and that most peasants' households have improved their standard of living as compared with the extreme poverty and even famine that they suffered during the collective period. Stone Mill

---

17. Huang, *Peasant Family and Rural Development*; Louis Putterman, *Continuity and Change in China's Rural Development: Collective and Reform Eras in Perspective* (New York [etc.], 1993). For the case of Stone Mill, see Wang, "Complex Households, a Fading Glory".

villagers finally have sufficient food to feed the family, but in the meantime urbanites have become wealthier and more modernized. Compared with the affluence of the urban Chinese, the poverty of the peasant Chinese reflects a social inequality that is deeply rooted in the demographic–economic structure of the postsocialist economy of the PRC.

By working in the city, adult children can contribute to improving the income of their parent's household. It is also the hope of the parents that by having nonagricultural jobs in the city (e.g. carpenter, mechanic, chef, or interior renovator), their children may never have to depend on agriculture to make a living. As summarized by a high school teacher in the village, "To be successful (*you chuxi*) is to study hard and leave rural society (*nongcun*). It was the case in the collective period, and it is still the same now."

Children, especially sons, are important in the economic and cultural lives of Chinese peasants. They are the embodiment and the means of continuing the family line. In Chinese rural society, individual identity can be said to be a self-centered, patrilineal kinship identity, which is related to one's patrilineal kinship roles as a son/daughter, a grandson/granddaughter and a descendent of one's ancestors.[18] In rural society, the socioeconomic status of the family is measured by the achievement of the younger generation. Parents place great hopes on their children and make a tremendous effort to support their endeavors. Traditionally, the economic strategy of peasant households, as exemplified in the case of the Qian family, was to keep the household consumption to the minimum level and expand the family farm. With sufficient land, their sons would be able to marry and live decently, the family line could continue, and the parents thus would be able to live up to cultural expectations.

Even though these family goals remain, the means to achieve these goals and the embodiment of them have changed in the postsocialist state. Since there is no private ownership of land, the family farm no longer exists as socioeconomic capital for the family to continue its bloodline. Peasants in the PRC are saddled with low economic status and the negative cultural identity of being considered backward. Being a hardworking peasant no longer necessarily brings sufficient income and social respect. Therefore, the urban employment of peasant children has become not only an opportunity to improve income, but also to enhance social status by having the children marry desirable partners and thereby earn the family respect from the community.

Supporting the urban employment of adult children has a higher priority among the villagers of Stone Mill than the goal of maximizing household income. Adult children who have graduated from high school could replenish labor to household production, especially to those households which are

---

18. Xiaotong Fei, *From the Soil: The Foundations of Chinese Society* (Berkeley, CA, [etc.], 1992), translated by Gary G. Hamilton and Wang Zheng, chs 4, 5, and 6.

able to expand the scale of production. However, nonagricultural employment is overwhelmingly preferred over work in agricultural production (*wunong*) to the extent that some parents have to limit the scale of household agricultural production. The case of Lanni illustrates the influence of this preference on the organization of household production.

Lanni and her husband are in their mid-forties and have a daughter and a son who have recently graduated from the local junior high school. The daughter has been working in a restaurant as a waitress and as an apprentice to a pastry chef, and the son wants to be a chef as well. Neither of them wants to work in agricultural production of any kind. Lanni's brother, who works in a city, is willing to finance the couple in expanding their orchard or starting a chicken farm. The couple has thought seriously about both plans, but they have finally decided against doing anything because neither the son nor the daughter could leave their city jobs to work for the family.

In order to help their children seek city employment and urban residential status, parents have also paid dearly. A few wealthy families (about fifteen) have bought urban residential status (i.e. a city *hukou*)[19] for their young or adult children in the local urban centers at a price of eight thousand yuan, which nearly equals an average household's annual income. A few parents have managed to support their children who passed college entrance qualification examinations. The cost of college tuition and stipend, at 10,000 yuan a year, has not only exhausted the parent's income and savings, but has put the parents in debt. Average families usually help and support their adult children in attaining employment in the competitive job markets of local urban centers. Each year, parents of new graduates make great efforts to find their children a job in nonagricultural sectors. Instead of improving their household income through the urban employment of their children, some parents have invested several thousands of yuan in their children's urban employment.

Those who cannot find nonagricultural employment do not settle for working at the household's agricultural jobs (*nonghuo*) either. It is not uncommon for these young people to refuse to be fully involved in agricul-

19. The *hukou* system, which was established in the 1950s, designates people as city or rural inhabitants, according to their status of residence. During the 1950s–1970s, the government exercised strict control over rural–urban migration and urban residential status (i.e. city *hukou*). One's rural residential status (i.e. a rural *hukou*), which was based on the rural residential status of one's mother, could hardly be changed. After the 1980s, the government began to ease its restrictions in changing residential status. In some areas, there were peasants who could afford to buy a city *hukou* – at a very high price, however. For more on the Chinese *hukou* system, see Tiejun Cheng *et al.*, "The Origins and Social Consequences of China's Hukou System", *China Quarterly*, 139 (1994), pp. 644–668; Mark Selden, *The Political Economy of Chinese Development* (Armonk, NJ, 1993) ch. 6; Sulamith Heins Potter, "The Position of Peasants in Modern China's Social Order", *Modern China*, 9 (1983), pp. 465–499.

tural jobs at home while their peers are working in the cities – they wait
and look for city job opportunities instead. Parents do not count on them
as standard full-time laborers in planning the household's agricultural activities, for they also hope that their children will soon find jobs outside the
village. Often one sees a jobless young man hanging around in the village
in trendy urban clothes, passing his time by playing cards or chatting with
people. Some help their parents with agricultural tasks in the orchard or
cornfield – however, this help is only temporary. To many young people,
wearing the plain peasant garb seems to symbolize the denial of their city
dream, to the point that some of them insist on wearing nice clothes even
when working in the field. The overt change in farm wear reveals the mindset of the young villagers, who stay at home yet aspire to city jobs.

DECOLLECTIVIZING THE HOUSEHOLD BUDGET

In rural China, the household (*hu*) is the basic domestic unit of production,
reproduction, and consumption, and is often under the management of the
parents, who are also the owners of the household property. The sharing of
family property, and often a common budget, is a distinctive feature of
Chinese household organization.[20] It is not essential that a household share
a residential unit; various household members can be placed in different
houses and at different locations when economic activities need to be carried
outside the home community.[21] Unmarried children, regardless of their age,
are members of the parents' household until they marry (for daughters) or
until the parental wealth is divided up among sons after they marry, where-
upon they start their own independent households. In the case of the Qian
family in Stone Mill's past, sons and grandsons working and living in
another village brought their income back to the household. In today's
Stone Mill, adult children commonly take jobs in the local town center,
Dalian City, and other places. Those who work in the local area may live
at home and commute to work; others live the city where they work and
visit home a few times a month or several times a year depending upon the
location of the city and the time schedule of the job.

Except for a woman's dowry and private room money (*sifangqian*), the
household traditionally had exclusive ownership of household property and
the income of its members.[22] Household members were supposed to turn
all of their income over to the household, leaving the household head to
make the consumption and production decisions. Although household

20. For Chinese household organization see Cohen, *House United, House Divided*; Maurice Freedman, *Chinese Lineage and Society: Fukien and Kwangtung* (London, 1966).
21. For instance see Cohen, *House United, House Divided*; Susan Greenhalgh, "Networks and
Their Nodes: Urban Society on Taiwan", *China Quarterly*, 99 (1984), pp. 529–552.
22. See Cohen, *House United, House Divided*; Rubie S. Watson, "Women's Property in Republican China: Rights and Practice", *Republican China*, 10 (1984), pp. 1–12.

members were expected to work their best to contribute to the household, the distribution of household property was based on the egalitarian principle of an equal share per stripe (i.e. each son and his patrilineal branch).[23] This contradiction between the unequal economic contribution of sons and the equal distribution among sons has created a structural basis for conflict among family members. Family conflict between or among interest groups – between generations or among brothers and their wives – has been a major theme of Chinese family life.[24] It manifests itself in the resistance and rebellion of those children, especially those sons who have contributed to the household more than other siblings yet receive an equal amount of family property when they marry and when the parental property is finally divided up.

In Stone Mill today, thanks to the wage labor jobs first attained in the 1980s, adult children's income from wage labor varies from 100–200 yuan to over 1,000 yuan a month. As the discrepancy in economic contribution between siblings increases, so does the dissatisfaction among those who have contributed more than other siblings. Especially those who have not been able to find urban jobs and then wander through the village streets to kill time anger their siblings who have worked hard and contributed significantly to the household's collective budget. In situations like this, parents are willing to support their jobless or low-income children, in the hope that this situation is temporary, but the other children are not pleased about it.

In the case of Fu's three sons, the eldest son had originally given their parents all of his modest earnings from his job as a plumber. His two younger brothers could not find city jobs and stayed at home doing nothing. Their parents encouraged the two younger brothers to keep looking for city jobs and did not ask them to take over the family's farm tasks, which caused the eldest son great dissatisfaction. However, as the two younger brothers began to work in a construction team and interior renovation business, respectively, they brought home income that was several hundreds of yuan more than that of their eldest brother. Foreseeing the discrepancy between their unequal economic contribution and their equal share of the family's payment to their marriages, the two younger brothers were unhappy with the parents' management of their income. Before long, the parents decided to let the sons manage their own income and pay for their own marriages.

As income differences among children has begun to widen, the collective management of a household has become more and more difficult. Beginning

---

23. See Cohen, *House United, House Divided*.
24. See *ibid.*; Maurice Freedman, *Lineage Organization in Southeastern China* (London, 1958); Maurice, *Chinese Lineage and Society*; Margery Wolf, *Women and Family in Rural Taiwan* (Stanford, CA, 1972); Yan, "The Triumph of Conjugality".

in the 1980s, parents often allowed each son to keep his own income or a portion of his income in order to save on his own for his future marriage. In Stone Mill today, it is common for children to keep at least a portion of their earnings under their own management. (In 1997, only thirty-five per cent of the adult children gave all their wage labor income to their parents; forty per cent kept a portion of their income, and twenty-five per cent kept all the income under their own management for their own consumption and their future marriage.) They often spend this private money on leisure activities in cities, or buying clothes that they would otherwise not be able to buy if all their income was under the control of their parents. They also accumulate their own savings for their future marriages. According to the egalitarian principle of wealth distribution, parents generally spend equal amounts of money on each son's marriage. If a son is able to contribute his own savings to his marriage, then the more he earns, the better equipped his new home will be.

Traditionally, the young couple would not own any conjugal property until after the division of the parental household. Since the 1980s, in Stone Mill as in other rural communities,[25] the conjugal wealth of the young couple at the time of their wedding has increased dramatically to include fixed property (a house) and household facilities (e.g. a television). Contributing to this new conjugal wealth are the groom's parents, the bride's parents, and the bride and groom themselves from their own wage labor income. A large amount of conjugal wealth enhances the economic power and independence of the couple at the time of their marriage. Compared with the collective economy in traditional households, the drastic increase in conjugal wealth is a structural change to the household organization that has economically facilitated the new custom of an early separation of married sons from the parental household, and thus the popularity of nuclear residence.[26]

It is the parents who have sustained the survival of the family and supported the economic improvement of their children, and who have now lost the advantages they had in the traditional household through the transitions taking place in the postsocialist state. With the decollectivization of household budgets, parents have relinquished part of their control over the socioeconomic lives of every family member, and they will hardly improve their chances of regaining it as sons marry, live separately, and manage their own financial affairs. Supporting elderly parents has been a Chinese family tradition that continues until today. However, by helping their children leave the village and live in cities or suburban areas, parents have lost the chance to get help from their children on a convenient daily basis. The struggle of these adult peasant children to survive in urban areas has also

25. See Yunxiang Yan, *The Flow of Gifts* (Stanford, CA, 1996), pp. 176–209.
26. See Wang, "Flying From the Nest".

Danyu Wang

allowed them less time and economic capacity to support their parents. Although some may be able and willing to support their parents, the egalitarian principle, which stipulates that each son contribute equally to parental support, has created additional tension among brothers. If one brother provides more parental support than the others, he will cause dissatisfaction among his siblings, because they will then feel under pressure to pay more themselves. The level and content of parental support, which is often adjusted to the lower-income brothers, is clearly discussed among brothers, who end up specifying in detail the amount of cooking oil, pork, and other life necessities that each son should provide. In the mid-1990s in Stone Mill, forty-one per cent of the couples who had one or both parents alive did not give their parents monetary support. Among those who provided monetary support to their parents, seventy-one per cent gave less than 500 yuan yearly, which equaled five per cent of the average household income. The living standard of elderly parents is much lower than that of their adult children.

FROM A GENDER-BASED TO A COUPLE-BASED DIVISION OF LABOR

In today's Stone Mill, as in many other rural areas,[27] agricultural production has become primarily the wife's responsibility, regardless of whether the household engages mainly in wage labor, in both agricultural production and wage labor, or primarily in agricultural production. The traditional inside–outside (*nei* vs. *wai*) division of household labor still remains, meaning women work at tasks inside and men outside the home; however, there has been a shift in both the boundaries and content of these categories of inside and outside that has been observed in other rural areas in China as well as in Stone Mill.[28] In Stone Mill, the inside–outside boundary, which used to be marked by the house, is now marked by the village – women work in the village at agricultural tasks and men take nonagricultural jobs outside of the village. This new boundary is reflected in the way a village woman named Lihua describes her work:

> I take care of work inside the home (*jiali huo*) – housework and tasks in the vegetable garden, the cornfield, and the orchard. My husband and our daughter work in factories in the town. I usually don't let my husband take time off for these inside tasks because he is paid by the hour. My husband takes charge when dealing with matters outside of home (i.e. the outside of the village) (*jiawai shi*) [...]. For example, he took care of finding jobs for himself and our elder daughter.

27. Martin K. Whyte, "Introduction: Rural Economic Reforms and Chinese Family Patterns (Symposium on Rural Family Change)", *China Quarterly*, 130 (1992), pp. 317–322.
28. Tamara Jacka, *Women's Work in Rural China: Change and Continuity in Era Reform* (Cambridge, 1997).

Husbands, on the other hand, bring home cash from wage labor jobs in addition to their labor in the household production. The husband's contribution to the household income is obvious and often significant. In 1997, among couples married after 1980 (those who are about age forty and younger), fifty per cent of the married men surveyed earned at least half of the household's cash income solely by their wage labor income. By taking wage labor jobs in towns and cities, men have also gained experience in a society beyond the village, and they can establish social contacts with co-workers and others who have access to cities and nonagricultural sectors. These social contacts provide husbands with information and access to wage labor opportunities, and thus to social and economic resources. Thus, husbands are able to secure their male authority as well as the role of "bread-winner" of the family.

As the generational factor comes into play in the analysis of change within the family, one observes an increase in the independence of the younger generation from their parents and their parents-in-law. After they graduate from high school and before they marry and start a household of their own, adult children work in the parental household as additional and somewhat temporary laborers. With the withdrawal of adult children from agricultural production and the prevalence of an early separation from the parental household, the traditional gender division of labor has been reduced to the current conjugal division of labor, centering only on the peasant husband and his wife. Changes in generational relationships in the family have enhanced the traditional gender division of labor on the more immediate conjugal level.

Although traditional gender division still exists, women have been able to extend their arena of activities to a new "inside" sphere, which includes both housework and farm tasks. With this newly expanded domestic sphere, they have begun to improve their participation in decision-making and in the control of household resources. An old saying expresses women's critical role in the traditional household economy: "If you hire incompetent laborers, you will be poor for a year. If you marry an incompetent wife, you will be poor for life" (*Gu bu dao hao huoji yi nian shou qiong, qu bu dao hao xifu yibeizi shou qiong*). In today's Stone Mill, the wife's ability to utilize her power in distributing household production and consumption resources has grown, and so has the household's dependence on the wife. A married woman makes decisions concerning daily household matters, both at home and on the farm, that were formerly decided by the husband or the parents-in-law in traditional households. Some of these women, especially those with husbands who work principally in wage labor jobs (e.g. Lihua), assume major responsibility in organizing routine agricultural tasks. This expansion of their economic resources has contributed to the young women's independence from the patriarchal authority and control of their parents-in-law, and enables them to sustain nuclear households as a new mode of family life.

The universal human need for survival is organized by the household in its own cultural ways under certain socioeconomic conditions. The cultural goal of maintaining family continuity, prosperity, and dignity has remained in contemporary rural China, yet it is pursued with a different set of strategies. The change in the household strategies from the expansion of land to a combination of seeking city jobs for children and improving household income, is the peasants' response to their socioeconomic condition in the postsocialist state. This new set of strategies has not only helped China' peasants to survive the impoverished life, but has also resulted in a reconfiguration of the generational relationships. Despite the prospect of not receiving much in return economically from their adult children while they manage the family household or later in their old age, parents have fully supported the city employment of their adult children, even at the expense of paying for their job searches and training. With the increased income and income differentiation among siblings, the household budget has begun to be decollectivized and the parental power in controlling the household has begun to be decentralized. The traditional mode of parent-centered household management has begun to change. In its place is evolving the rising independence of the younger generation.